Change Magic

The Evolutionary Approach to Organisational Change

Peter Freeth

Published by

CGW
PUBLISHING

2016

Change Magic

The Evolutionary Approach to Organisational Change

ISBN 978-1-908293-04-6

First Edition March 2003
Second Edition April 2008
Third Edition March 2017

CGW Publishing 2016

Published by:

CGW Publishing
B1502
PO Box 15113
Birmingham
B2 2NJ

www.cgwpublishing.com

www.geniuslearning.co.uk

Change To make or become different

Magic The use of special powers to make things happen that would usually be impossible

Ingredients

Change Magic

Change is an illusion.

Close up magic, when performed with a high degree of skill and dexterity, has the power to amaze, to take your breath away. And yet, underlying the performance are a set of simple, timeless, elegant principles which tap into our most fundamental human processes and can be assembled by skilled magicians into an infinite repertoire.

And no sooner have the audience uttered their "oohs" and "aahs" of wonder, the question on their lips is, "how did you do it?"

Great magic is based on a simple premise – that people only notice what they notice. Magicians use this to divert attention away from the secret pocket or palmed card. You can use this to effect change that is an elegant evolution of what works best in your organisation. By focussing your attention on "change", you are drawing people's attention to it and giving them something to worry about. By focussing your attention on results, outcomes and continuity, you allow change to go unnoticed.

Of course, there's more to it than this - Change Magic is also about effecting elegant, systemic change. Complex systems, including companies and people, have many interdependent parts. When problems occur, the cause is often in a different part to the effect. The effects, or symptoms, are often visible across the system, giving the impression that there are many problems. In fact, there is often just one single part of a system that needs a little drop of oil.

Change isn't something you do – it's something you notice after it has happened. Change is a comparison over time.

As a Change Magician, you will learn how to put change where it belongs – in the past. Change is just what you perceive when you notice a difference in your sensory perception over time. You look at something, then you look at it again an hour later. If it's different, it has changed. This means that people tend to notice some differences and not others. Some things change and others stay the same. In fact, everything changes and everything stays the same, depending on what you notice. This has a very important consequence for that corporate habit known as change management, and we'll talk about it later.

Change is a perception, not a process. We can look back at a period of history and call it the Industrial Revolution, but did people at the time call it that? We are in the midst of a revolution now, as society shakes off the bonds of industry and moves towards a more people centred way of building companies and business processes. We don't know what to call it, because we don't know what age it will lead us into. As hard as the futurologists and science fiction writers try, their predictions of the future are always constrained by the past.

One of the most important things about change is that people – and therefore companies – make it much bigger and louder than it needs to be. They make something out of nothing.

When Change Magic happens, you must be prepared for people to notice…nothing at all. There may be no elaborate project names, no logos on mugs, no ticker tape parades and no thanks. As a Change Magician, you will just perform your magic and move quietly on.

You don't need to follow the 6 step change process or the 19 stage coaching model. You don't need to learn any number of other people's habits, even though they may have been effective for other people, somewhere else, in a different situation. Change Magic is concerned with results, not process. Some people don't like this. If they can't see the steps of the process, they can't figure out what happened. The fact that they're living happier, easier, more successful lives is not enough. They need proof.

As Groucho Marx said, "Who are you going to believe? Me, or your own eyes?"

Change Magic presumes that you already have the means to change your systems and business processes, products and manufacturing methods, office furniture and stationery.

Change Magic therefore takes over when you have changed all of the things typically addressed by change management consultants and you find that there is still something missing. Change Magic takes over when change involves people, because you generally won't change people just by putting an activity in your project plan in between 'rearrange furniture' and 'order new business cards'. Consultants are often telling me that changing business systems is easy, the bit they always get stuck on is getting people to welcome that change.

Magic is also concerned with effect. No matter how the trick is really done, the audience wants to believe in magic or mind reading or levitation, or whatever the trick is designed to create the illusion of. Therefore the magician's greatest challenge is not to learn the mechanics of the trick but to perform that trick in a way that engages, surprises and delights the audience. In business change, we have the same challenge because the reality of successful businesses is much simpler than the management consultants would like you to believe. And yet simple things can still be difficult.

Change doesn't exist. Over time, we notice that things are different. We call it change, but a change never really happened. Things are different but change does not exist as a thing in itself. You can't put change in a wheelbarrow. You can, however take some things out of a wheelbarrow and put different things in it. The most obvious clue is in the word itself – change is treated as a noun, a thing, yet in fact it's a verb, an activity, an action. To change. I cannot change, I can only change what I think, say and do, and since you will only ever judge me based on what I say and do, you assume that I have changed. You will naturally confuse me with my behaviour, as everyone will do with you. When you push a door that's marked 'Pull', you're an idiot. When you don't get round to finishing off that work at home, you're lazy. And when you exceed your targets, you're lucky to have such a great boss. You just can't win! Well, of course you can't win, because it's not a competition, it's just a game, and in a game, you can change the rules.

Change Magic is not only about change. It's about magic. It's about people waking up one day and finding that things are bigger, stronger and better. It's about constant evolution. It's about people looking on in amazement and asking, "How did they do that?"

Reading this book once and then leaving it on a bookshelf to gather dust is not the way to get the best from it. Read this book and then take action. Don't sit around and think. Don't read another book. Go out and start making a difference, right away.

Why are you still reading? Go and do something!

About This Book

I've read many books by business gurus which actually comprise just one good idea padded out to turn something that's worth a good essay into something they can sell as a book. It's a shame, because it spoils the one good idea. Of course, they want to commercialise their own good idea or piece of interesting research, and you don't make a lot of money out of essays these days. You need books, models, training programs, acronyms and so on.

This book is packed full of ideas. So many ideas that you might not take them all in at once. You might find that these ideas start to change the way you see things, and when you come back to the book again, you'll notice new ideas and new significance as a result of that changed perception.

The other problem with many other books is that they reduce knowledge down to a checklist. So many habits, or a list of things to do, nice simple mnemonics. Easy to remember, but impossible to put into practice. You see, we live in a Google generation where we want easy, simple answers. If the solution to poaching an egg or performing open heart surgery isn't on the first page of search results, we're not interested.

If you're thinking that a mnemonic makes an idea or process easy to implement because you can remember the steps then I'll explain later why this is not the case. In order to really be able to do something, you have to learn it in a particular way, and fortunately humans are exceptionally good at that. I'm not saying that you shouldn't have a list, but just like the list of ingredients for a cake, it's not enough. Even the recipe isn't enough. If you've ever tried to emulate something created by a TV chef then you know that even copying a professional isn't enough.

Change Magic isn't about checklists or rules for what worked for someone else. It's a journey, and as you read the book, you might at times wonder where that journey is leading. At those times, bear with me. All will become clear.

You need to work a few things out for yourself. You need to write the recipe *after* you've baked the cake, not before.

So this isn't a book that will give you answers on a plate.

Plates are for cakes, not answers.

Change

Change can be defined as difference over time. You may think that's obvious, yet it raises two important points; that in order for a change to take place:

1. Things have to be different

2. Time has to elapse

Still waiting for the rocket science? I met a rocket scientist once. He was a very nice man, and his hobby was exploring the railway systems of the world. It turned out that rocket science wasn't that difficult after all. Back in the 1970s when flexible working practices were pretty much unheard of, he worked out a personal deal with his employer. He didn't have much of a social life, so he would work for most of his waking hours in return for being able to take 3 month holidays to ride on trains in Malaysia or South America. This was in America, where his colleagues were allowed 10 days holiday a year. This is just unthinkable in the UK where we expect between 20 and 30 days. So even 30 years ago, he figured out a way to get what he wanted whilst giving his employer and customers what they wanted too.

How do people know to respond to change? By noticing difference over time. People only respond to what they notice changing, and people notice things that:

- Are important or relevant to them
- You draw their attention to

This simple premise lies at the heart of Change Magic. If you don't want people to get upset by change, don't tell them about it as they probably won't notice anyway. Of course, your change managers want all the glory so they will tend to draw attention to what they're doing with slogans, mugs and focus groups.

In reality, you may have to change things that are important to people, but you would only ever change them for the better, wouldn't you?

The key is to stop telling people what will change. Just tell them what tomorrow is going to be like. They'll work out how to get there for themselves.

Big IT change projects are interesting because the people who resist the new systems seem to be afraid of change and seem to reject or sabotage it. In fact, this is a good example of the need to identify the right problem.

Here's a useful IT change belief for you:

People aren't afraid of change. They're just reluctant to spend more time learning how to work complicated computer software.

And be honest, who isn't? Twenty years ago, I used to pride myself that I could work any piece of technology without ever reading the manual. Twenty years later, two things have happened - technology has become more complicated and I've become less interested. I just want to take pictures with my camera - I don't want it to tell me the time or print 'Happy Birthday' in Japanese on all my photos. Consequently, the clock is wrong for six months in every year because I can't remember how to change it and I'm really not that bothered as I have a thing on my wrist that already tells the time.

Modern smartphones overcome the problem of resistance in an interesting way. Ten years ago, if I changed to a different make of mobile phone, I had to learn a new menu system, new features and, most importantly, I had to transfer all my contacts and data across. Today, all of my data and settings are 'in the cloud', which just means that all of my data is sitting on someone else's computer. When I get a new phone, I simply enter my login details and within minutes, my new phone is my old phone, minus the scratches.

Large IT projects are very complicated, which is why companies employ IT experts and consultants. Even 'simple' software upgrades become a logistical nightmare when implemented across thousands of computers.

For the meek end user, the computer system is a tool for their job. So to add to the logistics of software upgrades, we have the problem that the users don't want to give up access to their computers while the upgrade is taking place.

If you're involved in IT change then you might be thinking, "he doesn't know what he's talking about – IT change is not just about new computer software" and you would be half right.

Company car drivers know that, every 3 or 4 years, they get a new car. Some look forward to it, some resent having to clear out all their maps and sweet wrappers and most are happy to go with the flow. Why not tell your employees that they have to have a new computer system every 3 years? I've seen so much academic research about change that suggests people accept change when they expect it, yet we seem to be missing the simple point - just tell people to expect it!

If you want people to accept change, let them expect it.

This is even good advice for parents. Don't argue with them after bedtime or home time has already been and gone. Tell them, "ten more minutes", then, "five more minutes", then, "time to go now". It really does work, and it works for adults as well as children. Forewarning gives a sense of control, and control is what enables us to easily adapt to change in our lives.

In most big companies I've worked for, an unofficial rumour system was used to soften the impact of organisational changes. Trusted employees would be given confidential hints of upcoming changes. They would tell their trusted friends who would tell everyone else. Everyone would respond to the news which would be denied as rumour, thereby allowing the people who were upset by the change to get upset by it and then forget about it. Some weeks later, the change would happen and everyone would feel a sense of smugness that they secretly knew the change was coming.

This happened so often in so many different companies that it had to be intentional. Either that, or there is some utterly compelling human drive that makes it impossible for us to keep secrets.

Anyway, the point about change is this: people only notice what they notice. If you don't tell them about change, they will not notice the majority of what changes. If you tell them about what is staying the same, you are giving them a context or framework for the change that puts it into a realistic perspective.

The interesting thing is that our sensory systems are evolved to detect difference. You cannot be aware of the absolute temperature right now, but you'll notice if you start to feel warmer or colder. Therefore, in order for our sensory systems to detect change, we need to have a point of reference. And that is the key to Change Magic.

Companies always seem eager to tell their shareholders that the company is going to change radically in order to meet the challenges ahead. When the same message is given to employees, it's really no wonder that they get upset.

Shareholders, particularly institutional shareholders such as investment banks, want to see things change. If the new CEO hasn't made them a big pile of cash in his first year they want him out. Institutional shareholders even gang up at company AGMs in order to force CEOs out.

I wish I could remember who it was, but I can't so I'll tell you the story anyway; a few years ago a corporate CEO addressed institutional shareholders at a press conference and basically said, "Stop poking your nose into my business and trying to tell me how to run It. I don't tell you what investments to make so don't tell me how to run my business. I'm the CEO, and I'll run my business the way I want to, and that means I'll generate lots of profit for you". I liked it. It came at a time when many CEOs were under pressure from shareholders to make certain decisions that were good for short term profits, which make the fund managers look good. He publicly stood up for himself, and I like that.

When my first daughter was born, my then wife suggested I should drive more slowly as I was now responsible for more than just myself in the car. I suggested that there was nothing wrong with my driving and we then had a rational discussion on the subject, as you can no doubt imagine. My wife told me that she would be changing her driving habits and so should I, so I asked her how many accidents she had had in the last ten years. "None!" was her reply. I asked, "and you think now is the time to change your driving habits?"

You see the point, of course. Having driven perfectly for ten years, she perceived a change in circumstances that required a change in driving habits. Would that be more or less likely to lead to future accidents?

Statistics tell us that people who hire cars abroad are actually less likely to have accidents, because they are more worried about having an accident. People are actually more likely to have an accident near to their own homes, when they are feeling most complacent.

So change in itself doesn't exist. We become aware of a difference in our perception of something or someone. In change management, we aim to control that change process. In Change Magic, we aim to control the outcome and let the process take care of itself, with a little gentle guidance from a friendly Change Magician.

Culture Change

I recently visited a client to help him with some business planning. He took a piece of paper and started drawing the organisation chart and all of the different activities that he wanted to plan, including business strategy, business objectives, HR strategy and financial planning. One of the things on his piece of paper was 'culture change'. I asked him what it was and he said, "that's a culture change program that's been running for a few years".

Here's the top tip: if your culture change program has been running for a few years, it isn't changing your culture.

Companies use the term 'culture change' all the time when what they really mean is that they want people to do different stuff. Since they don't know what they want people to do differently, and they don't know how it needs to be different, it's impossible to define or measure the behavioural changes required. It's much easier to say that the behaviour of people in the company is part of an ethereal 'culture' that needs to change. No-one knows how to change it, but they'll know when it has changed, because it will seem different.

By and large, people do not want the rules to change. It's far easier to be specific about what you want people to do differently and to then tell them how to do it. Can you imagine how much money a lengthy culture change program might cost? Can you imagine the time devoted to it by people who could be doing something else?

I thought this was a perfect illustration of one of Change Magic's key principles – don't think about change, think about what you want to be different. Change is the scenery that passes by as you focus on your destination.

Evolution

This seems as good a time as ever to bring up Charles Darwin, because his theory of evolution by natural selection is very important to understanding how people adapt and change.

If you believe in the creationist theory of life on Earth then you can regard this chapter as a metaphor for organisational development rather than true. In that case, you might accept that evolution doesn't happen, therefore survival of the fittest is irrelevant. Since the species that exist today are here as a result of the intent of a higher authority, the same must apply to companies in which case you shouldn't be reading this book. You should just accept that things are they way they are because that's the way they're meant to be. Like all beliefs, this can be very useful as it means that if your company ever goes out of business, it wasn't your fault.

In my opinion, the creationist or 'intelligent design' theory seems plausible when you try to get your head round the immense periods of time required for Darwinian evolution. It's easier to believe that someone else put us here than it is to understand the slow, random, evolutionary path that led to me writing this and you reading it. Think of the differences between you and your parents. You are neither of them, yet both of them. You are different to them, yet the same. The differences between you and your parents may confer an advantage to your survival, they may not. You may have a mutated gene which makes you more resistant to a certain type of infection. However, your mutations may equally put you at a disadvantage. There is no way to tell, other than to measure how long you live and how many children you pass your mutations onto.

If you think there is any truth in the theory of evolution by natural selection, or if you just believe that evolution is possible, then read on. I do of course accept that many creationists believe that evolution does take place under the watchful eye of a higher power, a bit like the Inland Revenue or IRS.

Essentially, we have evolved into the dominant species on Earth - inhabiting every continent and ecosystem on the planet - because we have a very special capability that other animals do not have. We are able to adapt to our environment within the space of a single generation. When habitats change, either as a result of natural disaster or human intervention, many species are unable to survive.

That, and we also have opposable thumbs, which mean that we are the tool-making apes.

Most animals on Earth have evolved to exploit an environmental niche, which makes them specialists. More accurately, the environment has shaped their survival. Humans are not specialists. We can climb trees, but not as well as Monkeys. We can run, but not as well as Cheetahs. We can swim, but not as well as Sea Lions. However, we can climb, run and swim in the same day better than any of them.

I should just say that Humans are not necessarily superior to or more intelligent than other species on Earth, we're just more popular. The same is true in industry too. Many would say that Microsoft and Ford don't make the best products, but they certainly are popular. Being the best at your particular job isn't important – it's being the best at surviving that's important.

Some would say we're better at taking advantage of things. Either way, our knack for survival is a very good thing for you and your loved ones.

One thing that Humans do really, really well is communicate. Our ability to communicate powers our ability to adapt because we can share information with other Humans about our environment. Not only can we communicate, but we can also write down our communication so that it leaps over time and geography.

When a Chimpanzee invents a new tool, other Chimpanzees watch closely to see how to use the tool. When Humans invent new tools, we can write the instructions down and pass them to our children or to Humans on the other side of the planet. Symbolic language allows us to acquire knowledge faster than any other species.

So we, as a species, are where we are today because we are able to adapt quickly to a rapidly changing environment. We can eat almost anything, live almost anywhere and acquire new knowledge quickly from many different sources.

If you worry about how people will cope with change, stop it immediately. Your biggest concern should be how to give people enough change to keep them interested.

Darwin's theory of evolution by natural selection has some absolutely critical lessons for organisational change. Here are those critical lessons:

- Successful species do not suddenly evolve a huge competitive advantage. This requires a lot of energy and a generous helping of luck and is only a short term advantage as it is quickly copied.

- Successful species evolve by generating a huge number of design variations and the environment chooses the most useful or appropriate designs.

- Successful species are only marginally more effective at surviving than their nearest competitor, however they are consistent in applying this small advantage so the effects are cumulative over time.

- Successful species adapt quickly to environmental changes, so the most successful are those that can adapt within a single generation to those changes.

- Most species are highly specialised in exploiting a particular environmental niche.

- The human species is specialised for adaptation.

- Mass extinction affects those species that are reliant on a single environment which changes as a result of climatic or geological change.

- Species do not evolve towards a specific goal. They evolve randomly and are selected in or out by other species (predators) or by the environment (food and climate). As we look at highly specialised species today, we say that they have evolved "to" exploit a particular environmental niche. It's more accurate to say that the environmental niche has shaped the species that occupies it.

So, let's translate that into the language of organisational change:

- Don't waste time and money trying to predict what will work. Try anything and let your market decide for you.

- Don't waste time and money trying to jump way ahead of your competitors. They will copy you almost instantly and use your investment to better exploit their own market niche. Instead, invest in the development of what works and be prepared to act quickly if a particular idea proves popular. One step ahead is as good as a mile.

- Just do the basic things consistently well. As a consequence, doing the basics well also leads to cost and time efficiency - a double bonus!

- Decide what you are good at and then just get on with it.

Successful companies are not tied to a particular market or customer. No-one can predict massive global change so successful companies thrive in both good times and bad times. They are naturally adaptable, just like human beings. Fortunately, companies are made up of groups of human beings and so are equally adaptable, given the opportunity.

A Cheetah will hunt any of the species of Gazelle that inhabit the African plains. Do you know how much faster a Cheetah can run than a Gazelle? Have a guess – 10 miles per hour faster? 20? We know that the Cheetah is the fastest land mammal, able to run at over 60 miles per hour. Next time you're driving on the Motorway, imagine looking out of the window and seeing a Cheetah running alongside you to get an idea of how fast that is.

A bird of prey called the Lanner Falcon can fly at 80 miles per hour as it dives for its prey. With gravity on its side, the Lanner Falcon can sustain this speed much more easily than the Cheetah.

So, how much faster than a Gazelle does a Cheetah run? The answer is... just a tiny bit faster than the youngest or weakest Gazelle. The Cheetah is not trying to win a race. It is not trying to prove anything to the Gazelle. It is not trying to dominate the Gazelle herd. It's just trying to catch lunch. Why make it more difficult than it needs to be?

From wildlife programs, you may have this image of a Cheetah outrunning a Gazelle and leaping onto its back, like a lion. In fact, the Cheetah has a small claw on its 'wrist' that it uses to trip the Gazelle. Once the Gazelle is on the ground, the Cheetah goes for its throat.

A Cheetah is not a long distance runner – it will stalk its prey until it is close enough to sprint. The moment the Cheetah starts its run, its heart rate, blood pressure and body temperature soar. Many Cheetahs actually die while hunting as they over-exert themselves and suffer heart failure.

Fortunately for all of the big cats, once they catch something, they don't have to eat again for a few days as protein takes a long time to digest. Big cats are permanently on the Atkins diet.

Finally, if a Cheetah leaves its kill, it won't go back. Cheetahs don't scavenge, whereas all of the other African big cats will. So if a lion comes along and the Cheetah retreats for safety, when the lion has gone, the Cheetah will need to hunt again. The greatest threat to the survival of Cheetahs is man. No surprise there. But the reason is interesting – farmers are putting up fences to protect their land, which means that the Cheetahs don't have wide open plains to hunt in.

This is all very interesting, but what does it tell us about success in business?

Firstly, the Cheetah is not trying to prove its superiority over the Gazelle, it's just trying to eat one. It's not trying to run faster than the herd, just faster than the slowest Gazelle. In business, are you trying to change the world? Are you on a mission? Or are you simply finding enough people to work with? Or perhaps you're putting all your effort into getting from one meal to the next?

Secondly, the Cheetah isn't trying to outrun the Gazelle and pounce on it. It just wants to get close enough to trip the Gazelle up. Are you trying to give your customers too much? Or are you doing just enough to get their attention?

Thirdly, do you put so much effort into the chase that you risk everything? Or do you take it easy, avoiding the risk of a big chase and miss the really big kill?

Being the fastest land mammal does not make the Cheetah the perfect metaphor for business success, because the Cheetah is only successful in exploiting its niche.

In fact, the most successful hunter in Africa, besides man, is the wild dog. A wild dog is about the size of a Labrador and they hunt in packs, very efficiently. Some hunt while others protect, some attack while others defend. They all share in the rewards of that strategy. The wild dog is the most efficient hunter on the African plains. It's also the rarest and is in real danger of extinction. Even success does not guarantee longevity for you.

One of the most important contributions that Cheetahs make to the world is to make faster Gazelles. In turn, faster

Gazelles make faster Cheetahs. Nature corrects any imbalance in order to maintain the performance of the system. If baby Cheetahs are too much faster than their parents, they will hunt until the Gazelle population in their area is diminished to the point where the Cheetahs can no longer survive. The environment that the animals exist in creates the parameters for performance improvement so that the whole system evolves over time.

Every generation of every organism produces more offspring than an environment can sustain. The surplus are consumed by predators and scavengers, and just enough survive to maturity to ensure the survival of the species.

When the environment changes, the predators don't go away. A harsh winter might mean fewer berries, but there are just as many wolves, and that's bad news this year for the reindeer, and bad news next year for the wolves.

The presence of predators means that environmental changes ripple up the food chain. Conversely, when there are no predators, the ecosystem becomes bloated and loses its natural defences. Dodos became extinct because they had no natural predators prior to man's arrival.

Natural resources such as food, shelter and mates are analogous to economic resources such as money, customers and raw materials.

When an economy changes direction abruptly, as in the case of the 'credit crunch' of 2009, those natural resources become restricted, but the predators are still very much alive and kicking.

Of course, predators aren't the only threat in an ecosystem. An organism's own siblings compete for those resources, and the weakest or slowest may just not find enough food to survive.

Many business services providers such as trainers and consultants fed heartily on the financial services industry during the years of economic growth. When the news of the credit crunch hit the headlines, banks and other financial institutions cut their budgets overnight. Those suppliers who had focused exclusively on the financial market lost their incomes literally overnight.

Das globale Bankensystem wankt

Berliner Zeitung, October 9, 2008

Credit Crunch Hits Casinos Worldwide

Online Casino Reports

US mortgage giants Freddie Mac and Fannie Mae taken into public ownership.

The Guardian, September 7, 2008

An NHS helpline to help people struggling with stress has been launched following concerns about the mounting problems people will face because of the economy.

BBC, December 30, 2009

> Organic food sales fall in credit
> crunch. Shoppers bought fewer organic
> fruit and vegetables last year while
> the economy deteriorated, according to
> the Soil Association.

The Independent, April 7, 2009

> Lehman Brothers was tonight scrambling
> to secure a buyer after a week in
> which confidence in the bank has
> spiralled lower at a breathtaking
> pace.

The Guardian, September 12, 2008

> Accountants at PricewaterhouseCoopers
> have earned £322m in fees from the
> collapse of Lehman Brothers' European
> arm, a sum thought to be the largest
> ever earned from any single UK
> corporate failure.

The Guardian, April 14, 2011

Wow. People at Lehman Brothers lost their jobs, while PWC made £322 million out of their plight.

There's one other thing that Humans can do that is very different to what most other animals can do. We can create solutions that are fundamentally different to their problems. For example, if you can't get your new sofa through your front door you can take your window out. Most animals just apply more and more force to the problem. They tend to think linearly by extending the problem. Humans can think abstractly, creating solutions that are different to the problem.

A perfect example of this is Trevor Bayliss' invention of the clockwork radio which was inspired by a news article about the spread of AIDS in Africa. Apparently, people didn't know about the danger of AIDS because they didn't have batteries for their radios to listen to health information. No doubt you will have heard this story many times before. A linear solution would have related to new ways to distribute batteries. Trevor Bayliss' solution was to ask himself, "do we need this problem?" or, more specifically, "do we need batteries?"

In short, human creativity and problem solving is possible because we are able to think outside of the constraints of the problem.

Incidentally, I often wonder if Trevor Bayliss' idea worked because people were able to listen to health information on the radio, or just because it gave them something else to do in the evening.

Successful companies are not tied to a particular market or customer. No-one can predict massive global change so successful companies thrive in both good times and bad times. They are naturally adaptable, just like human beings. Fortunately, companies are made up of groups of human beings and so are naturally adaptable, given the opportunity.

Every business column and expert seems to be advising companies to specialise. We can see that animals and plants that exploit an evolutionary niche by becoming highly specialised enjoy a rich and predator free environment. Unfortunately, when the environment changes, the niche vanishes and the species dies out. Sometimes, no-one could foresee the change in environment such as the arrival of an ice age or a large meteor impact. More often, specialist species are wiped out by an environmental change caused by a more successful species - usually man.

Species that are highly specialised face extinction when:

- Their natural habitat or food source changes (think of the removal of hedgerows in Britain, or rain forests)

- A more generalised species moves in to their habitat (when the grey squirrel displaced the native British red squirrel)

- A predator is introduced to their habitat (when ship's cats started breeding on islands that the sailors visited, or when humans first arrived... pretty much anywhere)

The environment that companies survive in is mostly created by other companies. When they change, the environment changes. Some companies have a large environmental impact, and this doesn't necessarily mean large companies. If you exploit a niche, be careful. For example, when Apple faced extinction, the mass PC market would not have noticed. The specialised media market relies almost entirely on Apple Macs and so the loss of a relatively small player would have changed the whole market environment. Companies would have emerged to service and restore used Macs, Mac software suppliers would have expanded to move their software to the PC platform and training companies would spring up to retrain users. So, when you think of it this way, it might make you wonder how Microsoft benefited from rescuing Apple.

By supporting Apple, Microsoft were able to exert more control over consumer choice – until Linux came along. Alternative operating systems have been around for decades, so why was Linux so popular? Perhaps, by supporting Apple, Microsoft created an environmental niche for Linux to evolve in. If the Cheetah wiped out the Gazelle, something else would move in to exploit the Gazelle's old habitat. This raises interesting questions about the power of the consumer, and whether Bill Gates created Microsoft, or we did.

The constant in the computing system is choice. When someone removed choice from the system, someone else put it back again.

Essentially, any system will either rebalance itself or destroy itself. If a system isn't balanced then it is either spiralling out of control, consuming resources faster than it generates them, or it is spiralling downwards, failing to sustain itself. In a complex system like a market economy, there are enough individuals with a vested interest that the system will rebalance after even the most significant setback. Just notice how many market crashes the stock market has recovered from.

No matter what state you think your business is in, if it is trading then it is working. The people within it are adapting to the situation, not coping with it.

I have observed that people have no trouble at all getting what they want. What they have trouble with is wanting the right things.

Don't try to decide what your customers will want in five year's time. If, in 1995, you had told the mobile phone companies that a large chunk of their revenue would come from teenagers sending each other short, plain text messages using a strange new coded language, they would have laughed at you. The future was multimedia, and only corporate customers could afford it. SMS would never be a business application. Don't restrict your strategy to what you can see in front of you as you will deny yourself opportunities that lie around the corner.

Business plans are very important for many reasons. Just try not to confuse planning with knowing what to do. By all means, write a nice glossy business plan that will impress the bank manager, CEO or shareholders - just keep this simple alternative business plan in your mind which, coincidentally, is the model for successful evolution and also the mental model used by any successful person:

- **Decide what you want**
- **Do anything**
- **Notice what works and what doesn't**
- **Keep doing more of what works**

Is that it? Yes! This isn't rocket science - just Change Magic.

There is an old rumour that scientists once claimed that bees should not be able to fly because their wings are too small to generate enough lift. This is a great example of thinking that is constrained by a problem. It turns out that bees' wings don't work like aeroplane wings. Their mathematical model did not fit the case of the bee, therefore their deduction was that bees can't fly. Of course, we know that bees do fly very well, so we know that there is something wrong with the model. To be fair to the scientists, they realised that too. The whole story seems to have started as a conversation at a dinner party which a journalist turned into something with a slightly different meaning. Fancy a journalist doing that. Fancy it even being possible. Hmm... I wonder if that would be useful for a Change Magician?

The truth is that scientists never said that bees couldn't fly, they said that based on our current understanding or aerodynamics, they shouldn't be able to fly, yet they can. Even in 2015, scientists are still understanding how insects fly, and the aerodynamics of very small wings which of course work very differently to very big wings.

Anyway, the first clue is that the point of reference is a model - a generalisation of something that was true once, somewhere else. If your model doesn't fit what you can observe you may be inclined to think that either a) your observations are flawed or b) your model is flawed. In fact, there is a third choice - your model is fine but just doesn't apply in this case!

For viewers watching in black and white, here's that insight again. If what you measure does not fit your model, it does not necessarily mean that either your measurement or your model is wrong. It could just mean that your measurement is simply not fine enough. We can never measure something smaller than our smallest unit of measurement.

As with all generalisations, business models are statistically valid, meaning that they may apply to all companies some of the time or some companies all of the time. They don't help you to pinpoint which companies they apply to at which times.

Trial and error is a logic tool for selecting logic tools. Trial and error is not a good way of choosing the best way to work with people, because they have good memories, so the situation is never the same twice.

Knowledge becomes a constraint when it replaces possibility with certainty. When a problem lies unsolved you don't know what solution will work because it hasn't happened yet, so you take a gamble based on previous experience. This is another example of generalisation at work. If I only gave you one piece of advice for problem solving, it would be to resist the temptation to be certain. Embrace doubt.

Oh, you might be thinking that my business plan is actually a vision or a mission statement. If you're not, well done. If you are, go to the back of the class. Haven't you been paying attention?

With the bees, it turns out that they rotate their wings in a special way, a bit like a helicopter. The scientists who claimed that bees shouldn't be able to fly didn't know this because they weren't looking properly. Does this mean that if your business is working, you shouldn't worry why, you should just make the most of it? No! It means that if the reason why your business is working isn't staring you in the face, you're not looking properly, or perhaps you don't want to admit it to yourself?

Cheetahs don't have sharper teeth or better camouflage than other big cats. They can, however, run a great deal faster. The reason for a Cheetah's success if obvious. It's simple and true that the simplest answer is usually true.

The Cheetah is an interesting example to use because its numbers in the wild are diminishing rapidly. The Cheetah hunts alone and needs a lot of wide open space to hunt in. Farmers are planting crops and putting up fences which limit the amount of hunting space available. Lions hunt in packs and will often chase Cheetah off their kills. Leopards drag their kills up into trees to protect their lunch from lions and hyenas. If a Cheetah is chased off its kill, it won't return to it. Man is disrupting the Cheetah's natural habitat and since the Cheetah is a highly specialised hunter, it is having difficulty adapting.

The ecological balance of African big cats is an interesting metaphor for corporate behaviour. Is your company a lion? A pack hunter that relies more on power and reputation than performance? Is it a leopard? An ambusher, protective of its prey? Is it a Cheetah? A high performance niche player being driven out of its market and unable to change? Is it a hyena? Happy to pick up the leftovers? Perhaps it's man? Dominating the landscape and adapting to exploit the environment?

If the reason for your success isn't glaringly obvious, your vision may be blurred by too much knowledge and not enough curiosity.

Coming back to Darwin, or Lamarck, or the other people who had the same realisation but without the publicity, the most important thing to bear in mind is that evolution is a dance between the organism and its environment. The environment exerts the pressure to change, the direction, and the organism adapts randomly.

Here's another way to think about it. Have you ever sifted flour, or sugar, or soil in the garden? Or perhaps you've tried to get sweets into a jar? Anyway, a situation where you shake something to get it to settle. What's happening? You're agitating the jar or sieve and what's inside is jiggling around randomly. With no gravity, it would float off in all directions, but the force of gravity exerts a steady downward pressure and you get sieved flour or a jar of neatly packed sweets.

If you don't believe me, get a jar or jug of some sort, put some stones in of different sizes and some sand on top, then jiggle it and see what happens. In this instance, gravity provides the direction, just as water or temperature or altitude provide the direction in an environmental niche, and just as technology, cost or knowledge might provide the direction in your environmental niche.

So there, in a nutshell, is the secret of success in a competitive market: jiggle.

Don't read this bit

Problems, Problems

I don't want to dwell on problems, but let's face it, the only time you really want to change something is because you have to in order to solve a problem. Change is always externally motivated. Come on, be honest, even when you wanted to change something about yourself, it's because of some external feedback, wasn't it?

Let's define a problem as, "An arrangement of a system which prevents that system from efficiently achieving its purpose". Some problems are fun, like crosswords and IQ tests, so we call them puzzles. Some problems are not fun, like diabetes or stress or not earning enough money to cover all of your debts. And what we all have a tendency to do is devote our time and attention to problem children, the quiet ones who just keep their heads down and get on with it and who don't get attention because they obviously don't need it.

Whoa! Can you hear yourself? You're giving attention to the problems which demand attention. They don't demand solutions, they demand attention. Once you know that a child is being naughty just to get attention, what do you do? Carry on giving that attention? Probably, yes but ideally, no. What you really ought to do is cut off the attention and only give attention to the behaviour that you want to encourage. And so it is with corporate problems too. We put effort into turning round failing companies, failing teams, failing projects. We send failing, incompetent managers on training courses. We focus on closing skills gaps. It's so wrong.

Many traditional problem solving methodologies have one major drawback - they concentrate on the problem rather than the solution. You are required to gather information about the problem to find out "why" it happened.

Looking in your rear view mirror is far less useful than looking out of your windscreen.

Learning why you have a problem is not useful. Learning how to recreate that problem is very useful. If you use a process to uncover why you have a particular problem, then you will simply end up with excuses - reasons why the problem exists - justifications for the problem. If you want to look for excuses, don't read this book. If you want to learn new ways to create solutions that go over, around and beneath the problem - if you want to create solutions that are genuinely well balanced, involving all of your natural talents and experience - if you want to learn to think differently, then this book is for you.

All too often, corporate consultants ask managers why they think there's a problem, summarise this as a root cause analysis and then propose a solution. What they don't do is test the problem, as in recreate the conditions for the problem and see what happens. In other words, they don't intentionally create the problem to see what happens. Some people do, to be fair. IT professionals will 'stress test' systems to identify a problem, but it seems that whenever the problem involves people, the scientific method goes out of the window.

Albert Einstein famously said, "You cannot solve a problem with the same thinking that created the problem."

The question for many people is, "Everyone keeps telling me to think differently, but exactly how do I learn to think differently?"

So, your first task is to declare the problem irrelevant. If your reaction is "But I can't do that!!" then this is not the book for you. If your reaction is one of relief, then read on. Problems are a signpost to the past. They point to where you have been, and to where you do not plan to go again. Problems are useful in that they allow you to rule out one course of action from the infinite variety of possibilities that lie ahead.

Throughout this book, we will not focus on problems, we will focus on figuring out *what you want instead*.

Problems don't define the solution any more than the past defines the future. If you want to get different results, do something different.

But what?

Think Different!

The manager of a well known professional sports team delivers a lecture on change management and team building to corporate audiences. He probably delivers the same lecture every time, although I've only seen it once. In it, he tells a story of a businessman driven to the limits of endurance. He only turns his life - and his business - around by learning to think differently.

The message of the lecture is "Think Different!"

The question on the listener's mind is "How?"

From birth, your thoughts have been confined to the inside of your skull. Apart from those people cursed with the gift of telepathy, you have only ever experienced your own thoughts. Language gives us a glimpse into the thoughts of other people, and it is but a fleeting glimpse. Language cannot convey the rich experience of your inner world, and this leads to a great deal of misunderstanding.

Does your front door open in to the left, or in to the right? How do you know the answer to that question? Did you see your front door? Maybe you moved your arm as if opening your door and watched which way your arm moved. Ask your friends or colleagues this question and find out which they do - or maybe they do something different altogether.

What's the point of this? Well, watching how people recover memories is part of learning how people think. By learning how people think, you are learning how to motivate, influence and communicate far more effectively than ever before.

Don't be too concerned with profiles and categories. It doesn't really matter who is a what. It only matters that you understand the myriad, breathtaking ways that people's inner worlds can be constructed.

Here is a map.

You might easily think this map represents the whole world, yet it is really only a small part of it.

The words you choose to label this bit of the map are irrelevant.

What might be more important is knowing how that part fits into the complete map, and how learning about other people's maps can help you to reach your destination more easily.

If you don't know how big the map is, you'll forever believe that the part that you can see represents the whole world. This constrained thinking was prevalent until people started sailing across the oceans and discovering new lands. Almost every language on Earth uses a different string of letters to represent the same place. The English say England and the French say Angleterre. What's important is that we both know that the world is bigger than just England.

The more interpretations that you build into your map of the world, the more complete and useful it will become. This won't happen if you continually judge other people's maps as being wrong because they're different to yours. After all, two different maps can't both be right can they?

Think of a street map of London and a tube map of London. Which is right? If one is right, the other must be wrong! Of course not, and by using both you get twice the useful information. Think of maps of experience in the same way and you'll find things much easier.

How does this apply to learning how people think? Well, we won't dwell on all the different, proprietary psychometric profiling techniques. Labelling how people think is not always important. It is more important that you simply appreciate that there are different ways that people can think, and that other people think and process information differently than you do.

We all think in different ways, all of the time. You don't have to sit down and learn a new way to think - you are already capable of thinking in different ways to suit different occasions. You will typically have a preference, and that is what these test tools reveal.

Labelling someone as a Pragmatist, a Critical Parent, an ENFP or a Red-Blue is meaningless in itself.

I used to work with a marketing manager who would begin a meeting with suppliers by saying, "I'm an ESTJ so I'm very judgemental" and then go on to use that as an excuse for being rude and arrogant. Another huge British company put everyone in a particular group through a profiling exercise and then ran training courses to help people understand their profiles and interactions with other people. What happened was that all the people who hated each other now had a legitimate reason for the politics and back-biting, so relationships actually got worse as a result of people knowing they could never get on with people of certain types. You might say, "it was just implemented badly" whereas I would say, "People will adapt to make the situation useful to them, and that's exactly what happened."

Is there any point in labelling people with an arbitrary name for a thinking mode? Is it more useful that you learn the skills necessary to influence their thinking modes to support your desired outcome?

Some people insist that there is no such thing anyway, and some people are absolutely certain that their profiling method is "true" and that all the others are "wrong". What we can learn from this is that all of the published profiling tools are simply filters - ways of thinking about thinking. None of them is complete or true, they are each designed to filter a particular aspect of that strange thing that we call "personality". If you are looking for four different kinds of people, you'll find them everywhere and prove your model "true". If you look for 6 billion different kinds of people, you'll find those too. It's like they say - there are two kinds of people in the world - those who think there are two kinds of people and those who don't. For the most part, profiling in this context is about generalising, and that is only useful as a way of making data easier to understand. It doesn't make the data "true", it just makes it less complicated. Personally, I'm always generalising.

Profiling tools tell you more about the author or profiler's views of the world than about the people being profiled. This is a recognised problem with many psychometric tools termed 'type indicators'. These tools define a series of categories or types which a person is fitted into. Well, who decided that there are only a certain number of types of person? It's like saying that there are egg recipes, and there are potato recipes, and that's that. So where do we put Spanish omelette?

So, the challenge is not to "think different", but to recognise that you already can and do "think different". It's what you think about that makes the difference.

Concentrating on the problem itself tends to make the problem bigger. By focussing attention on it, people notice more about the problem, find more reasons and causes for it and make it more serious and immobile than it ever deserved to be.

This is a common situation during change management programs. By concentrating on the change itself, they lock the company inside it. The company is unable to enjoy the benefits of change because it's forever changing.

Don't think about the change. Start thinking about how things will be different. Remember that change is just what you perceive as difference over time. Since you know that everyone will perceive difference differently, you know that anything you think about change will be different to what everyone else thinks. If, instead, you concentrate on how you want things to be, the change becomes incidental.

Useful Ideas

In order to get the best out of this book, I suggest that you bear in mind a few thoughts:

Nothing is true

The concepts of true and false, right and wrong are of no use to us in solving organisational problems. It doesn't matter who is right. It doesn't matter which idea is true. The world is full of people telling you that their idea is 'right' and all the others are 'wrong'. These beliefs only lead to arguments because everyone is right, from their point of view. Everything is true, depending on what you believe.

Instead of words like 'true' and 'false' or 'good' and 'bad', think about ideas as being 'useful' or 'not useful'. You will then stop worrying about what is right and instead concentrate on what will get you the results that you want. You will also find that you can evaluate new ideas more easily as you no longer have to keep their owners happy. All ideas are valid, and they may or may not be useful in the current situation.

Usefulness must in turn relate to purpose. My computer, which I am feverishly typing away on right now, is very useful for writing books. It is utterly useless as an ornament in a fish tank. So a thing cannot be useful in itself, it must be useful for a purpose. If we don't know what something is supposed to do, we can't evaluate it. Let's take an underperforming salesperson. He's useless. Is he? What's his purpose? To do just enough work to not get fired? In which case he's doing a fine job. But if his purpose is to sell a certain quota of products and services then his behaviour is not fit for purpose, though that still doesn't mean that he is useless.

Once you accept that all ideas work, given the right context, you have to shift to a completely new evaluation criteria for deciding which idea to put into practice.

Nothing in this book is true either, it's all made up. Yet even though none of this is true, you might find that it's exactly the way things are. You might find that everything in this book works in the real world. The important point is that you will find it works by putting it into practice, you won't just take my word for it, and you won't confuse statistics and research with your own experience, which is far more important for you.

There are many other change management methodologies around, and a common problem with them is that their advocates try to convince you that their methods are true, so you end up with unrealistic expectations. All of these approaches are just generalised models of reality.

This is a very important point to bear in mind, so here it is again:

All models are generalised interpretations of reality. Whilst they may be useful, they are not true.

When a model aeroplane becomes complete and accurate enough to fly and carry passengers, it's not a model any more. It's an aeroplane. The corporate development world is full of the latest management, leadership, coaching, creativity and change models as if someone have finally found the answer – an answer that only they have been clever enough to discover, through their painstaking research and desire to make lots of money. You have to remember that a model is never a replacement for the real thing. A coaching model cannot be used to coach. I know that's an awful shock for the people who love their favourite model that they learned on the training course. Equally, a recipe, in itself, isn't enough to cook something.

One example is the popular GROW coaching model, which most people think was created by Sir John Whitmore but which seems to have been created by Graham Alexander. Coaching schools teach people to coach using the GROW process, but the problem is that a real coach would never use GROW. It's like saying that you can get from Manchester to London by going via Birmingham. Yes, you might go through Birmingham on the way, but if those are the only directions you give someone, they will quickly find that Manchester is not next door to Birmingham, they have to go through some other places too. And it depends on what you mean by 'through' and 'Birmingham'. Which parts of Birmingham? Which roads? Therefore, GROW may form part of a much bigger and richer map of a coaching interaction if we choose to look at the interaction in that way. These models are not actually 'true' in any real life situation, although they are useful for popularising an approach through an easy to remember and appropriate sounding acronym. I doubt if the FAIL model of coaching would have been as popular.

Language is itself a model of experience, so the word apple can create a very rich sensory experience inside your head, but you can't eat the word. The same goes for change models, organisational models and behavioural or personality models. The models are only useful when their generalised version of the world makes it possible for you to comprehend a complex situation. Aside from this, you should not rely on models to predict the future, as they only hold true in a generalised version of the future.

Chaos theory tells us that complex, iterative models are useless in predicting individual events. In English, this means that in any complex system we have no way of knowing how events will conspire against us. The further we look into the future, the more unreliable our predictions will be.

Therefore your survival depends on your ability to adapt, not your ability to predict. You cannot predict the future from a business theory, but you can learn to adapt to it.

Theories are a generalised model of the past. They cannot tell us anything useful about the future. As the people who look after our hard earned money are keen to remind us, "Past performance does not guarantee future results".

Conversely, the question in the minds of business leaders and shareholders is, "What does the future hold?"

When my daughters were born, all the doctors and nurses wanted to predict exactly what was going to happen. They told us to the day when the baby would arrive, how it would arrive, how big it would be and so on. Unfortunately, as that day got nearer, the baby had other plans and so the medical staff kept on revising their predictions. At no point did we need reassuring, yet the doctors acted as if their job was to know exactly what was going to happen.

Prior to the birth, the medical staff have no way of knowing what will happen, how big the baby will be or which way it will come out. However, once things start to happen, doctors and midwives come out of secret tunnels and respond quicker than a quick thing. Even when they don't know what's going to happen, they know exactly what to do once it does, and they do it even quicker than a really, really quick thing.

We were not reassured in the least by their random speculations. What reassured us was their capability to respond to any eventuality, and their clear focus on the well being of the baby and the mother to the exclusion of everything else.

When your shareholders or employees ask what will happen, you can be honest and say, "I have no idea, but when it does happen we'll be ready for it. For now, we'll focus on what's important".

So, don't worry too much about truth or accuracy, as both are highly subjective. Only concern yourself with what you want.

So much money is spent by companies trying to decide what is the 'right' thing to do that they never get round to doing anything. So much time is spent trying to find out what is 'true' that the question no longer matters.

Only do what works

Take action. Stop thinking and start doing, and take the trouble to notice if what you're doing is working. If it isn't, stop doing it.

Most of this book contains information that is useful or relevant for most people. If you find yourself reading something that isn't useful for you then stop reading it! Read something else instead!

If you find yourself trying harder and not getting any further, then consider that what you're doing isn't working and do something else. By doing the things that work, you will conserve all of your energy for being successful.

This might sound obvious, but you would be surprised how many people just carry on trying harder without ever trying something different. Many of these people make matters worse by trying too hard, and that becomes a problem all by itself.

It can be difficult to let go of a habit, so I suggest that you stop from time to time to ask yourself the following question: "Am I doing this because it's the right thing to do, or am I doing it because I'm doing it?"

Do not ask, "Will this work?", ask, "How will we make this work?"

You are already closer to your dreams than you think. If you ask whether something is possible, you must consider the possibility that it is not which means you don't have to dig any deeper. When you ask how it's possible, you have to explore more options in order to achieve the result. Asking how will lead to more creative solutions, because you're not giving people the option of a careless, easy, dismissive answer.

There is no substitute for knowing what you want.

It may be useful to point out the things that are wrong, the things that are missing, the things that don't work. Unless you know what you want instead, that information is academic at best. Knowing what you want can make your goals clear and easy to achieve.

Many people go through life knowing exactly what they don't want. That gives them no useful information for getting what they do want. If you're in any doubt, call a decorator and ask him to paint your bedroom 'not blue'.

Many companies talk about 'lack of focus' or of 'not having a clear strategy'. Knowing that you don't have these things is not useful. Take time to decide what it is you do want before you take action.

Words like 'focus' and 'strategy' are so vague that they are useless as a way of directing behaviour. You need to be very specific about what it is you want someone to do, which implies that you first have to know yourself. Often, companies and individuals are motivated to change by a situation that they do not want to stay in, so the incentive to change is there, but not the direction. Change motivated by moving away from something tends to be random, directionless and ultimately unhelpful. So, first acknowledge the situation and then ask, "What do we want instead?"

Finally, don't be shy about what you want. If it turns out to be something that you think other people might not like then hiding that will only make matters worse. So be honest – what's the worst that can happen? Are you afraid of getting what you wish for?

Remember – all of these ideas are neither true nor false. They are merely useful in helping the people in an organisation to change.

Wave functions

Do you know what this is?

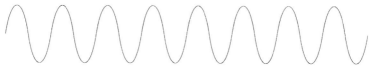

It's a wave. A wave is a concept used in physics to represent the flow of energy. If you were to look closely at a violin string, you would see it taking up this kind of shape when vibrating at a certain frequency - producing a tone that we can hear. So a wave represents a physical position of a medium over time. The violin string appears in a position at a single instant in time, but a microsecond later it will be somewhere else. We know that the string's position is limited by its flexibility, so at any moment in time we can't predict exactly where the string will be, we can only know the area that it will be in, and that area is a wave function.

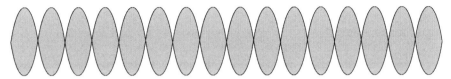

The wave function for a violin string is defined by the note being played, known as the string's vibration frequency.

For years, physicists talked about elementary particles like protons, neutrons and electrons. They behaved like particles. You could fire one electron at a phosphor screen and see a brief flash of light. When you fire enough electrons at a phosphor screen you get a reality TV program, or at least something of equal entertainment value. But then, in other experiments, they behaved like waves. So are they particles or waves?

Advances in our ability to observe on a smaller scale show that the assertion that an electron is a particle is true, or false, and saying that it is a wave is also true and false. A bit like saying that an elephant is big or small. Both true, depending on whether you're an ant or a blue whale.

Quantum physics sees an electron as a probability cloud, meaning that its component parts are somewhere within a space defined by its physical properties, but we can't say exactly where they are at a given moment in time. So an electron has a wave function. If we look at its wave function, we could treat it like a particle. If we want to treat it like a wave, we could pick an arbitrary path through the space that it occupies.

Why am I telling you this? The companies which train coaches and tell you that you have to stick to their proven method, and all the people who say you have to stick to the agenda, that you have to use GROW, or GONAD, or whatever their model is, are talking about wave functions.

I have always said that we can guarantee the end point or the route, not both. And when we're talking about something as complex as a system of people, that means we can guarantee the outcome or the process, not both. I can guarantee to get the client the result they want, but I don't know how I'll get there until I'm there. Or I can guarantee to use GROW, but I don't know what end the result will be.

If you look back at the sine wave, the points where the line crosses the zero axis are the points that we can predict given the frequency of the wave. These are called nodes. But once we have left the node, we have no idea where the energy will be until it reaches the next node. Where we go between those nodes is anyone's guess, within the range of routes that sit inside the wave function.

If we were defining a road journey, we could say with certainty that your journey would begin at your house and end at my house, at which point I would have to call the police and report a stalker. We couldn't say what route you would take. Some people will contest this by saying that you could give someone a prescribed route and be certain that they would end up at the right place, and this is a typical line of thinking in this example.

You see, the problem is twofold. Firstly, knowing that you will turn left on the High Street and right at Acacia Avenue is simply not good enough. Where exactly will the car be positioned? When exactly will you turn? How long will you wait at the traffic lights? None of these are important in an everyday sense, so we have learned to ignore information at this level of detail.

When we apply this thinking to the complexity of an organisation, typical consultants will think at a higher level of detail. Their thinking will be 'good enough'. They will give you a lovely proposal. For example, they might use Kotter's change model which is based on Lewin's research which goes back to 1951, and it looks like this:

All seems fine, doesn't it? It reminds me of the sales trainers at a telecoms company who taught the sales people the AARDVARK sales model. The first step was 'Access' which meant that the first thing you do is gain access to the CEO. Oh! Is that all I have to do? It's so obvious now you've said it. I'll just ring him up and tell him to buy something from me.

You'll notice a hint of sarcasm there, which is pretty much what all the sales people thought.

You see, the steps of AARDVARK, or the Kotter model, or any other model comprising steps is a series of nodes. In between those nodes, anything can happen.

We need to look at these models as a way of observing change, not as a way of making change happen. If you follow the series of steps above, you will not find it easy to implement culture change.

Critically, we need to look at these steps or nodes, not as instructions of what to do but instead as signposts for where we'll be, or even points at which we will check our current position according to a set of criteria. So we bumble along through our culture change program, and after a couple of months, we stop and look to see who seems to be taking charge, and we call those people our 'guiding coalition'. What usually happens is that the guiding coalition is chosen from influential managers who don't have any time for or interest in the project, and other staff who have too much time on their hands because they're not doing their jobs but who lack the skills or experience to actually make a difference. The result is a change project team which achieves nothing.

Later, instead of saying that we must now 'empower employees', we stop and take a look at who already is 'empowered', whatever that means.

In the 'Structures, Processes and Interfaces' chapter I'll tell you more about the idea of focusing where we start and end instead of how we get there in the context of business processes.

One of the main problems I find with the traditional approach to change is that the end result is actually hardly any different to the current culture. The change program makes the change seem much bigger and more significant than it actually is, and if you let people get on with it, you will find that they naturally evolve best practice anyway.

In reality, you don't actually want a change program. You don't even want a change, and you wouldn't know what to do with one if you had it. Change is not a thing, it is a difference in perception over time. Instead of concentrating on the change, concentrate on the end result. Specifically, concentrate on how you'll know when you've reached it.

So at the start of a coaching session or change project, we are sitting at a node, a fixed reference point. The client sets the frequency and we're then off on a journey until we get to the next node and can say with certainty where we are. Coaching models, like all models, are just models - scaled down representations. Like the diagram at the top of the simple sine wave, a violin string will never actually look like that because it's a 3 dimensional physical medium, and the waves can flow any way they like. It will look like the wave function, and our brains interpolate a simple sine wave because that's what we always saw on Tomorrow's World.

We can create a probability cloud, a wave function, where it is more likely that we will do some things rather than others, but we can't predict exactly what will happen until it does.

This is why Change Magic's primary focus is on the end result. Let's not try to predict how we're going to get there, because that prediction will inevitably be wrong when we look at it in sufficient detail for it to be useful. 'Turn left at the High Street' is not nearly enough detail for introducing change into a system as complex as a business, so above all else we have to keep our focus on the end result, look ahead and be positive.

Interference

If you remember your science lessons from school then you may remember interference, or Moiré patterns. Whenever two signals of different frequencies are mixed, an interference pattern emerges. With light, you see bands of dark and light. With sound waves, you hear a regular 'beat'. The pattern wasn't there in either original signal, it's there as a result of the interaction between the signals.

Neither signal 'caused' the interference, it's just there.

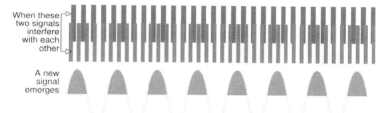

When these two signals interfere with each other

A new signal emerges

The pattern is there because of our sensory ability to detect it. We hear the beat because our ears work that way. We see the stripes because our eyes work that way. We notice the patterns that arise from the difference between the original signals. The new interference pattern is only a function of our sensory perception, it doesn't exist in itself.

You could say that when two sources of information are combined a third source is created which is different to the original two and totally unique. Neither original signal 'caused' the interference, it's just there.

Sometimes, we see things only because we look for them.

Catalysts

For those of you without a scientific or chemistry background, I should just explain what a catalyst is. Probably the most familiar application of a catalyst is in the catalytic converter of a car, which helps turn toxic carbon monoxide into slightly less toxic carbon dioxide.

A catalyst is a substance, often a precious metal, that accelerates a chemical reaction. It doesn't seem to take part in the reaction, although it may exchange parts of itself with the substances directly involved in the reaction on a second by second basis. If you look at a catalyst over a long period of time, it does not change. The catalyst can work by lowering the temperature necessary for a chemical reaction to take place. The reaction would happen naturally without the catalyst, it would just take much longer.

So, the interesting thing about a catalyst is that it doesn't appear to be involved in the reaction, yet it clearly plays a very important role in it. The catalyst may exchange parts of itself to help speed the reaction along, but it doesn't give anything away permanently. The catalyst is no different at the start of the reaction to at the end of it.

A catalyst accelerates change without becoming involved in it.

Possibility

Do you ever say that you *can't* do x, or y, or z, *because...*?

In fact, anything is possible, as long as you understand that it has a cost, a consequence and a commitment.

Cost

What you want to achieve has a cost, and it will probably cost more than money. The cost is the price you have to pay in order to get what you want, and the cost might include time, or something that you have to stop or give up.

Consequence

Whatever you achieve has a result; a consequence. It isn't good or bad, it's simply what happens as a result of you achieving an outcome. Whatever you do, no matter how well planned and well intentioned, will have consequences. You have to be prepared to live with those, because they are a strong indication of the nature of systemic change.

Commitment

In order to get what you want, you have to stick to it. You have to find a way or make a way. There's no point giving up half way. Too often, people in organisations will start working on something, start making a change, and then give up too soon when they think it isn't working. The strange thing is that it is working, it's just not doing what you expected as quickly as you would like. Maybe you weren't prepared for the cost? Or the consequences are not what you had anticipated? That's no reason to give up.

Anything is possible if you are prepared for the cost, consequence and commitment.

Dead Ends

Problems set a framework which constrains what you are able to think about. If I ask you to tell me your favourite colour, you are unlikely to answer "haddock" because I have framed your range of responses by my question. Questions are phrased using an interesting linguistic structure called a presupposition. In fact, all language contains presuppositions - they are the unspoken truths that make the language understandable. The question "What is your favourite colour?" presupposes that you know more than one colour and that you have a favourite.

Presuppositions are like a code book which allows us to communicate using short messages. I don't have to explain in detail what a cat and a mat are, and what sitting involves, I can use the short version and presuppose the rest.

You would be unlikely to answer 'haddock' because 'haddock' is not a linguistic label that we might associate with the sensory experience that we label 'colour'. In short, haddock and colour are not part of the same branch of our mental hierarchy.

What about 'coffee'? Or 'blueberry', or 'cinnamon', or 'cream'? They are in the same category as 'haddock' – edible things – as well as being labels we could use to describe colours, particularly if you're choosing a new colour to decorate your living room.

What about 'bumblebee'? It's a living creature, like a haddock, but also the name of a colour which I recently spotted in my local DIY shop.

You may have heard in the past that you can ask open or closed questions, and that some questions are "leading questions". Well, here's a surprise for you, so make sure you're sitting down. All questions are closed, and all questions are leading questions. It's a matter of how much they lead, and in what direction. Since your questions are going to lead people anyway, you might as well make them useful.

Sales people are taught on sales training courses to ask 'open' questions such as "tell me about your furniture requirements for the new office". This is still a closed question, because it defines the answer. It's broader than "do you want some chairs?", but the key to getting people to really open up does not lie only in the way you phrase the question.

Our everyday language contains presuppositions which are often interpreted by people unconsciously and randomly, leading to unexpected results. It's quite common to hear, "you look nice in blue" interpreted as an insult and, "oh, you're still here" interpreted as a confirmation of impending doom. A colleague of mine used to say things like, "I've been thinking about how we should reorganise ourselves in the team" which sent some of my other colleagues into frenzies of panic about the latest reorganisation that they knew nothing about.

I heard a great story from a dental nurse about parents who don't take their children to the dentist because they are scared themselves. One mother finally plucked up the courage to take her daughter to the dentist. The girl was naturally open minded and curious and, as she sat in the chair, her mother said, "don't worry……it won't hurt".

I can almost hear you thinking, "hang on….WHAT won't hurt?"

Because language is a simplified, distorted, shorthand version of what we are thinking, we leave out all the important stuff that must be true in order for the sentence to make sense. The mother probably made some awful picture in her head, crossed it out and told her daughter not to worry. That picture never existed in the girl's head until her mother put it there.

Sometimes, you end up telling people things that they don't need to know. Stop it immediately!

So, language can direct your attention to a particular subset of your overall experience and thereby constrain your ability to think freely. Since Change Magic requires that you have access to all of your experience and talent, you need to be able to recover yourself elegantly from the confines of problem thinking.

When you're locked into a particular pattern of behaviour, the question of the behaviour being an appropriate response just doesn't occur as it's outside of the framework of the problem. The behaviour has become part of the environment and the only question that remains is, "how hard do I need to do this to get results?" Of course, no frame of thinking is truly open because it's always constrained by the frame 'things that can be thought about by a human mind', however some frames are more open than others. We often refer to people as being 'open minded' or 'closed minded' when what we are really referring to is whether other people agree with us or not.

As we get more constrained by problem thinking, the frame that constrains our thoughts becomes smaller and smaller. When you start thinking about a problem, your end goal becomes fixed. You could continue trying to solve the problem without ever realising that the end goal is no longer important, or is no longer what you want, or has already been achieved by someone else.

So as you progress through a problem in this linear way, ruling out certain courses of action and devoting more energy to what you think will work, you become more and more constrained by the problem until you are unable to think of anything else. You have boxed yourself in to the problem, locked yourself into a cage and excluded any alternative ideas that may work more effectively.

There is always a lot of pressure on people in organisations to "think out of the box". It's perhaps reassuring to realise that you don't need to think out of the box. You just need a bigger box.

In order for you to solve problems efficiently, effectively and easily, you must open up your thinking, not allow it to be closed down. That may be easy for me to say, as I don't have your problems. That's very true and fortunately for you, you won't have your problems for long either.

Before we go on, I should explain what I mean by "efficiently, effectively and easily":

- Efficiently - using only the time and resources necessary to solve the problem

- Effectively - solving the problem so that it stays solved

- Easily - making it look effortless to a casual onlooker, to develop your reputation as a Change Magician

To continue opening up your thinking, here's another useful belief:

If what you're doing isn't working then do something else.

This is contrary to the popular belief that if what you're doing isn't working then you're either doing it wrong or you're not trying hard enough. Does speaking louder at a foreigner make your native language more comprehensible? Does a repetitive, circular argument get you any closer to an agreement?

Years ago, my brother bought my parents one of those realistic fake family history documents where they look your surname up on the Internet and then tell you your family history, coat of arms and motto. Apparently, our family motto is "We succeed against adversity". We joked that our family motto, according to our father's example, should be, "We succeed by hitting it repeatedly with a hammer and shouting 'Jesus wept!'"

I realise that this may be a dilemma for you, whenever you can't think about doing something else because you're too busy doing something that isn't working. Fortunately, there is a deceptively simple solution. You are only constrained by the problem when you're thinking about the problem.

People get used to doing things in a certain way, and when groups of people get together, they can get stuck in habits, long after they have forgotten why they started. Regular project meetings, for example, often take place because it's time for a meeting rather than because there's something to report on. Sometimes, this is valuable, because regular updates create a rhythm that can keep a project on track. Sometimes, it's less valuable.

I suggest that you begin every meeting with this question:

Are we doing this because it's the right thing to do, or are we doing it because we're doing it?

This page is not blank

Parts

Many nations recognise, in law, the rights and responsibilities of a company as if it were a person. The similarity does not end there.

When an entrepreneur starts a new company, he or she performs all the functions of that company. If he is starting a plumbing firm, he buys materials, fills out tax returns, visits the bank, finds new customers and occasionally does some plumbing.

As his business grows, he hires an office administrator, more plumbers, buyers, finance staff, sales people, marketing people, managers, and finally a board of directors. Not bad for a plumbing firm!

A company grows by adding people since there's too much going on for one person to cope with. The person who founded the company is capable of doing all of these jobs, he just doesn't have the time. We can say this because he performed all of these tasks when the company was small enough to allow him the time to do so.

Let's take the case of someone setting themselves up as an executive coach or consultant. Their skills might include:

- Empathic
- Flexible
- Questioning
- Gains trust
- Objective
- Feedback

It's important to add commercial and business skills to this list. We focus on the technical qualities of the coach, but the coach needs some other skills to get into a position to use their technical skills. First, the coach needs to be able to find clients and form professional relationships with them. Even a coach operating within a company with a 'captive audience' needs these skills – perhaps even more so, to overcome the resistance of buyers who believe they have no choice and will therefore resist it.

You could think of a coach's skills as operating in layers, with some skills needed before others can be employed.

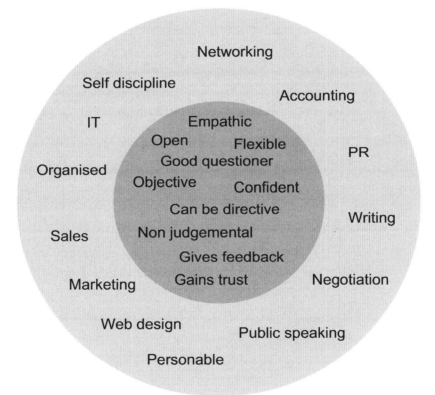

You'll recognise that there are skills in the outer layer which are common to anyone running a business, and this is a mindset that successful coaches have. Not all coaches, or people running businesses, have accounting or marketing skills, so some of these skills are often outsourced to people like accountants, lawyers, marketing consultants and so on.

In the way that we see small businesses grow, either the coach can focus on coaching and outsource the outer layer, or the coach can concentrate on building the business and outsource the inner layer, by hiring employees or associates. Both types of business model function well to give the business owner more of what he or she wants from it. A lot of coaches do a bit of both, outsourcing a function like accounting or web design and also working with a small number of associates or partners.

You could also think of people as being made up of parts. You have a creative part, a reflective part, a kind part, a mean part, an energetic part, a part that wants pizza and a part that wants to go to the pub - and so on.

A company is made up of many interdependent parts and a person is made up of many interdependent parts too.

There are many tried and tested models for working with personal coaching and change. The most useful models treat the person as a whole. They recognise that you cannot change part of a system without affecting the whole system. If you change part of a person, those changes propagate throughout the whole person.

Similarly, if you need to make changes in an organisation, you cannot change one part without that change having wide reaching effects throughout the organisation.

We can summarise this with a useful belief:

Changing one part of a system changes the whole system.

The changes may go unnoticed if they are neutral or beneficial. We only tend to notice the changes that occur elsewhere in the system if they have a detrimental effect on individuals. Remember, it is not companies who notice these things - it is people.

Many approaches to organisational problems attempt to seek out the cause of the problem and implement a 'cure'. After the management consultants have moved on to their next project, the employees are left to live with the long lasting effects of the 'cure' as they ripple throughout the organisation.

When you break the handle off your favourite mug, it's not a mug any more - it's a pen holder. Think of the mug as being part of a system which includes you, the mug and some hot tea or coffee. You can't pick up the mug when it's full of hot liquid any more, so the system breaks down. It's easy to say that the mug is still a mug, because the particular application means that we generalise our sensory experience. It still looks like a mug, therefore it must still be a mug. Taking this a step further, when you drop the mug on the floor and it smashes into pieces, is it still a mug? What about when it was a ball of clay in the factory? Was it a mug then? The thing that you call a mug only becomes a mug for a period of time. You are only you for a period of time. Time changes all things.

Our comprehension and use of language is interwoven with our entire experience, and software programmers have a hard time replicating it. You can teach a computer to recognise that a table is both "a table" and "wood". When you smash the table up, you know it's still wood, it's just not a table any more. Programmers can't teach computers this concept, and I think there's a simple point they're missing. Up to a certain point of smashing, people still think it's a table too. If you go down to your local council tip on a Sunday morning, you'll hear people say, "Look! There's a perfectly good coffee table that someone's thrown away. All it needs is three new legs and a new top".

At what point does an organisation change beyond recognition, and up to what point do you hang onto to the way things used to be, because things still look the same? All the company needs is a few more customers, and some new products, and some new employees, and it will be as good as new.

Change tools are readily available which treat a person as a balanced system - an ecology. They result in long lasting, positive change. They avoid the unforeseen side effects of a 'cure' which is only directed at the 'problem'. In short, they work, and they work quickly.

Just as there are many models for personal change, there are also many models for organisational change. What is wrong with these models is that they assume there is a problem that needs to be fixed. They assume that the problem lies with a particular function, part or process, and that by reorganising that function, everything will be better. It will not. Everything will be different, but we cannot predict that it will be better. In order to know that's it better, we have to make measurements and comparisons.

There's another reason that managers reorganise functions and teams in order to improve performance – because that's the only thing they have the power to change. They can't change the company's products or services, they can't change the market environment, they can't change other teams, they can't change corporate policies, so they do what they can with what they've got, and fiddle with job titles and responsibilities.

What is different about Change Magic is that it assumes the following as a useful belief:

Companies are not broken.

If companies were broken, they would no longer be companies. They would no longer be in business.

When working with people, it is useful to believe that they are not broken either. They already have what they need to make their own changes. When people have difficulty, it is usually because the resources they need are not available to them in the context of the problem. For example, someone who has no trouble managing conflict with a customer cannot use the same skill with their manager.

Think of the worst problem you have ever had. Were you 'broken' at the time? Did you need fixing? How could you move past this problem if you had been broken? If the problem once seemed impossible to solve, how did you deal with it? The answer is that you found a way that worked for you, and that the passage of time may have played a part in changing your perspective of the problem.

If we translate this into an organisational model, a company has all the resources necessary to make the changes it needs. It cannot be lacking any major parts, otherwise it would never have grown to its present size. Its parts must be working in some sort of balance, otherwise they would not be working at all. If it were broken, it would have no way to function without external intervention. Some sort of mechanic or engineer would have to fix it.

There are many government funded organisations that only survive because they are heavily subsidised or given grants. We could say that these businesses are on life support. If we pulled the plug, would they survive? And don't worry, I'm not talking about the social infrastructure of the country – I'm talking about businesses that are set up for the sole purpose of siphoning off funding that the government makes available for schemes such as careers advice and work placements. I've seen a couple of these organisations very close up, and what I found was that the people there wanted to 'sell' their services far more than anyone actually needed them.

When an organisation is surviving on life support, we might have to ask the tough question, "is it providing a service that people need?"

Assuming that you accept this for a moment, what can be the cause of organisational problems? We'll come on to this later. When working with individuals, another useful belief can be applied to the concept of 'parts'.

Every behaviour has a positive intention.

Positive doesn't necessarily mean good or morally acceptable. It simply means that every behaviour is motivated by an intention to achieve something. So, in this belief we have two meanings. Firstly, people don't waste energy for no reason. Secondly, people take action to get things, not to lose them. When people lose things it's a side effect – an accident. It's not the original intention.

Sometimes, a person may alternate between different patterns of behaviour, as if one part gains control, then another, then another. This is a very useful analogy for what happens when people try and fail to give up smoking or lose weight. Smoking has advantages, otherwise the

Parts

person would never have started. Therefore, if the person gives up smoking those advantages will be lost. If the person doesn't consider this, there will be a constant battle between the parts that benefit from different aspects of smoking or not smoking. A common side effect of smoking is state control, so some people smoke to calm their nerves. If this person gives up smoking, how will they control their emotional state? In a therapeutic context, this is known as secondary gain. In an organisational context, I've heard it called all sorts of names but it really comes down to the same thing - that habits or situations that we call "bad" and want to avoid have some positive benefits too. As a species, we can easily adapt to exploit these positive benefits, making it much harder to avoid the "bad" situation.

When these parts communicate effectively with each other or with some central control part, the person will be aware of all of their conflicting needs and will manage their time and resources effectively. Good dieters can manage their meals and still allow themselves treats. Organisations that have effective internal communication tend not to have much internal conflict.

When parts are not in communication with each other, problems arise because each part adopts behaviour which satisfies its own needs. Many dieters will fast for a while then go and indulge themselves, leading to another fast. Self employed consultants describe a 'feast and famine' market situation because they do not communicate with each other about the real, ongoing state of the market. Companies with poor internal communication generate conflicting information and appear to be badly coordinated. This is not malicious or intentional - it is simply the most reasonable way for each part to act when it has no or limited communication with other parts.

A behaviour can only be evaluated in comparison to its context and purpose.

A salesperson goes to a customer meeting, drinks coffee and chats for hours. At the end of the meeting, the commercial relationship is no further forwards, the customer has still not committed to buy anything. Is the salesperson ineffective? If his aim in the meeting was to close the deal then maybe, yes. However, if his purpose was to tie up the customer's valuable time in order to shut out a competitor then his behaviour was very effective. And if his meeting was in the Middle East or North Africa then his meeting was extremely effective. I once sat with an IT manager in the Office of the Presidency in Egypt for four hours drinking tea. Four hours. Until he finally told us why we were there.

The weirdest thing was that the reason for the meeting was for him to ask a technical question – a ridiculously simple question. A question which I didn't actually know the answer to. I used his phone to call the product manager in the UK who answered the question immediately. I passed the explanation onto the IT manager.

A waste of time? No, he was utterly delighted. I thought he would be disappointed that I couldn't answer the question, in fact he was even more impressed. An expert from the manufacturer had travelled all the way to Egypt to visit him, an expert so powerful that with a single phone call, he could command one of his minions to provide the necessary information. He didn't value what I knew, he valued who I knew.

So behaviour only makes sense when we also evaluate its purpose and the context within which it exists.

A part that is unaware of its relationship to other parts can only act in its own self interest.

If you thought you were the only person in a burning building, you would run for the door. If you knew there were other people in the building, you might behave differently.

Managers often complain about teams operating in 'silos', distinct from one another and even competing with each other. But if they are unable to communicate openly, what would you expect.

"Why" is the wrong question.

Asking 'why' will lead to reasons, justifications. Asking 'why' will not help solve the problem. There is no useful information in a person's motivation, because we can generalise all motivations into "whatever makes a person take action". Therefore, whatever the reason was, we can be certain that it was a good one.

Why do we ask why so much? I have a theory, as you might expect. As we grow up, one of the most important things we use language for is acquiring rules about the world. When you ask someone "why", the answer is expressed as beliefs or behavioural rules. When we ask "why" we are learning other people's behavioural rules. As a child, this is very important and is necessary for our survival in any society. As an adult, we have enough of our own rules without needing to learn other peoples'. In fact, as a business coach, the thing I spend most time on is getting people to forget rules that are no longer useful.

Asking "why" tells you absolutely nothing about real cause and effect, it only tells you about mental processes and behavioural rules. These are very useful things to know about, but for different reasons.

Knowing the cause of the problem will not help you to solve it.

Knowing why a thing motivates someone is not useful information. Only knowing how that person gets motivated will help you. Let's say the same thing in a different way. If you want to motivate someone, you will need to know how to motivate them. Knowing why you want to motivate them will not make it happen.

So, it's pointless to try and understand why a person did what they did. We only need to accept that they had a good reason for doing it. If you can't find the good reason it's either because you're not looking properly, or because you have different values to them. If you start to question and contend their justification for a particular decision then this is a good indication that your values do not match up. Fundamentally, the information and criteria that you gather to make a decision are different. When you say that they made the wrong decision, what you are really saying is "You made a decision, but you arrived at it in a different way to me. By not being able to read my mind, you have failed to meet my expectations".

How many past arguments would have been resolved more easily if you had said this instead of "You're wrong, that was a bad choice".

What is important, above all else is this: How do you help this person to do something different? Often, we get into a rut of behaviour and when we don't get our own way we just try harder and harder and end up feeling very frustrated.

~

Let's apply this whole group of new ideas to an organisational model. Every part of an organisation acts with a positive intention. That intention may not be immediately obvious to a casual observer, especially one with different values or motives.

For example, the sales department sabotages the marketing department's aims to launch new products by not talking to customers about them. Is their intention to harm the marketing department? No – that's a side effect.

Their intention is more likely to be to protect their own interests. They simply haven't given any thought to the way that their actions affect the marketing department – and why should they? These two parts are not connected well enough to permit the transfer of this kind of information.

Remember - A part that is unaware of its relationship to other parts can only act in its own self interest.

Therefore, the sales department will take action to preserve sales success. A new product might as well be a competitor's product because it takes the customer's attention away from what the salesman needs to sell. Therefore the sales department is acting in the best interests of the company, because it is unaware of its relationship with the other departments, who are also taking action in the best interests of the company.

In this example, the marketing department may be blamed for failing to bring a new product to market. They may in turn blame everyone else for obstructing them. Everyone does the wrong thing for the right reason. We tend to observe other people's actions and infer their intentions from what we observe, so based only on what they can observe, marketing would be right to think that everyone else is obstructing them. Whether they are right or wrong is, of course, irrelevant. The issue here is how to change the situation.

If the only time the sales and marketing people meet is at new product launches, then you can see how their distorted view of each others' roles is to be expected.

Remember that watching what someone does will not necessarily give you any information on how they do it. This also means that watching people and observing their behaviour gives you little insight into their mental processes. Firstly, they are not the same as yours, even for similar behaviour, so your own experience is largely irrelevant. Secondly, if you want to influence people's behaviour in order to effect change, you must influence those mental processes, not the behaviour itself.

Finally, in certain situations, enquiries and detailed investigations of what went wrong are very, very important. Where safety or mechanical processes or components are concerned, Change Magic is not an approach I would advise you to use. Where a problem is mechanical or procedural in nature and you want to stop the exact same problem from happening again, Change Magic will not help. Change Magic is not designed to help you find causes, only to help you get different results than you are getting now.

Change Magic works where the components of a business process have free will, are autonomous and communicate with each other freely. In other words, Change Magic is an approach that works well with people and not very well with machines.

On the other hand, many companies (and consultancies) try to apply business process methodologies to people, and that doesn't work either.

In this context, Change Magic can help you to easily introduce the new attitudes or procedures that are necessary in order to solve a mechanical problem. It's really just a simple case of using the right tool for the job.

Talking about tools, it's worth thinking for a moment about purpose. A screwdriver and a hammer can both do the same job, but they are not the same thing. A chisel can be used to hack up a lump of wood, in the hands of an amateur, or it can be used to create a beautiful piece of sculpture, if in the hands of a craftsman.

Actually, that's not entirely true, because that judgement requires us to compare the end results to some frame of reference and decide that one has more merit than the other, and that doesn't make much sense. If what I wanted was a hacked up lump of wood then the amateur's attempt is more fit for purpose. So I mention this because tools such as coaching tools and psychometric tools are not, in themselves, useful in the same way that a screwdriver is not, in itself, useful. It becomes useful when combined with a screw and someone to screw it. So any tool needs a purpose and an operator, and every part is a part of something else.

This sentence is

Growing Pains

What we typically see in organisations that grow in an organic way is something like 'growing pains'. There doesn't appear to be an obvious event such as a merger or acquisition, yet many issues are the same as those faced by organisations facing 'step change' as a result of a merger. Scaling a business puts strain on people, and those people will respond in whatever way they naturally and individually respond, which makes it inherently difficult to plan or provide a solution for.

Traditional change management approaches are designed to work with a change event such as a merger, where differences can be benchmarked between the two organisations and a roadmap put in place to integrate the two.

The merger date is known in advance and the board can set a timetable for business integration so that managers can prepare their teams. This makes it easier to provide an off the shelf solution for change management, business integration and people development programs.

When a business scales organically, we need a higher degree of individual focus, and a much greater capacity to handle the human dynamics of change within those individuals and their managers.

As businesses grow, pressure is typically exerted from the people who carry targets, often in a sales capacity, and is transmitted through the organisation. The different lines of pressure converge on a small number of people who then suffer from two simultaneous problems; greater focus on the importance of their role and greater demands on their time. Everyone is looking at them, and they have to perform better and faster.

Therefore, the simplest approach is to remove one of these problems. Traditionally, managers would do this by hiring more people or offloading work, either within the organisation or externally to an agency or outsourcing provider. Rarely are the sales people told to sell less.

By the way, this implies a scarcity mentality – we have to sell more while we can because it might all end tomorrow.

Essentially, the structure of many organisations is based on a risk/reward rule. The greater the risk, the greater the reward. If you are willing to carry a target, you get paid more. If you are happy to beaver away at the bottom of the pile, you get a smaller reward but lower risk. The problem with this comes when the workflow for each individual becomes real-time.

A manufacturing business would need the production people to make something for the sales people to sell. It wouldn't matter how fast the production people worked as long as there was a sufficient stock of products. Production and sales are disconnected in time.

In a bespoke manufacturing business, production and sales are connected in time. The sales person needs the specific product being built, so there needs to be a much closer relationship between sales and production, or through the whole supply chain.

One approach is to organise horizontally by team rather than vertically by function. The advantage is a close connection between the people who each play a part in serving the client. The disadvantage is that it can become parochial, so sharing resources is less likely to happen and you lose the benefits of mass production.

The options are fundamentally to structure the business for mass or bespoke production, depending on whether you need the different functional components to be directly connected to each other.

Coming back to the idea of growing pains, when companies grow organically, they suffer from all the same problems as are experienced during inorganic growth, but since there's no specific event causing the growth, it's hard to get managers to treat it seriously and devote resources to it.

If you were to compare your organisation now to how you want it to be in, say, 5 years' time, you would see a difference, I presume. And if you regarded that difference as a merger or acquisition, you could start planning for change. So how about that? Instead of letting people struggle on until something gives, plan to change.

Cloning is not growing

You started life as a single cell, and over time, that cell divided into two identical cells, then four, and so on. The DNA molecule which contains the instructions for building our bodies is very clever. No doubt you've seen the 'double helix' diagram, what you may not know is what happens when cells divide. The whole molecule unzips down the middle, leaving two long strands, just like the zip on your favourite cardigan or lounge suit. Each of these long strands then rebuilds a new 'other half' so that two identical DNA molecules are produced, which now contain complete instructions for building new cells. Well, mostly identical, apart from some copying errors. Sometimes, those copying errors result in the early demise of a cell, and sometimes they turn out quite well and are passed on to future generations of cells. Sometimes, those copying errors are passed on too prolifically, and we call the result 'cancer'.

Not only do you live in an evolving system, your body is evolving from the inside too, within your lifetime.

Since you start life as a single cell, how do you now have arms and legs and other useful parts? Why aren't you still nothing more than a big ball of identical cells? How did you end up with over 200 different types of cell in your body?

The answer is that at around 5 days after fertilisation, your cells began to differentiate. Your DNA contains the instructions to make all of the different cells in your body, and so different genes contain the instructions for different cells. Based on the chemicals that are present around the ball of cells, different DNA instructions are read, and different cells are produced. Amazingly, these cells fit together so that you, mostly, don't end up with a toenail growing out of your ear.

We could say that for the first five days of your life you are a clone, a ball of undifferentiated cells.

Does that remind you of our start-up company? What if our plumber grows his business by simply working with other plumbers? As soon as more than a few plumbers are working together, they start to hit problems. Who coordinates their diaries? Who allocated work to them? Who invoices customers? Who pays them? Very soon after the birth of the company, we need to see differentiation take place in order for that company to survive. Without differentiation, the plumbers will say, "What's the point of this? I might as well go back to working by myself".

Let's take an evolutionary leap forwards and look at larger companies. Some managers are control freaks. They believe that their team only functions because of their awesome leadership, and if their team fails, it's their team's fault. They forget to mention that, if they have a team of unskilled bozos working for them, that's kind of their fault too. Isn't it a manager's job to develop their team?

A need for control is a sign of an underlying insecurity. Your desk is probably not chained to the floor because you don't expect anyone to walk off with it. However, you might not leave your wallet lying around at work. We only secure the things that we think we might lose, and our perception of risk varies depending on the environment.

Our control freak manager is terrified of failure, so he thinks that the only way to ensure success is to keep a tight grip on operations. If only his team would do exactly what he told them to do, everything would be fine. When they don't do what he told them to do, they're stupid for not listening. And when they do exactly what he told them to do but it doesn't work, they're stupid for not doing it properly.

He can only blame his team for failure because the alternative is literally unthinkable – that he is a failure. A useless, worthless, unlovable, failure. An outcast, rejected from society. And no-one wants to feel like that, do they?

In a later chapter I'll talk about the problem of categorisation, which is essentially what has happened here. The manager has restricted his self-judgement into two poles; success and failure. He can't be a failure so he must succeed, at all costs.

We tend to grip something most tightly only when we realise we're about to lose it.

Often, especially in smaller, organically growing businesses, managers think that this 'tough guy' approach is actually what works. Of course, the employees know that's not true. What's happening is this: the boss thinks, "my company is successful because I'm a tough guy and I don't take any nonsense from anyone". We look for cause and effect in the world, and as a result we have rituals and lucky charms. The boss thinks that being a control freak is what makes the company successful, but the company is growing and he has long since run out of hours in the day that he can personally supervise everyone. So he has to take the uncomfortable step of hiring subordinate managers.

What does he do?

You know the answer – he hires clones. He hires people who are just like him. Only he can ensure success, but he can't physically do everything, so his next best option is to hire in his own image.

What he creates is a clique of like-minded middle managers who take the credit for success and blame their stupid team for failure.

This environment will typically have higher levels of staff turnover, stationery theft and unauthorised absence.

In other words, disengagement.

I am sure that you recognise this working environment.

Competency based interviewing processes are designed to prevent the problem of hiring people who are like you, but the reality is that most hiring managers will still hire who they like the look of, even within a competency framework, because the interview process is still almost entirely subjective.

"Can you tell me about me a time when you demonstrated leadership skills?"

"Yes, I remember once when I was an awesome leader and I was great. The end."

"Fabulous! When can you start?"

You would not be here, reading these words, if your cells had not begun to differentiate.

Differentiation enables you to multi-task, and it enables you to withstand injury or disease.

An undifferentiated company or team is at risk of failure from underperformance, simply because it has multiple people, looking over each others' shoulders, doing the same things. Duplication is inefficient, and inefficiency will ultimately be driven out of any business, either by the management consultants or by your customers and competitors. Or you. You could do it, too.

Information and Patterns

Since we're covering a lot of basics here, we should chat about information for a moment. It's a very fundamental idea, especially to someone who is interested in making change easy.

Just take a moment to look at this page – don't read every word yet, just look at the page overall. When you have done that, turn to any other page in this book. What differences do you notice?

Lots of scientists and philosophers have pondered the location of your personality. Is it in your brain? Your whole body? Perhaps it's even somewhere outside? Perhaps it exists only in the perceptions of the people who know you? Anyway, let's just pretend for a moment that what you regard as your 'personality' is a series of decisions and perceptions that emerge from activity in your brain. A scientist might observe that someone could lose an arm or a leg in an accident, or even have an organ like their heart transplanted and still retain their personality, whereas if they lose their head, their personality seems to disappear too.

Anyway, the famous Nobel prize winning physicist and all round cool dude, Richard Feynman, said something in one of his books that relates to our purposes here. In "What do you care what other people think?", he talks about the idea that the atoms in our brains are constantly decaying and being replaced. We know that our skin and blood, for example, are being replaced, but doctors tell us (probably incorrectly according to new research) that nerve tissue does not regenerate. But what Feynman is talking about is not the nerve cells but the atoms within them. The atoms are being replaced, yet the connections that represent our memories are still there. Your whole library of experiences, your very identity and personality reside, not in any physical place but as a pattern, an organisation of connections.

This is the fundamental idea that you need to understand – the difference between medium and information.

This page differs from the other one you looked at in that the physical medium is organised differently. It's made of the same kind of paper, it has the same kind of ink on it, and it probably has about the same amount of ink on it. And yet it is not the same. The difference does not lie in what the page is made of, it lies in how that material is organised. That organisation forms a pattern that is recognisable by a human, and that pattern conveys meaning. The information resides partly in the page and partly in your mind, where your pattern recognition "software" can be found.

Do you see how this is a vital idea for us to understand? Even the biggest and most challenging change is not really a change in medium, it is a change in information, a change in the way the medium is organised.

Here's another way to get your brain working on the idea. Butterflies and caterpillars are the same information, represented in different physical forms. When a caterpillar crawls into its chrysalis, it doesn't just grow wings, it dissolves into a chemical goo and reforms as a butterfly. It reduces back to the raw information from which both forms of the creature emerge.

Which came first, the chicken or the egg? Neither, because they are the same thing. They are both physical manifestations of the same data – the instructions carried within the chicken's DNA. The egg has a chicken in it, the chicken has an egg in it. Therefore, we should first ask "which chicken, and which egg?" Unless you mean "the egg" as a generic concept, in which case there were eggs on the planet long before there were things that we would recognise as chickens.

If you mean an egg that a chicken hatched from then clearly the egg came first. If you mean an egg that a female chicken laid then clearly the chicken came first. Except there was a time when the chicken wasn't a chicken – it was a ball of cells dividing. Some time later it would become a chicken, with an egg inside it.

If you mean any chicken and any egg then I'm afraid that's too general a question. Negotiators would call this a 'One Truck Contract'. In other words, you sign a contract to hire 'One Truck' but what you end up with is not the truck you saw when you signed the contract. It would be like buying a house – and not getting the one you looked at.

How does this relate to information? Because if we only look for material differences then we may be looking in the wrong place. The egg and the chicken are made using the same information, and represent the same information applied at different times. The body of the chicken didn't come from the egg – it came from the sunshine, the air, the water and the corn. The information to turn sunshine, air, water and corn into chicken is the thing we should be interested in.

We are, in part, pattern matching and meaning making machines. We are able to seek familiar patterns in randomness; faces in rocks, animals in clouds, familiar music and voices in a crowded room.

We don't look at a chicken and say, "There's a pile of sunshine, air, water and corn", even though the atoms are all the same, just arranged differently. We label the way that the components are organised, the pattern.

Here are some shapes for you to look at:

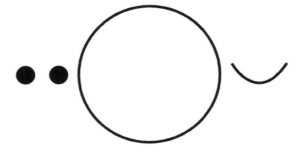

Do you notice anything familiar?

What if we take the same content, the same elements, and arrange them in a different pattern?

It's a Space Hopper! Or an engagement ring? Or a leaf's view of a slug?

Let's rearrange the components again:

It's tempting to say that what you see is different, yet what you're seeing is the same, and the changed relationships imply a new meaning. The shape you see arises from the pattern, not from the components. It's obvious when you think about it – what you see as an eye now still isn't an eye, it's still a black circle. In fact, it's not even a black circle, but now we're getting picky.

The two pages you looked at are the same, if we think generally about their physical construction. Yet the physical medium's organisation is very different, and that's where the information lies.

It's easy to look at the world around us and just label things as they "are" rather than how they "seem". This is a problem, because we then confuse things with their labels. You know that you can't eat a menu, yet some people act as if an agenda will guarantee a successful meeting. We can call a part of your body an arm, but that doesn't mean you could easily separate it from the rest of you – even accounting for a very vague definition of where your arm ends and the rest of you begins.

If you're with me so far, you're looking around you and thinking, "Ah! Of course! This explains so much!".

If you're still struggling to understand what this means, it's OK, it's a tricky thing to get a head around, because it's the same head that created this mess in the first place.

Before you learned to understand and use a symbolic language e.g. English or any other spoken or written language, you lived in a world of raw sensory information. You didn't need to label something as a lollipop to know it tasted good, and you didn't need to label something as cabbage to know that the best place for it was all over the kitchen floor.

As soon as you started building a map of the world outside of your senses, you started adding symbolic labels to that map. You learned what things are called, and you learned how to organise those labels into hierarchical categories. As you got older, you began to interact more directly with the map and less directly with the sensory world that it represents.

Many years ago, my then wife and I were driving in Spain and she was navigating. The road numbers on the map bore no relationship to the roads we were driving on. She was getting frustrated because we should have been on the N something and I was saying we were on the M something. She was looking at the map, confused, telling us what we should be seeing – a lake – and the road we should be on.

In Spain, the road numbers can, and do, change, and they might not be accurate anyway. But towns tend to be in the same place, so I suggested that rather than telling me the road numbers to look for, she should tell me the towns to head for, because I was fairly certain the Spanish government wouldn't have moved them. And finally I suggested that instead of telling us what we should be seeing, she look out of the window at the beautiful view.

Have you ever looked at a map in that way?

Maybe you have heard, "He's in a world of his own!"

The words you are seeing on this page only make sense to you because you have learned to identify patterns of ink on paper and you have learned to assemble those patterns into some kind of meaning.

If we change just one aspect of the physical medium, like this:

It becomes unintelligible

That says, "It becomes unintelligible". The information was the same, but the physical medium changed.

We can change it the other way, too:

By standing far enough away from the chicken and the egg, we can no longer tell the difference between them. By looking closely enough, we can no longer see the difference between them, or the sunshine, air, water and corn that they came from. The atoms look much the same. We can only form a collection of atoms into a pattern that we can call 'chicken' or 'egg' if we look from just the right distance.

Are you following? It means that you exist as a pattern of information. Everything you see and attach meaning to is a pattern of information. It isn't "good" or "bad" – it's a pattern that you have attached those labels to. Even the good and bad feelings that go along with those perceptions are labels that you have learned to attach to a particular set of nerve impulses. To others, you have attached the labels, "headache", "ice cream" and "love".

As soon as you start to see the world around you as the world within you – the world of labels attached to a map that are as arbitrary as Spanish road numbers – you can see how easy it is to change those labels and in doing so change the world. You might be thinking that changing the map doesn't change the world, but what if everyone has the same map? If they all make the same change in that map, and they start behaving as if that new map is correct, doesn't that change the world?

So you see, we create the world as we know it by projecting our map out onto it, so by making changes in those perceptions and projections, we begin to change the world itself, we make our wildest dreams come true, because as Willy Wonka said, "We are the music makers, and we are the dreamers of dreams".

These are not words, they are
    spaces where light isn't

Information and Patterns
101

Structures, Processes and Interfaces

Most organisations today are organised in some sort of hierarchy. Usually, people are grouped by similarity of job function but sometimes they are grouped by geography or by the type of customer that they work with. They might even be grouped together by a common interest such as a project and reorganised as new projects arrive.

When you look at a typical organisation chart, you'll see that everyone has a job title. Whilst these may sound descriptive, they're usually far from it. All sorts of people have job titles like consultant and executive, and so you could instead ask a question which the organisation chart does not answer for you - "What do all these people do?"

You will then find that some of the people in this organisation are doing jobs very similar to people in other parts of the organisation. People are administrating processes or managing other people in a number of places in the organisation. You might say that you only have one marketing department, or one customer service department so instead look at the behaviour of someone in the marketing department, and in particular, think about how their behaviour and skills are similar to those of people elsewhere in the organisation. Someone in marketing might process information, make decisions and talk to customers in much the same way as someone in customer service. The process is similar, yet the difference in content is what we notice most. We confuse what people *do* with what they *can* do.

When growing an organisation, it can be useful to think about whether you are adding capacity or capability. Whenever you add capacity (by hiring more sales people) you also add capability (because they all have different experiences and skills). Sometimes, that extra capability doesn't get fully utilised because the focus is only on capacity.

This replication of behaviours that we see in companies is something that we do not see reflected in individuals. You have evolved to be extremely energy efficient.

You have very few redundant components. Whilst you have two lungs, two kidneys etc. remember that under normal operation these organs load share - they each do half of the work. They do not overlap. One lung does not process air that the other has already processed.

With respect to the analogy of 'parts' that we have used to describe the organisation of your brain and your capabilities, there is again little overlap. You will find that you have many ways that you can achieve something, but that is not the same as overlap - it is what we call "behavioural flexibility". Overlap is when you have lots of competing activities that achieve the same result. Flexibility is when you have choice over those activities.

You are at your most powerful and potentially successful when you have behavioural flexibility. If you always drive to work and the car breaks down, you are stuck. Your behaviour is likely to be restricted by the frame of the problem - you might call the breakdown company, you might go and try starting the car again, you might kick it. If you are focussed on the outcome (getting to work) instead of the strategy (getting the car started) then you will have access to a huge repertoire of behaviour - walk, get the bus, call a taxi, phone a colleague, work from home, cycle, skateboard etc.

This behavioural flexibility is far more useful in helping you achieve your goal than focussing on the problem with the car.

Let's have a look at an organisation structured by job titles.

By focussing on what people actually do (and this is quite a simplification) we can start to understand how this organisation survives and we can also recognise some areas of overlap.

Overlap means wasted resource, time, money and increased frustration for the people involved in the overlap.

You may or may not already know this, but here's a little history of why the finance departments in many large companies are so big. In the old days, HR was called the Personnel Department. They hired people (which involved lots of paperwork), paid people and then fired people (which involved more paperwork) so originally, Personnel was a Finance function because Personnel was mainly concerned with payroll. It's only recently that companies have thought about developing people and caring for them. Back in the old days again, companies bought computers to do payroll and finance spreadsheets, so the IT department was originally the person in Finance who knew how to switch the computer on, and where to kick it when it broke down. Of course, all the administrators that a company needed in the old days were the ones who did payroll and finance paperwork, so they ended up in the Finance department too. Before desktop computers came along, every manager had a secretary who was responsible for making the tea and working the typewriter. Some companies had 'typing pools', huge rooms full of, mainly, women who knew how to work typewriters.

In those days, companies didn't really put much effort into marketing. They didn't have PR strategies or branding focus groups. The marketing people just asked customers whether they still liked beige and then told the factory to make more beige things. The sales people were totally separate to marketing because they just went door to door, asking if anyone wanted to buy beige things. The marketing people were responsible for finding out what customers might want, the sales people were responsible for making customers want whatever the company made. Or, more likely, the sales people were responsible for standing in the vicinity whenever a customer wanted to buy something, and for then buying the drinks afterwards. This situation is very different today, where there is much more alignment between sales and marketing and where the sales people only buy drinks if they really have to.

In any case, the point is that organisational structures are often rooted in ancient history, much like the sales peoples' expense accounts. The kind of organisational problems we see today often occur because organisations break one of the first rules of Change Magic - they do things because they are doing them, not because they're right.

Let's view the company organised by the order in which certain activities take place:

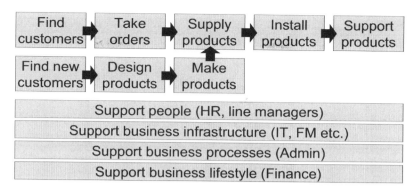

From this point of view, we end up with an approach which will be familiar to anyone who knows about supply chains or business process re-engineering.

Both of those methodologies are fine for dealing with areas of simple overlap or practical inefficiencies within a single part of the company. Neither of those approaches works well with the complex situations we are working with here. There's nothing specifically broken in the organisation, therefore an approach which seeks out problems is doomed to find them, fix them and cost a lot of money in the process.

The problems are, in a sense, caused by the belief that there is a problem. Have you noticed that itch yet? Or that ache in your leg? Or that noise that your car makes occasionally?

A business process approach also has a tendency to try to force departments or job functions into a supply chain that they may not fit into. As you can see, the IT department isn't actually part of the supply chain at all, or it's integral to it, depending on how you think about it. Here's a different way to think of a supply chain:

Functions like sales and manufacturing are links in the supply chain. Functions like IT, Finance and HR are the fabric of the chain itself.

Methodologies such as Business Process Re-engineering, TQM, TOC, Six Sigma etc. are filters. They are designed specifically to help you find a particular kind of problem and deal with it. Whether you knew you had this problem before or not, and whether this particular problem is relevant or not, you will now be overrun with consultants who can fix it for you.

WE HAD ONE OF THOSE TROUBLESHOOTERS IN.

HE WAS TROUBLE SO WE SHOT HIM . . .

Now, you may say "How can this be true? Sometimes, there is definitely a fault in a business process" and yes, that's true. A piece of paper may go to the wrong place and get lost and a customer order is not fulfilled. The question is, how does a persistent fault arise? In a machine, faults usually arise because a component breaks. Components break because of loads placed upon them. There are two possibilities - either the component has a flaw, or it was not designed to cope with the load placed upon it.

Electronic and mechanical components have a useful service life, during which their reliability can be predicted. At the beginning and end of a component's life, it is more likely to fail. At the start of its life, it will fail because of factors like manufacturing defects. At the end of its life, it will fail because of wear and tear.

Engineers represent a component's lifespan with a graph like this:

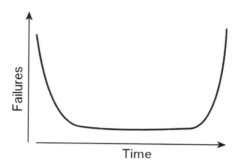

It's called a bathtub curve. Who says engineers have no sense of humour, eh? Anyway – a component is more likely to fail early in its life, like a person who is getting used to the job, or perhaps hasn't had their proper induction training. It is also more likely to fail at the end of its life, like a person who is getting bored, or whose skills are not being updated with new learning. In the middle there is a useful service life.

You may still be thinking that there are real, physical problems that must be analysed and processed. There was recently a TV program in which business owners are sent to work on the factory floor for a week. In one program, the CEO of a bakery went to work with the people on the production line. Time after time we saw the production process grind to a halt with causes ranging from machinery failure to a packaging machine having been installed incorrectly so that it had never worked properly. A gap between two parts of the machine meant that packs of buns fell into the gap and jammed the machine.

These are clearly physical, business process problems that you can only solve with the help of consultants. Not so. The maximum period of downtime was about a minute. In every case, the team of production staff fixed the problem and carried on. When the dough mixing machine broke, they took the dough out and mixed it by hand. They taped a piece of cardboard over the gap in the packaging machine. Clearly, there are other problems here - the gang of middle managers knew about certain problems and lied about them to the CEO. When challenged, they offered to set up working groups to look into the problems. In other words, they saw their job as insulating the boss from bad news and were just trying to keep the lid on long enough for someone else to sort it all out.

In the case of the packaging machine, the middle managers had spent a huge amount of money on a new machine that had never been set up properly. The original, functional machine sat next to it, switched off. The CEO asked the middle managers if they could just switch the old machine back on to maintain production, and they said they would set up a working party to look into it. A working party! To walk over to a machine and press 'start'!

You might be thinking that this would never happen in your business, so if you like, I'll come and point it out for you.

The point is this: When properly aligned and motivated, people will naturally resolve the most complex and potentially show stopping problems, all by themselves. When people are misaligned and demotivated, there's a major calamity whenever the photocopier is out of paper. Therefore the smooth running of any business is mostly down to people being left alone to sort problems out and only partly down to business processes. When people know what they need to do, they just get on and do it. They don't set up focus groups. They just get on with it.

When business processes don't 'work', you must consider the possibility that this is intentional, the people involved don't want it to work because that involve them having to do more work. Nothing happens by accident.

When business processes break after a long period of perfect operation, we might say that a person has made a mistake - either because of high workload or because they have a flaw. Perhaps they always make a certain mistake, but the system corrects for it under normal loading conditions.

When a particular business process gradually increases the load on the system over time, perhaps as a result of growth, there comes a specific moment when a component breaks due to excessive load - just like in a machine. Is it possible to predict this and change the component or the process before it breaks? In the case of machinery, this is called stress testing. Excessive load is simulated, although as far as the machine is concerned, the load is quite real.

Therefore, when stress testing a business process, the load must be real in order for the people involved to perform as they would in a high load situation.

Bear in mind that, up to a point. business processes may be inefficient but they do work. The issue here is one of overlap or failure caused by growth. If you address that situation then you will never need business process tools. I'm sure you already have a method for stress testing your business processes, and this is not the subject of this book. The problem under discussion here is the overlap between parts, not a fault in a single component.

Often, these process methodologies are based on fault finding procedures for production lines. They have evolved from procedures that were applied to mechanical components that did not have free will, were not creative and did not communicate with each other.

Most importantly, when we stress test machines, we do them no lasting harm. Yet we subject our people to real, ongoing stress, even though we know it's wrong, because they don't say, "enough is enough", and that stress causes permanent damage.

The root of the problem for our discussion lies in the communication between parts, not within the parts themselves. When these business processes contain people, the system becomes self correcting. Communication between the parts of the system allows for information about faults and potential problems to be shared. You don't really need to make this happen. You don't need an employee suggestion scheme - you just need to pay attention.

For example, if a customer tells you that it would be much easier for them to place orders if your order forms had a box for their reference number, just let the person who takes the order make the change. You don't need a change management project for this. The layout of the order form is totally arbitrary, it's only a way of gathering information from your customers. There are some pieces of information that you need, but aside from that, why make it a big deal? Just listen to the information and act on it straight away.

The people who 'own' your corporate documentation would recoil in horror at this suggestion. We can't go changing order forms willy-nilly! What if someone was unfamiliar with the new layout and didn't know what to write in the box marked "Name"? Heavens above!

Global corporations like to have harmonised business processes, but this is a complete waste of time. They acquire local businesses, merge them together, change their names, impose corporate processes and expect them all to operate as one. Which doesn't happen. Historically, it takes a complete generation of staff for a culture to settle in this way, meaning that all staff in the organisation have joined after the merger or acquisition.

The harmonisation of business processes following mergers and acquisitions is a massive cost to growing businesses, and it is an absolute waste of time. Here's why, using a telecommunications analogy.

The International Standards Organisation, back in the 1980s, realised that in order for global communication networks to grow, they had to be able to talk to each other. The old system involved, essentially, someone in a grass hut holding two telephones together. Today, you can dial a mobile number, anywhere in the world, be connected within a few seconds and enjoy the same connection quality as if they're in the next village to you, i.e. fairly awful.

In order to achieve this kind of interoperability between the hundreds of equipment manufacturers and disparate signalling systems, the ISO devised the 'Seven Layer Model' which defines not how a system should operate but how it should interface. Each manufacturer is free to figure out how their own technology should do its job, as long as it follows the basic rules to communicate with any other system. Shiny modern systems can then interface with creaky old systems, and calls can still be connected.

Communication standards define the minimum level of interoperability, so for example, your computer can connect to any wifi network in any coffee shop anywhere in the world. Some manufacturers develop features such as enhanced error correction, traffic management or security, but these features are only available if you use only equipment from that manufacturer, so you'll tend to see them in private, corporate networks rather than in public networks.

Moving this analogy back to our order form, we don't care how the customer facing staff take the customer's details as long as they use a standard interface for the next stage in the process. Maybe that standard order form is the shared interface, maybe it isn't. The point is that you don't need to harmonise processes, let each ecosystem do what it has evolved to do, and create interfaces that allow those ecosystems to interact efficiently.

In most jobs, certain things have to happen in a certain order, often because of physical and chemical processes which only work in one direction. The baker can't put the dough in the oven before he has mixed the ingredients. The sales person can't win the business before he's contacted the prospect.

In some jobs in some companies, people have much more flexibility about what they do between these points or nodes, and those are not the laid back companies with pool tables in their cool offices, they are the companies who carefully measure activity in order to improve results.

For example, let's consider the role of a sales person. Let's assume, for the moment, that the sales cycle looks like this:

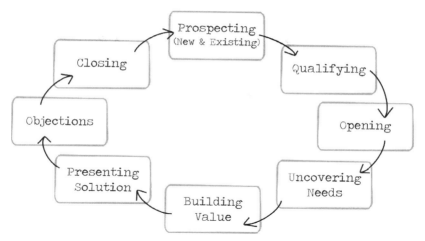

We know that if a sales person skips a step, he will create problems later on. If he doesn't 'Qualify' a lead, he'll waste time on unproductive meetings. If he doesn't 'Build value' then he'll get price objections later on.

Do we dictate exactly how the sales person builds value? Do we dictate the exact questions that she asks to qualify an opportunity? Some companies do. You can spot them using a simple test. If you feel like the sales person is reading from a script, then they probably are.

The building of value must be based on the prospect's specific needs, otherwise we're talking only about generic product features. The sales person is focused on what they want to sell, not what the customer wants to buy.

Instead of scripting the conversation so that any idiot can do it, we need to measure activity at the nodes of the cycle. How many prospects are currently at the Qualifying stage? How many at the Closing stage? By measuring this kind of activity, we end up with metrics such as the conversion rate, which tells us how efficiently our sales people are progressing projects through the sales cycle. If the conversion rate is low then there might be problems with the quality of leads, the qualification criteria, the skill of the sales person in uncovering needs and so on. Based on market conditions, we can create a baseline or benchmark for what we think our conversion rate should be, and if there's a deviation from that, we can find out why. If the rate drops, we know we have a problem to address. If it increases, we know that there's something we might be able to learn from and replicate.

Many small businesses measure their sales performance using only one metric – their bank balance. The problem is, by the time your bank balance falls, it's too late because your sales cycle needs a certain amount of time to complete.

By measuring activity at the nodes, you might find that in order to win one project, you need 10 at the 'Qualifying' stage, and for that, you need 20 at the 'Prospecting' stage. So if the sales person hasn't generated 20 new leads this month, you know that in 6 months time he won't be winning any orders.

Often, sales people are only measured on order value for this year, or quarter, or month, or week, or even day. The company doesn't care what they do as long as they win deals. This focus only on the 'successful' end result leads to disengagement and unethical sales behaviour. Someone told me recently that she received a call offering her two free mobile phones for her family or friends. She asked what the catch was, they sales person said there was no catch, it was to reward her loyalty. Out of curiosity she continued with the call, pressing the sales person on the issue of hidden costs, who eventually revealed that the 'free' phones would only cost £15 a month.

The sales person gets measured on sales, not net sales. The UK's distance selling regulations give customers a mandatory 14 day cooling off period. The scam works like this; the sales person lies in order to get a customer to order the phones who only then realises that they're not really free, so the customer returns them with no obligation. The sales person still measured a sale because returns aren't tracked back to their sales figures.

A few years ago, I worked with a company which delivers public sector contracts in the UK such as 'return to work' schemes, running Job Centres, training, managing benefits payments and so on. Each office had a monthly target to get job-seekers back into work, and each successful placement was called a 'start'. A typical target would be 25 starts in a month. The incentive for the job-seekers was that they would lose their unemployment benefits if they didn't at least look for a job. The company would place a job-seeker into a job, and the job-seeker would be kicked out after a couple of hours. They might have been lazy, disengaged or even drunk. By lunchtime, the job-seeker was back at the office, and the recruitment staff would place that job-seeker into another job that same afternoon. Again, the job-seeker would be kicked out after a couple of hours.

The net result was that the company failed to place this person into a job. However, the job-seeker had in fact started two jobs, so this counted as two starts. The company hit its targets, the job-seeker got their unemployment benefit, the government can say that it has helped so many thousands of people back into work, and everyone is happy. Everyone knows that the system is corrupt, but it benefits everyone, so that's OK.

When you give people targets, they will do the minimum necessary to hit the target.

And why do anything else? The Cheetah isn't trying to lap the Nürburgring in under 10 minutes, it's only trying to run just fast enough to trip up the slowest, weakest Gazelle.

If, instead, we measure activity at node points, at interfaces, make comparisons over time and look for ways to improve then we can create systemic change. We cannot set out to improve something, we can only set out to change the way we do it. If you set out to improve something then you are limiting your flexibility from the start. You will imagine what you think will work, dismiss out of hand what you can't imagine working, and pursue limited options. However, if you set out to change something and measure the effect of that change then your options are almost limitless. You have no way of predicting what will 'work' and what won't, so don't even try.

You cannot improve anything, you can only change it and then measure it

Millions of years ago, a bunch of cats didn't get together and create a working party to analyse the best ways to run faster. They didn't hire consultants. They didn't have a steering committee. They just changed slowly and randomly and let their customers decide which modifications worked and which didn't. Humans thrive in every climate on the planet. When the environment changed, we adapted to it by paying attention to the information that was all around us. We watched other animals and we learned the best places to find food or shelter. Some cultures still know where to find water in the desert by watching and paying attention.

Your business can adapt and thrive too, just by paying attention and letting people make the changes they need to make. If this doesn't fit with your quality policy, you may need to rewrite your quality policy.

In this context, quality does not mean producing something in the finest way possible – it means uniformity. If you are making cars with wobbly wheels, as long as all the wheels wobble you're conforming to quality standards.

You may also have seen business models based on the belief that everything should be organised around its value to the customer. This leads to vertically oriented organisations, whose hierarchy comes from customer focus rather than business process focus.

In a vertically oriented structure, you will often see different sales teams for transport, manufacturers, oil companies, telephone companies and so on. This presumes that the only people who need to understand the customer's business are sales people!

Everyone has a view as to whether horizontal or vertical structures are right and it is the subject of many other books.

My personal experience is that neither is right, they are both appropriate sometimes. This is based on many years of personal experience of seeing companies constantly re-organise from one to the other with no significant benefits arising from the change involved. As you will by now have realised, either structure is just a pattern that you might notice - just a model. Neither really exists. In all cases, there are people who talk to customers, and other people who support them. The organisational structure is just a pattern overlaid on the communication infrastructure of the organisation. It doesn't really exist at all, except as a result of us looking for it in order to draw nice organisational charts that make it look as if we're thinking about how to make the business run better.

Constant re-organisation is wasteful as it's based on the belief that the success of the company depends on who people work for and what their job titles and cost centres are.

Let's stop and think about that for a moment. We are saying that by reorganising a company we will improve its performance. By having parts of the organisation aligned with other parts we will make the company more productive. What we can learn from this is that people who constantly reorganise their companies are starting to get an intuition of what the problem is, but they don't know what to do about it. Therefore they constantly change the only thing that is within their power - the structure of the company.

Re-organisation is an example of a solution that's applied before any information has been gathered about the problem. It's also the favourite of many managers in large companies who essentially don't have the authority to do anything more useful.

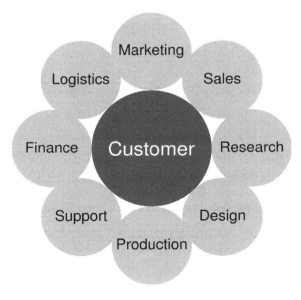

This metaphor of the customer at the heart of the business is a useful one for getting people in a large organisation to focus on what is important i.e. the person who pays the bills!

Often, the reality of this metaphor is that the sales people should define strategy for the organisation. Clearly that's not the answer either!

Here's another version of that same model, with a small variation. It recognises that the customer is not separate to the company - the customer is part of the company, part of a process.

The customer both generates the need for the company's products and is the receiver of them.

Is a customer's buying team part of their organisation or yours? Is an account team part of your organisation or your customer's?

So what's the conclusion here? Management consultants could come in, look at your business and suggest you restructure and reorganise, as they often do. This might fool you into thinking that organisational structure actually matters.

What reorganising aims to achieve is getting the 'right' structure so that people can be more effective, yet it is usually the very presence of a structure that prevents them from being effective. Structures tend to constrain communication, perhaps because of team meetings. The very meetings that managers hold in order to open communication also serve to restrict it.

I used to request cross-representation at team meetings, so someone from marketing always attends the sales meeting and vice versa. If you're going to hold a monthly or weekly team meeting, shouldn't you also hold a cross-company meeting on a similar schedule? Otherwise, you isolate teams from each other.

Here's another curious thing. Sales people are in a team. Marketing people are in a team. Designers are in a team. Managers are in a team. They each hold their own team meetings. And yet, if we look at the actual flow of business critical information, it flows sideways across that structure. The grouping of people by job title has placed barriers across the organisation. And why should all these people sit in different teams?

"So that it is easier to manage people, by grouping them in teams"

Of course, that presupposes they need managing. Perhaps we could structure the organisation purely around workflow. Here's an idea:

When you introduce a new product, organise anyone who is involved into a team. Don't waste time with dotted line responsibility back into their usual teams. This is their usual team, their only team. They spend all their time together.

But what if sales people sell more than one product? And don't the finance people need to sit across the organisation? And doesn't this then isolate products just as the traditional structure isolated roles?

Of course, any good plan has its ups and downs. The point is this: Don't organise teams based on the way you have always done it. Don't organise people so that they're easier to manage – that's analogous to putting them in cattle pens. Organise them so that you shorten business critical communication lines as much as possible. If getting products to your customers is business critical, shorten that line. If generating spreadsheets for internal circulation and disseminating information about the use of the coffee machines is business critical, shorten those communication lines.

Here's the important point: businesses don't fail because the strategy is wrong - the strategy is never wrong. Having a plan is a good thing, independent of what that plan contains. I know you're already thinking of examples to disprove that, and I'm not asking you to believe it anyway. The important thing for you to bear in mind is that business ideas don't fail because of the strategy; they fail because the execution of that strategy is inconsistent. You might say that sometimes the strategy can be misaligned with the market conditions, for example you can't sell snow to Eskimos. And yet people do indeed sell sand to Arabs and coals to the people of Newcastle, because they are able to understand and satisfy the needs of those customers.

As I said, you might point to the airline or supermarket price wars as being counter examples, to which I would respond that being cheaper is not a strategy, it is a reaction. If it were a strategy, their whole business structure would have been organised around reducing cost of sale, and the price war wouldn't have put them out of business. If the business is structured around the rule that an airline ticket costs $500 and the price war drives that down to $100, what do you think is going to happen? Reacting to your competitor's pace is always a bad idea. Surely you've read enough management books to know that by now?

No matter how sound and considered the strategy is, if its execution is inconsistent it will fail, or at least not turn out how you had imagined. Therefore, the structure of the business should be clear – organise people so that they execute the strategy with decision making lines that are as short as possible. Having short decision making lines speeds up decision making, which makes you responsive, which makes you adaptable, which makes you successful. Simple.

As I'll explain shortly, there is always a delay built into the feedback that we get from the outside world.

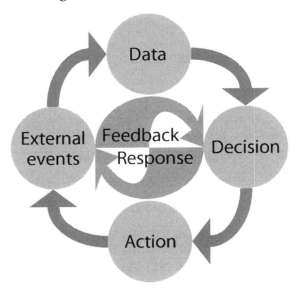

An organisation in the UK has about 70 people in the marketing department. They found that several layers of managers delayed decision making to the point where they were missing significant opportunities linked to current events. So many levels of management had to be involved in every decision that they never made a decision. Consequently, they got rid of all of their managers. They now have 70 people in one big, flat team.

When it comes to day to day marketing issues, anyone can take action within their area of responsibility. They can act fast because they have shortened the decision lines.

The problem they now have is that democracy has become a hindrance. Decisions that are about anything except for day to day marketing stuff are made by committee. When they buy services such as training for the department, all 70 people have to be involved in the decision to make sure that everyone's happy.

So what am I saying? That there's no such thing as the right organisational structure? Yes – because structure is an organisation of perception, not an organisation of reality. Go and ask anyone in any business if they only do what's in their job description. Ask them if they only get work through their manager. Ask them if they ever do something they shouldn't really be doing just because they think it's better for the customer.

I've just spent the morning in a bank, and the people I was with were saying that they all have to do bits of someone else's job, because those other people are lazy and don't do what they should be doing. Well what should they be doing that they're not because they're busy doing what someone else should be doing?

Do you think it might be a good idea to get rid of job descriptions, or at least move the boundaries? The situation is causing unnecessary frustration simply because of some words on a piece of paper called a job description which is in conflict with what these people believe is right for their customers.

Of course, job descriptions aren't really the problem, the problem is badly written job descriptions. A list of tasks is not a job description, that is a script. A good job description will define responsibilities and measurements, which equate to wave functions and nodes.

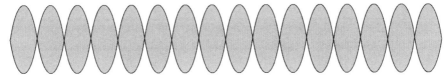

The job description essentially defines that within these boundaries you can do whatever you believe is right to arrive at these measurement points.

Properly written job descriptions are therefore vital in creating autonomy, which leads to increased engagement. Autonomy doesn't just mean that we are left to do our jobs, it also means that no-one else muscles in on our job, so job descriptions define distinct roles within an organisation, so that we don't have two people trying to do the same thing, which is ultimately demoralising for both of them.

We are a social species, so left to our own devices we will organise ourselves into some kind of structure. Some people took their particular need for a particular structure and imposed it on some other people who didn't care and called it an organisation, which is itself a collective noun or a nominalisation. We'll revisit these ideas later on, for now let me explain briefly.

A collective noun is a word to describe a group of something. And not just a group, the collective noun implies behaviour. A murder of crows, a shoal of fish and a crowd of football fans. An organisation of people? It implies a behaviour.

Nominalisations are verbs turned into nouns; stopped actions, still pictures, frozen moments in time. To organise – that's a verb, a moving process. An organisation – that's stuck, a thing.

As a social species, we will organise ourselves somehow. As a social species with a collective commercial purpose, we will find roles for ourselves, see stuff that needs doing and get on with it.

Business psychologists have observed human behaviour around roles in groups, and they have observed the processes of groups becoming established. Well, dogs sniff each other out, why would you be surprised that humans have the same social rituals? Go to any bar on a Friday evening to see mating rituals in action, and go to any job interview or business meeting to watch the same thing happening but without the sex and alcohol. Although, having said that, I have been to some interesting business meetings…

In large businesses, especially in regulated markets, rules and procedures dictate what people do. Except they don't. The rules and procedures dictate what people write down in reports, but those people still organise themselves around what they believe needs doing for who they think is the most important person.

This creates two structures, one appears in the organisation chart and relates to job titles. The other is informal and relates to lines of informal communication and influence.

I know that I should fill in these three forms to get a new pencil signed off by finance, but if I go straight to Fred and ask him over lunch I can save myself some time.

I know that I should fill out this documentation, but if I go to Sally and make her feel really guilty and stressed, she'll do it for me.

Influence is not all about cosy friendships and golf, you see.

Jim Holden wrote a book and created an approach to sales called "Powerbase Selling". Guess what the powerbase is? It's the real decision making hierarchy in a business rather than the one that's written in the organisational chart. And if you want to sell big complicated stuff, you have to understand it.

What I'm saying is that any business has a formal structure and an informal structure. The formal structure defines how things should work, the informal structure defines how things do work.

People, mostly, need a sense of purpose in what they're doing. When you hire good, well meaning people who need a sense of purpose, they will look for work that they believe is important. They will quickly learn the unspoken rules, because that's what we're all really good at, and they will get on with something that they think they should be doing. After some period of time, left to their own devices, they'll start to wonder if they're doing the right thing, and they'll ask someone who they think will be able to help them. And so if you leave people to their own devices, they figure things out for themselves. They figure out what it is you really want them to do, regardless of what their job description says.

So why bother with the formal structure at all? Instead of putting effort into getting people to go through the proper channels, overlay the proper channels onto the way that it really is. Sure, Fred and Sally end up doing all the work, but they do anyway! Isn't it better that you no longer have people who sit around doing nothing all day just to fill out your headcount budget?

It's all very well for everyone to go through Fred and Sally but as the business grows you need more of them, they can't do it all themselves. If you are hiring people who are generally amiable, then just by the laws of nature, their workload will spread out evenly as each person gravitates to the person they like best.

This isn't rocket science, you already know the score. The point I'm still making is that the way it is *is* the way it's supposed to be, not the other way round. Not least of all because it evolved that way, naturally, and evolution is an ongoing dance between an adaptable organism and its environment.

Perception

The world is not the way you think it is. There's the first surprise. This relates to the useful belief that nothing is true, in that nothing is the way it seems, and therefore it can only be true for you based on the way that you currently think the world is.

Here is the scary part. You create the world around you so that your beliefs are confirmed as true. You distort the world so that it seems exactly how you'd like it to be. If you don't like the way things are, remember that you made them that way.

When you walk into a meeting room, expecting to see confrontation, you will see the body language and feel the atmosphere. You will think, "I knew it". When someone else walks into the same room expecting a group of people to work together to resolve some thorny issues, they will see, hear and feel something very different.

Their eyes and ears will receive the same information as yours, but something will happen inside their minds that leads to a very different result, and this is the process of perception. We don't respond to what the world is, we respond to what it means.

You don't feel prickly or fuzzy because of a loved one's words. You feel that way because of what those words mean, because of what they imply. We respond to what people don't say rather than to what they do say. We read between the lines. We know what someone really meant to say, even if they didn't say it. And all of this we do so that people behave in the way we expect them to.

This has some very important and fundamental implications for what we're talking about here.

Do you recall that I said that people only notice what they notice? Their sensory filters remove anything that isn't worth noticing and it is thereby removed from the process of creating meaning.

Just last week, my mother said, "No one has been to visit me". Over the course of the next ten minutes, she told me that my brother had been the week before, and also Uncle Ron, and also my sister.

"So no one has been to visit you then?"

"No"

"No one except me, and Jeff, and Kathryn, and Ron"

"That's right"

So she excluded those minor details from her experience because they contradicted her belief, which in turn was driven by her need for me to feel sorry for the fact that no one ever visits her. Apart from everyone.

It's important to bear in mind that she isn't doing this consciously. Her unconscious is protecting its map of the world by only reporting information to her conscious mind that conforms to that map.

No doubt you have had similar conversations, and when you provided counter examples, you were told, "Yeah, but that doesn't count because…"

We literally build a world around our beliefs, and we are completely unaware of any information that may contradict them. Like a computer virus, our beliefs hide by masquerading as reality.

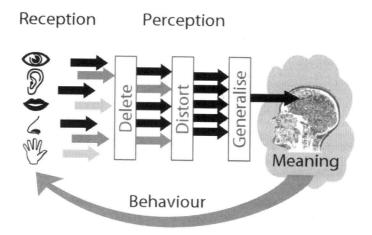

Reception   Perception

Delete   Distort   Generalise

Meaning

Behaviour

To make matters worse, our beliefs reprogram our sensory filters to confirm our beliefs, which in turn create meanings that lead to behaviour that perpetuates our beliefs.

Imagine that you are terrified of walking into rooms full of strangers. Consequently, you don't go to networking events. When you walk into a room with people in it who you don't know, you delete the ones who you do know, distort the ones who are looking at you out of interest into ones who are glaring at you and then see only a room of people either glaring at or ignoring you. You walk out of the room having talked to no one, and as a result you make no new contacts. This behaviour supports your belief that networking doesn't work for your business, because you never make any new contacts at networking events. You make this true by making sure you never talk to anyone!

Now imagine that you look forward to these events. Imagine that you're the kind of person who is naturally open minded and chatty. You don't go out of your way to meet people, you don't start talking to people on the train or anything like that, but in the right environment you do enjoy meeting a few new people.

When you walk into that same room, you see a few people glance in your direction as they naturally would when someone new arrives. Perhaps they're curious? Perhaps their current conversation is really boring and they're hoping you'll go over and rescue them? As you look around the room, you see a couple of people you recognise and make a mental note to say hello to them, although you don't want to get stuck with them as you're here to make new contacts. You get a drink, and a conversation starts up with a couple of people waiting to get coffee. At the end of the event, you walk out with a few new business cards in your pocket and you feel quite good that you have the ability to network and meet interesting new people. This behaviour supports your belief that networking does work for people who are prepared to make an effort.

Finally, imagine that you love meeting new people. For you, a networking event is a golden opportunity to expand your network because you know that the most important thing is the number of people who you are in contact with. Spreading your net wide means you have a far greater chance of meeting the few people who will be most valuable to you. When you walk into the room, your goal is to get a business card from everyone in there. You spend a few minutes with each person, gracefully closing the conversation or pulling in someone you had been talking to a few minutes before. By the end of the event, you have spoken to most people and have quite a handful of business cards. You go away to sort through them, follow up with a quick email saying how much you enjoyed meeting them and make a note to keep in touch with the ones who were most valuable to you. Your behaviour supports your belief that networking is the only way to develop your business, and it's something that you can be really good at if you relax and enjoy it.

Different beliefs drive three quite different patterns of behaviour within exactly the same physical environment.

I imagine you can see how this is relevant to change. People perceive their current situation in a certain way. Their sensory filters become accustomed to that. Their beliefs lead to their behaviour which tends to keep things the way they are. When someone comes along and says that things have to change, it means that something has to change in their perception, belief or behaviour.

Traditionally, companies will go straight for behaviour change. They will write out new business processes and print them on mugs and posters. They will offer incentives and bonuses. They will even punish non conformity through performance reviews and below average pay rises. Trying to change behaviour directly in this way is quite tricky, because people will be aware of the change and will be aware that what you want them to do is wrong, because it contradicts their perceptions and beliefs. This is exactly the approach that gets people all tied up in change management theory and resistance to change.

If, on the other hand, we focus on changing beliefs and perceptions, we will find that behaviour changes naturally, because the constant in the system will be maintained; namely that people always do what is 'right'.

Out of perceptions and beliefs, which is easiest to change?

We could say that changing perceptions will lead people to change beliefs which will change behaviour.

We could also say that changing beliefs will lead to a change in perception which will change behaviour.

An essential part of Change Magic is an approach to changing both perceptions and beliefs, depending on which is easier to get at in a given situation. Both will have the same effect – a change in the meaning derived from that situation and therefore a change in the behavioural response to that situation.

At no point do we need to worry about people's behaviours. If what they are doing works, then what they do will continue to work because it is appropriate to the situation. When the situation changes, their behaviour changes.

Remember that we can define culture as 'language + rules' and we could use the word 'rules' interchangeably with 'beliefs'. Therefore, we could define the culture of an organisation by mapping out people's beliefs, which is exactly what happens when we model a culture, which is something that I explain in my book 'Genius at Work'.

We could also therefore change the 'culture' by changing the rules or beliefs that define that culture. Traditional change management consultants think that changing beliefs is hard, so they don't try. Instead they introduce new processes and mission statements. In a way, printing posters with the organisation's new values is an attempt to change the language, which is part of the culture. But I would suggest that without changing the underlying beliefs, that change in language won't stick.

And since changing beliefs is easy for a Change Magician, we don't have to worry about printing posters.

This sentence is not true

Collecting Data

One of the most important 'head office' activities in a business seems to be turning data into a representation of business activity in the local office, store or supply chain.

Since every number in every system is gathered from an activity in the business, this involves turning those numbers back into a mental image of the original activities.

This is essentially the same process of deletion, distortion and generalisation that is present in human sensory perception where the stores or branches are analogous to the body and sensory organs, and the head office is analogous to the brain. Internal data capture and communication systems are analogous to the nervous system.

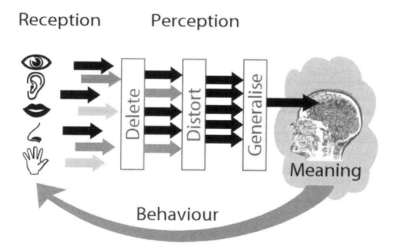

This is also similar to the process used to create the digital music that you'll find on your portable music player.

The infinitely variable original musical signal is coded as a series of numbers, which take up less storage space. Those numbers do not accurately define the original signal, but they're close enough that most people can't tell the difference, especially through tiny headphones in a noisy environment. The numbers are then converted back into an analogue signal which we perceive as music. Unless it's what your children listen to, in which case it's not music like we used to have in the old days, with a tune you could whistle to and lyrics that you could understand.

The recreated musical signal is not the same as the original, but most people can't tell the difference.

This metaphor is important for two reasons:

1. There is always a time delay between data, decision, action and feedback. Shortening this time enables higher quality feedback, more accurate behaviour and therefore better decisions that increase the organism's chances of survival.

2. The process of deletion, distortion and generalisation means that the organism responds, not to reality, but to an approximation of reality that is only as accurate as the organism's ability to handle the amount of data generated.

If we view an organisation as a large scale organism, we can see that the same two issues of information handling exist.

1. It's not the big that eat the small, it's the fast that eat the slow. Response time is critical in a changing environment.

2. Simplifying data makes it less accurate, so you can either hire more people to process more data, or invest in more IT systems to process more data, or base decisions on the most useful generalisation, accepting its limitations. Believing the data to be 'true' is probably the greatest risk of all.

A notable generalisation is that of a company's typical customer – a generalisation produced by market data which seems to drive decisions and strategy. The question is therefore not how to gather more data on more customers to create more accurate typical customers, but what the ideal customer will be in the future in order to achieve the business strategy. Whilst this is still a generalisation, it is one which guides organisational behaviour towards the future rather than into the past. In other words, if you accept that your market data is always out of date and inaccurate, you can either spend lots of time trying to gather more accurate data, or you can organise your behaviour around what you would like the market data to tell you.

For example, if you want to figure out if you would make money by selling product X, you might go and ask the finance people to do some analysis. You might find out who else sells X and how much money they make, you might find out what other products are available like X and how big the market for X is. They all seem like sensible questions, don't they? They sound like every company's market analysis approach. The problem? By the time you gather the data, it's already out of date.

Of course, if your competitors aren't selling X, or if they already have the market for X stitched up then that's valuable data, right? It saves you making a costly mistake.

Unfortunately, the most costly mistake is in making a decision based on what other people were doing last time you looked.

Our sensory organs respond to change. Press one of your fingers onto your hand with firm, constant pressure. After a few moments, your experience of the pressure fades as your nerves cease transmitting information, because there's nothing new to report.

And if that wasn't bad enough, not only do your nerves cease transmitting, your brain stops receiving. As something else distracts you, your ability to perceive becomes very selective. In extreme cases, you injure yourself in a dangerous or exciting situation and don't notice until later.

Our ability to perceive difference is the foundation of our ability to gather information. Difference is the basic unit of learning, because in order to learn, we must perceive difference. All of our sensory receptors and processing centres require change in order to activate, so we become desensitised or habituated to a stimulus when it doesn't change over time. Our senses don't work without difference. If there's no difference, then what we're experiencing is something we already have experienced. No difference = no learning.

Furthermore, since our point of reference is in the past, we tend to compare the future to the past and find the past to be better only because it is more familiar.

Feedback in an electronic system seeks to maintain the current state, and since feedback gathers information about what was created in the past, the system will tend to resist change.

Therefore, a useful approach is to change the perception of the current state in order to engage that feedback mechanism in using the future as the point of reference rather than the past.

Let's look at that another way. Let's compare the question, "Could we sell X?" to the question, "Could we redecorate our living room from green to blue?"

| Could we sell X? | > | Do we sell X now? | > No > | No, we couldn't |

You might be thinking, "But our market research is more accurate than that, because we have control groups, and proper trials and we collect data objectively"

| Could we paint our room blue? | > | Is it blue now? | > No > | No, we couldn't |

Strange, isn't it? So many businesses pride themselves on data collection that it would be unthinkable for that data to be misleading. After all, the data should accurately reflect reality, shouldn't it? And therein lies the problem. Data is not reality. Even reality isn't reality. As John Lennon said, "Reality leaves a lot to the imagination".

Data is a cut down, simplified, distorted and out of date approximation of reality, and if you base major decisions on that then your actions will never be quite what's needed to get you to where you want to be.

Some of the biggest companies in the world base key strategic decisions on historical data analysis. I know because I have worked for some of them, and seen the effects. Here's one example.

Company A wanted to find out if it could sell product X. The marketing people made a big list of all the manufacturers of X. They then set about a lengthy due diligence investigation to make sure they would make the right decision to work with a reputable supplier. After six months, they had still not approved a supplier, even though a customer was ready to take the service and.. wait for it... even though one of those suppliers already supplied product X to company A for its own internal use, serving about 100,000 users.

The marketing people concluded that there was no market for this product, even though they were amongst 100,000 people using it, every day, just in their company.

You want another? How about this:

Company A supplied a service to one company B, who added some other bits to it and sold a packaged service to its customers. Company A's sales people sold the service to company B and hit their sales targets. Meanwhile, company A failed to deliver the service, so company B couldn't deliver its service to its customers. Company A still insisted that company B pay the huge bill. This created cashflow problems that put company B out of business. The service people said that they were right not to provide the service after all, because company B was obviously not stable.

One more for luck: In the 1990s, mobile telephone operators said there was no future in text messaging because no business user would want to type a text message instead of making a call, and with messages limited to only 160 characters, what could you send that would be of any importance? In 2005, the SMS market in Europe alone was worth around €18Billion. 7.8 trillion SMS messages were sent in 2011, and in 2013, worldwide SMS revenue topped $150 billion. Around half of that is made up of messages that you receive not from other people but from robots! That's robots as in software at your bank mocking your balance, or from a courier company saying that they threw your parcel over your garden fence.

One of the side effects of SMS was that, because it only allowed 160 characters, it created a new form of language – txt me l8r m8, ruok, gr8 and so on.

If the mobile operators had instead asked, "How do we make money out of SMS?" then one answer might have been, "create a new shorthand language so that the 160 character limit isn't a problem". But since the question was, "Can we make money out of SMS?", the answer was, "No", because the answer was based on data gathered from the billing systems that gathered data from voice calls. If no-one was sending text messages, how could the data have answered the question?

And in any case, who would want to learn a whole new language, just to be able to send text messages when they can send an email? Ridiculous idea.

"I think there is a world market for maybe five computers" - Thomas Watson, founder of IBM, 1949

"Some day, every town in America will have one of these" - Alexander Graham Bell, speaking about the telephone.

"There is no reason anyone would want a computer in their home" - Ken Olsen, founder of Digital Equipment Corporation, 1977

"The Americans may have need of the telephone but we do not. We have plenty of messenger boys." Sir William Preece, chief engineer of the General Post Office

"It does not meet the fundamental technical requirements of a motorcar." Lord Rootes, on taking the Volkswagen factory and designs as war reparations in 1946. Over the next 58 years, more than 21 million Beetles were sold.

"Everything that can be invented has been invented." Charles Duell, Commissioner US Patent Office 1899

"This "telephone" has too many shortcomings to be seriously considered as a means of communication. The device is inherently of no value to us." Western Union internal memo, 1876

"Airplanes are interesting toys but of no military value." Marechal Foch, Professor of Strategy at the French War Studies College

"Louis Pasteur's theory of germs is ridiculous fiction." Pierre Pachet, Professor of Physiology at Toulouse, 1872

"The wireless music box has no imaginable commercial value. Who would pay for a message sent to nobody in particular?" David Sarnoff's associates in response to his urgings for investment in the radio in the 1920s

"We don't like their sound and guitar music is on the way out." Decca records rejects the Beatles,1962

"Who wants to hear actors talk?" HM Warner, Warner Brothers, 1927

"Who's been sleeping in my bed?" Daddy Bear

"Mind that bus – what bus – splat" Arnold J Rimmer

You might be thinking that I obviously have no understanding of business strategy or market data. You might be thinking that this is too simplistic a view, that you can't just base business decisions on where you want to be, you have to look at the facts.

Looking at the facts means looking back in time – always. Looking at your aspirations means looking forwards in time.

The past always seems safe, because you remember it and therefore you're certain of it. It might have been tough, even horrible, but at least it's behind you. The future, on the other hand, is always uncertain and must therefore be regarded with caution.

But what if, and you might think it's a big what if, you had more influence on the future than you thought possible? And what if everything you know about the past is a lie anyway? What if you had the ability to commit to a course of action and, in doing so, increase the chance of success?

Don't worry, I'm not about to get my crystals and scented candles out. History books list countless companies which were successful in spite of the rules and the data – Virgin (can't compete with the traditional airlines), Disney (no-one wants to go to a theme park), Nokia (should stick to making rubber boots) and so on. However, since I first wrote that, Nokia has disappeared from the market, acquired by Microsoft, chewed up and spat out. Market dominance is no guarantee of longevity.

Just remember that when someone says, "That won't work because…" they are telling you that it won't work in the future because (cause and effect) it didn't work in the past. If you didn't do it in the past, that's probably why it didn't work. Every new idea that becomes reality changes the world and the environment that makes new ideas possible, so it's not quite fair to say that something won't work, only that you don't know how to make it work, based on what you currently know.

Every significantly new invention, by definition, must create a new market for itself. Therefore, neither data nor dreams hold the answer; they merely reflect your attitude to risk.

"Will this work?" versus "How do we make this work?" - choose your question carefully.

Measuring Results

Research from the Association for Consumer Research on "Market Orientation and Customer Service" found a very strong connection between five links in the chain of events that connect service to profit:

However, other studies have found no significant connection between service and profit!

So is there a connection between service and profit or not?

The answer to this might be found in another research study from the University of Maryland, entitled, "Linkages between customer service, customer satisfaction and performance in the airline industry"

This research found that the connection between service and profit is 'non-linear', in other words, it's not a direct connection, where more customer service = more profit.

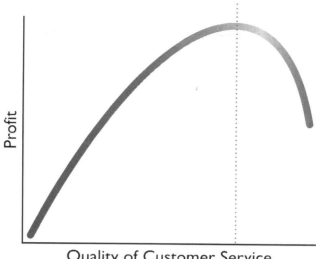

Quality of Customer Service

Better service leads to increased profits up to a certain point, and then it doesn't matter how much better your service is, your profits decline because the customer doesn't care and that extra service costs money.

Can you think of instances where a supplier did something that they thought was good for customer service, but which made absolutely no difference to you? Perhaps you were offered a discount when you didn't ask for one? Or you were given free drinks in a restaurant because of a delay in serving you, when you were actually glad of not being rushed? You're happy to take the discounts and free drinks, but they didn't make you a more loyal customer.

Research in 2013 from the Miller Heiman Research Institute found that companies that measured customer-focused behaviours had an average increase in profitability of 13% compared with other companies.

This performance gap increased to 25% when combined with measurements of sales practices.

Examples of the behaviours measured include:

- We consistently use a formal process for measuring customer satisfaction and loyalty

- Our salespeople have a solid understanding of our customers' business needs

- We clearly understand our customers' issues before we propose a solution

- We have relationships at the highest levels with all our most important accounts

- In an average week, our sales force definitely spends sufficient time with customers

Let's put these three pieces of information together.

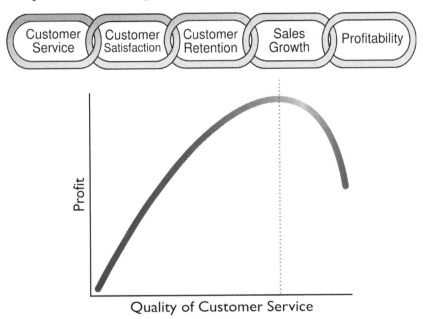

| Measure customer service behaviour › | 13% profit increase |
| Measure service and sales behaviour › | 25% profit increase |

It's very important to note that this is relative to the customer's expectations of service. The 'optimum service level' depends on the company's brand image which in turn creates those customer expectations. Clearly, Rolls Royce's customers expect something different than Casio's customers, but the same trade-off applies to both; once that optimum level is achieved, doing more for your customers adds no value at all, and may even be counter-productive on top of being a waste of time and money.

This connection between expectation and delivery could perhaps be summed up with:

Your customers are happiest when you do what you say you're going to do

Why is there a connection between measuring activity and improving results?

Perhaps because, when you measure people doing the right things, they tend to do more of those things, because once they know they're being measured, they want to excel.

Measuring activity also allows you to **give feedback before it's too late**!

What do you think happens when you measure activity and also give recognition for the right behaviours and results?

At the start of this chapter, I showed you a feedback diagram, represented as a cyclic communication flow within an organisation.

The faster the feedback, the more adaptable you are to your environment.

What's It All About?

As a species, we have evolved a tremendous capacity for processing sensory information and organising, storing and communicating it. We have developed a complex symbolic language that continuously evolves new components (new words, computer icons, logos etc.), new meaning (bad, cool etc.) and new formats (mobile text messaging, email, music etc.) to share our filtered sensory experience with other members of the species.

Part of the way that we resolve the incredible volume of sensory data into language is by equating our ongoing experience with stored, generalised experiences. This is the process by which we extract meaning from the events in our lives.

So, the human inclination to find meaning isn't just a recently developed need - it's an evolutionary demand, driven by the way that we code and label experience in order to generate language.

Sometimes, our ability to instantly find meaning in events is a conscious process, so we are aware that it is happening. More often, it is an unconscious process and so in a changing environment, it is the meaning that we must change, rather than the event or experience itself.

Something that you may hear very often in office gossip is that someone is being favoured by "the company". If you ask, "how do you know?" you may get an answer like, "because they've just moved the photocopier".

The film 'Office Space' is a lovely observation of the minutiae of office life, with poor old Milton reaching the end of the tether after his desk is moved, one too many times.

Moving the photocopier is just one of a sequence of events that proves that the company is making changes that favour a particular employee, such as taking the tomato soup option out of the vending machine, or making Fridays a casual dress day.

Maybe these changes are an example of favouritism? Some people get discouraged by this, others figure out how to become a favourite. It's only a matter of perspective.

In between our sensory organs and our conscious awareness lies a filter that works in three ways. It deletes by simply ignoring information that is not relevant, such as the sound of a telephone ringing when you're lost in a book. It distorts information so that it becomes more familiar, so a restaurant where you spent a romantic evening doesn't seem as good when you go back. Finally, it generalises information to make it less complicated, like when people say, "you're always doing that".

Here's the process by which we all create meaning from the patterns that we notice:

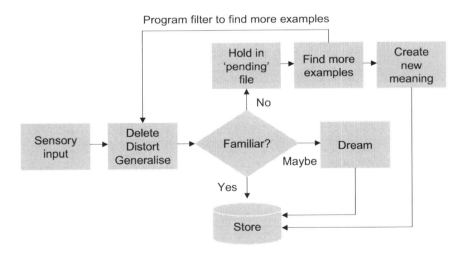

You might recognise this as the process of 'confirmation bias', a phrase which has become more widely used in recent years.

So, there are a number of elements that will cause you a problem if you try to directly challenge the meaning by saying, "no, x doesn't mean y". Firstly, the sensory data has been filtered and now only represents a simple, diminished version of the real sequence of events. Secondly, each example that supports the meaning strengthens it and also programs the filter so that the person notices more and more examples. This is what happens when you buy something that no-one else has, only to then find that everyone has one. You can use this same process to be more successful by programming the filter to select opportunities for you to achieve your goals. Thirdly, as the new meaning gets stronger, it embeds itself not just into long term memory but into the person's belief system. The new meaning becomes "true" at the same level as "the sky is blue" or "I do a good job".

How long will someone hold a suspicion in their mental 'pending file' before it is deemed to have been proven? How many examples do they need to verify their suspicion? The answer is that there is an answer, and that it's unique to each person. If you know someone who always gets three quotes before buying something, or who will always take two weeks to make a decision then you know the answer for that person.

So, if you try to challenge the person's interpretation of the situation directly, they are quite likely to say, "I don't believe you because....." and then they'll list why their interpretation is true. Their reasons will be so convincing, you may even start to believe them yourself. Why is this?

Because they didn't sit down and write those reasons, they were created by a mental processing system. As they list their reasons, they sound plausible because they are expressed in a form of language that feels comfortable to your brain. It's hard to resist this, so the good news is that you can use this to your advantage. If other people can do this to you randomly and unconsciously, it must follow that you can learn to do it consistently and consciously. There are examples of how you can do this throughout the book, but you should pay particular attention to the chapter on logical levels.

Sleep is a very important part of the problem solving and learning that you do each day. In the past, psychoanalysts tried to assign meaning to dreams and thought they were an expression of subconscious, suppressed desires. Your dreams don't mean anything, they're just part of a learning process. Learn to use sleep as an important resource.

All too often, people in companies sit around meeting room tables trying to force decisions. They say things like, "this is really important, we have to make a decision before we go home". If a decision is really that important then it's worth sleeping on.

And if you are going to sleep on it, remember the old Polish saying, "Sleep faster, we need the pillows".

I thought that putting messages on
these blank pages was a good idea
when I started, now I'm not so sure

Failure

It's inevitable that we have to talk about failure, because the fear of failure is a huge motivator for people in organisations. So much so that the pressure of targets, deadlines, shareholder returns and regulatory investigations creates stress, stress related illnesses and the early demise of people who are, apparently, your greatest asset.

In a recent coaching session with the manager of about 80 staff in a large American company, my client said that he has never failed to hit a target. He told me that after 6 months in his role with coaching support and adopting my advice to delegate everything, build a team culture and invest in internal development, his shipping figures have gone from -24% to +19% of target, and his orders have gone from -9% to +2% of target. A very impressive turn round. However, he told me that his boss will not allow him to fail. At the end of every quarter, my client will do anything to hit target, and so far, he has.

We established that he is motivated by a fear of failure, and if his boss has figured this out then his boss could be manipulating him to hit target by playing on those fears. This would be immoral, manipulative and just plain wrong. In spite of all this, unethical people will identify your fears and use them to exploit you.

I asked my client if he thought that his boss was manipulating him to make sure he always delivers good results, which in turn make his boss look good.

"Yes!", he replied.

So his plan is to intentionally fail at the end of the next financial quarter. Just a little bit, to see what happens.

The problem with the avoidance of failure is that it's based on utterly arbitrary definitions and targets. Why should a sales target be £1million? Aren't targets calculated using market and pricing data? Aren't forecasts based on intelligent analysis? For targets to be such nice, round numbers, someone, somewhere is sticking a wet finger in the air, and that is simply not fair. If you're going to make up my target, I'll make up my sales data.

We focus on and reward success. Exam grades, university places, job hunting, promotions, pay rises, cars, houses, consumer electronics, we are attached to success, but you must understand that success is extremely dangerous.

Self help gurus are fond of saying, "There is no failure only feedback", which is itself a corruption of a therapeutic concept that all results that a person achieves are valuable, whether they seem to get the person closer towards their goal or not. Remember, a servo control system, which is what you are, needs feedback in order to achieve its goals. When you are 'successful', there's no feedback, because what you did was exactly what you thought you would do, and the only way that you can do exactly what you thought you would do, that things can turn out exactly as you planned, is if you are playing so far within your limits that you have no chance of failure.

So if we're going to say that there is no failure, only feedback, then we must also accept that there is no success either, only feedback.

I'd even suggest this: Failure is the ONLY feedback.

We all present an image to the world, an image of perfection, of how we want to be seen and judged by others. Even someone who says, "I don't care what other people think of me" is presenting an image.

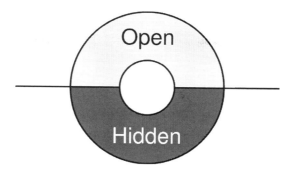

We believe that the image that we present is all that people see, our 'light' side, and that we are very good at hiding our faults, mistakes, bad habits and evil thoughts from others, our 'dark' side.

The reality is that everyone around us can see both sides, all of the time. So how is it possible that people don't run away, don't avoid you because of your terrible dark side?

It's because they don't care. They have their own problems to think about.

In our dark side, we hide our fears and insecurities. We hide the mistakes we make and the aspects of ourselves that we think of as bad or negative, but we only judge ourselves this way because we have learned to. In reality, behaviour is neither good nor bad, it is only effective at getting the result, or not.

Without mistakes and failures, we have no source of feedback to correct ourselves. If you're trying to navigate in the car, what happens when you take a wrong turn? Do you stop immediately and refuse to drive any further? Do you blame someone else for giving you the wrong directions? Do you blame the road signs? Or do you simply turn around and correct your mistake?

Feedback is neutral, it's just information. We attach judgement and meaning to the feedback, so we learn to seek out 'good' feedback and avoid 'bad' feedback. We learn that feedback is a judgement on our value as a person.

Of course, this is ridiculous. When you were a child, you didn't know any better, but you're not a child any more. Whether you see feedback as a criticism, or praise, or a weakness, or a strength, what you are actually doing is distorting the feedback. You are changing the feedback so that it confirms what you already know. If you believe that you are weak, you will hear feedback as a weakness. If you believe that you are strong, you will hear feedback as a strength. It is neither, and the only danger is in the judgement, the distortion.

Our brains, like many of the automated systems that you provide to your customers, are 'servo systems', they direct behaviour towards a goal. Imagine a toy car which has a very simply arrangement of a motor, wheels and some kind of sensor to direct it towards a target. The car's guidance system doesn't need to be accurate, it only needs to keep focus on the target. The car's path will look something like this:

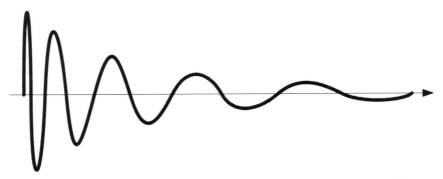

The car is 'off course' for most of its journey, yet it still gets there. That's what your behaviour is like as you direct yourself towards your goals. Sometimes, it will feel like you're moving backwards, but that doesn't matter. What matters is that you are moving.

Of course, we don't simply head towards our goals, because we have other forces that act upon us. Most of us can't head off to a tropical island whenever we want, we have jobs to do and bills to pay, so we find a way to balance our lives. If we don't weigh up the different aspects of every goal, we ignore some of the factors that could lead to failure, with the result that we don't end up where we wanted to be.

The past and the future are illusions, tricks that we play on ourselves to explain where we are right now and to give us a sense of control over our lives. The past and future are lies. We change the past to suit ourselves, and we pretend that the future will definitely happen, just because we think it will. The only truth is in the present moment, and what you can do right now.

Remember...

Failure is the ONLY feedback.

Companies

Before we go any further, it's just worth pointing out a simple yet often overlooked fact about companies.

Companies don't exist.

We take some pieces of paper filed in a vault somewhere, some magnetic patterns in a computer and a building with a word written on it and we call this collective hallucination "a company".

A company may be a legal entity, but it is not a physical entity – it is an organised pattern of information.

Why mention this? Because we can't blame companies for anything. We can only blame people.

When someone says, "the company wants me to do this", then ask, "Who wants you to do that?"

When someone says, "the company says this", then ask, "Who says that?"

You get the point. Companies don't make decisions, and neither do people. A person makes a decision which other people may or may not then agree with. A company does not support an idea, people do.

You can't change a company, but you can change what a person does. When you change the behaviour of a number of people, and that change in behaviour affects the measurable outputs of a business, that's Change Magic.

We all hear phrases such as 'culture change' or 'reorganisation' or 'restructuring', but in every case what it boils down to is changing what people do.

Culture change is an interesting example, as people involved in culture change are often heard to say, "it's not what people do, it's how they do it that's important". So, as an example, the customer service people may operate a functional customer helpdesk, but they don't look happy while they're doing it. We just need to clear up this simple mistake right now. In culture change situations, you are not changing the way that people work, you are again changing behaviour. Talking to a customer with a smile is a fundamentally different behaviour to talking to a customer with a scowl. It's not just a different 'way' of talking to a customer, it is fundamentally different and is driven by totally different mental processes. Culture change is just another euphemism for behavioural change.

Human beings like to complicate things. They like to say that change is difficult and takes a long time, because they don't want to admit that they could themselves have changed a long time ago. Most of all, they want to maintain their excuses for not doing what they're supposed to do by making simple things complicated.

You can avoid falling into this trap simply by being honest with people. What makes this hard for managers is that they rarely, if ever, tell people what their jobs are. Receptionists are told to answer the telephone and make sure people sign the visitor's book, yet that's not their job! The job of a receptionist is to embody the company's brand image and to know everyone in the company and how they can help the people who call and visit. Take a look at your own job description - did anyone ever tell you what you were really supposed to do, or did you have to learn that by trial and error?

Managers don't like to tell people what their jobs are because they don't want people to refuse to do things that aren't in the job description. Without trust, people will be awkward regardless of their job description. With trust, your staff will do almost anything for you.

One of my clients has the vaguest job descriptions that you can imagine, comprising a list of tasks in a retail store. Tasks are not the same as responsibilities. Consequently, staff only worked when they were being watched, because all store activities were the manager's responsibility.

A manager's primary purpose is to delegate responsibility, so a manager who doesn't delegate everything is failing in their duty.

Later on, we'll be looking at the importance of good management practices as well as ways to influence how people think so that they choose to change what they do.

Think of the word 'company' as a collective noun meaning "a group of people working together for mutual, commercial benefit".

Systems

A system is a collection of interconnected parts that together produce a specific outcome. Every system from the Amazon Rainforest to your washing machine has the same basic structure:

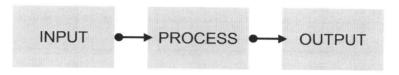

So that's quite easy. You are a system. Your inputs include food, oxygen and water and your outputs include heat, motion and children. You could call your process "Living".

Most systems are highly complex, in that the overall system has many inputs and many outputs, not all of which are obvious. Most importantly, man made systems such as washing machines and companies seem to generate many new outputs which are not part of the original design.

A washing machine could have the following process structure:

The designers of the machine intend the output to be clean clothes, but some other outputs are unavoidable (dirty water) and others are unintentional (vibration). The output of heat is something the designers try to design out of the system, as excess heat production equates to inefficiency.

As a process, the washing machine uses heat, detergent and motion to transfer dirt from clothes to water.

What about companies? Well, we could spend the next 100 pages listing all the inputs and outputs of a typical company, so here are a few to illustrate the point:

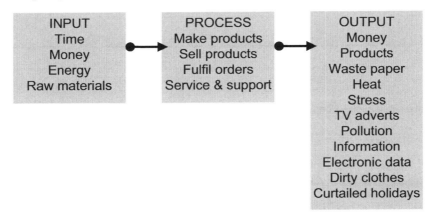

So, in the process of setting up a company to make washing machines, print money or sell furniture we end up with a large number of outputs which weren't intended and which don't explicitly contribute to the core business process.

If a washing machine is a tool for removing dirt from clothes, you could say that a company is a tool for removing money from customer's pockets. This is a good thing, because if your company did not remove money from your customer's pockets, it would end up in the washing machine and be no good to anyone.

Many consultancy firms exist to make your business more efficient by taking out excess waste, heat, pollution and people. By reducing the production of these unwanted by-products, more of your company's energy is devoted to core business processes.

Not as many consultancies concentrate on the other by-products such as stress and lost weekends. These by-products are sapping your company's resources as surely as stationery theft, yet they are frequently ignored by the business process re-engineers as being "soft issues", because they don't know what to do about them.

Many people focus on the "big things" of organisational change - the processes, contracts, procedures and environment. Fewer people realise that these things don't really matter at all because they are incidental to the real organisation - the people. It's too easy to think of the people as being part of the business when in fact the people are the business.

Consider these words:

▫ Business	▫ Partnership
▫ Organisation	▫ Association
▫ Company	▫ Team
▫ Corporation	▫ Department
▫ Firm	▫ Division

And think about how those words describe entities that exist independently of the people within them. Now tear that thought up, throw it away and replace it with this idea:

Those words are simply collective nouns for groups of people.

Just like a herd of cows, a flock of seagulls and a murder of crows, a company of people is just a way of describing a group of individuals with a common interest in a way that tells you something about the way that they behave collectively. Imagine some fish. Now imagine a shoal of fish. Different?

Coming up with new collective nouns is a seriously fun way of pinning down intangible behaviours. How about an empowerment of coaches? A confusion of middle managers? A slick of salespeople? The collective nouns you come up with say a lot about your preconceptions and are a very useful tool for flushing out the beliefs and values of individuals in a team.

For example, how do you imagine a team operating differently than a division? It's an interesting word, isn't it?

How does a confusion of managers behave differently to a group of individual managers? By coming up with collective nouns, you are unconsciously noticing the behaviour of group dynamics - a very useful thing to do in an organisation.

I ran a competition for people to come up with their own collective nouns so I thought I would share some of my favourite entries with you, to demonstrate how useful this idea is. I just want to point out that these are not necessarily reflective of my personal opinions!

- A babble of partners
- A conspiracy of support staff
- A sabotage of IT staff
- A hindrance of help desk staff
- A squabble of teachers
- A scribble of art directors
- A seizure of support workers
- A waddle of tourists
- An algorithm of analysts
- A kettle of builders
- A dusting of cleaners

- A waste of refuse collectors
- A high jump of human resources
- A cacophony of call centre operatives
- A mire of PMO staff
- A verbose of salesmen
- A snoop of PAs
- A clone army of junior managers
- A fleece of consultants
- A wad of investors
- A thicket of engineers
- A loss of consultants
- A worry of health and safety experts
- A bevy of publicans
- A crash of driving instructors
- A brace of dentists
- A clutch of mechanics
- A galaxy of astronomers
- A hush of librarians
- A synapse of NLP Practitioners
- A whinge of Systems Engineers
- A giggle of cabin attendants
- A contradiction of experts

Try it with your own team and see what happens.

There's a business process model called Theory of Constraints which works by removing the barriers that limit a system's performance. The basic premise is that cutting inefficiency is limited by the number zero, so you can't have any less than no inefficiency. On the other hand, there is no limit to the amount of money that you make so it's better to have an inefficient business that makes huge amounts of money than an efficient business that makes quite a lot of money.

Of course, neither approach is 'true'. If we take the model past its common sense limitations, we could say that a washing machine that has a drum that can wash all the clothes in the world, but which vibrates so much it changes the rotation of the Earth is better than a normal size washing machine that doesn't vibrate.

My belief is that most people want washing machines that are practical, efficient and quiet. The model works within the bounds of common sense - for example, if you can afford a Ferrari then you shouldn't be worried about its fuel economy. If you can afford to shop in a designer store, you don't need to ask the prices.

As a business, if you're making lots of money, you shouldn't be too worried about waste. When profits fall, that's the time to cut costs. Every business should be efficient all the time. A fall in profits should be tackled by more aggressive marketing or new product launches. However, this isn't a perfect world. When you're feeling well off, you buy luxury goods like home cinemas and those product lines that the supermarkets sell that seem to be standard products in a shiny wrapper with an exclusive sounding brand name. When you're feeling a bit short of money, you buy only the basics. You may even buy those product lines that the supermarkets sell that seem to be standard products in a plain wrapper with a basic sounding brand name. You could say that the sales of luxury goods are a side effect of the economic system rebalancing itself so that people have no more or less money, whatever the economy is doing, within the limits necessary to sustain a lifestyle.

People like to splash out when they're feeling flush. Businesses like to splash out too, and for the same reason. Waste isn't a sign of inefficiency. It's a sign of prosperity.

I've worked in many companies that went through hard times. The same signs told me, each time, that it was time to move on. The rented plants went back. The coffee machine was no longer free. A memo was sent out asking people to use both sides of photocopier paper, which might be interesting after the office Christmas party. For most of January, letters would go out to customers with someone's bottom photocopied on the reverse. Still, these short term measures make good business sense, don't they?

I have one concern about this, which is that one of the resources that gets wasted in an inefficient business is human energy. No-one likes to feel that their contribution isn't valued. We all like to think that we are important in the scheme of things, and that we make a difference. If your manager said, "you're useless, but the company is so rich I can't be bothered to fire you" then you may be quite within your rights to feel demoralised. Ultimately, companies don't make money - people do. Therefore, it is important that companies are efficient where people are concerned.

You may be surprised at how many companies work hard to move people away from what they love doing – turning engineers into sales people or managers, for example. Career progression seems to be based on your manager's own criteria rather than your own. Of course, if no-one ever told him that not everyone is motivated in the same way, why would he do anything else?

One thing I often hear said is, "people are our greatest asset". What does this mean? Does it mean that the majority of a company's working capital is tied up in the cost of people, and that they will be depreciated over three years, after which time they can be written off against tax?

When a person's talents and abilities are being fully exploited by a company, the company is getting maximum value for money, or return on investment. When the company stretches the person beyond their personal boundaries, the person grows or learns, so the company gets even more value. In other words, the asset appreciates in value.

This isn't all one way. When a person is given the opportunity to develop and grow, he or she is able to fulfil intellectual needs that lead to a sense of fulfilment, satisfaction and personal growth. If you're familiar with Maslow, you'll recognise this as the highest human need. Whilst you may think that Maslow's hierarchy of needs is outdated, it's difficult to deny the observation that hungry people tend not to spend time in libraries, unless they're trying to eat the cookery books.

Your business is itself a complex process with many unintentional outputs. You can either choose to reorganise the company to reduce those unwanted outputs, or you can find value in them like the companies that make office ceiling tiles out of the ash from power stations.

A good way to start is to think back to the day the business started and ask, "what is this process designed to do?", in other words, "what is the company designed to do?

Maybe the business was designed to produce a house in Florida, or more time with your family, or to bring your passion to the world.

Everything else, no matter how important it seems, is superfluous. Stress, pressure, lost weekends, late nights preparing reports and presentations are all just unnecessary by-products of your business. You can stop producing them if you want to, and that will lead to greater improvements in business efficiency than reorganising the sales team again. Best of all, these improvements are entirely under your control. Even this simple idea gets overcomplicated with corporate mission statements that say things like, 'world class' and 'thought leadership'. What utter, utter, nonsense. No company was ever established to be world class or deliver shareholder value. It was designed and created to make money. Why be afraid of saying that? We all need money to live in this commercialised world, because the local supermarket doesn't accept favours as legal tender.

Systemic Change

So, when one part of a system changes, the whole system changes. This is obvious with small systems because it's easy to see how any one part is connected to the other parts.

Here are some metaphors to help you understand the idea of systemic change - how one part changing changes the whole system.

If you change just one of the little ridges on your front door key, it becomes a different key. It doesn't fit your front door any more, but it may fit someone else's. There's nothing wrong with it, it's just a key to someone else's door.

When someone wins the lottery, their life does not change. Imagine the typical story of someone living in a council house with huge debts winning £10 Million. They spend the money on things that they know how to spend money on - things that are framed by their experience. They buy a big house, a sports car, go on holiday and take all their friends, then realise that the money's gone and they don't have the long term income to support the big house and the sports car. One year later, they're back in the council house because their lifestyle has not adapted to the money available. In fact, their lifestyle has corrected the imbalance by removing the money.

Imagine you live in a three bedroom house in a nice part of town, and that you do as much as your can given the salary and free time that you have. You go on two holidays a year and you have a relatively new car. You get promoted and your salary doubles. The first thing you do is adjust your lifestyle, maybe shopping somewhere more expensive, maybe eating out more, so that your lifestyle can correct the imbalance. At some point, you'll probably move to a bigger house so that you end up with as much free money as you had before. Your lifestyle has adapted to the extra income. You don't just have more money, you have a bigger house, a newer car, you eat out more, you have more "stuff" around the house and you might even spend time with different friends in different places. Your lifestyle has adapted to the extra income in order to restore balance.

This example also shows that systems and therefore systemic problems have an element on which they balance. In this example, it's the amount of disposable income.

Imagine someone who wants to go on a diet. Over the years, they have dieted successfully and then put weight back on. The process is that one day they decide to go on a strict diet and enforce it rigidly. After this, they won't eat with other people or go out to a restaurant for fear of temptation. These lose weight to the point that they feel happy with themselves, then have a treat to celebrate. Having had one treat, they've broken the diet and they start to gain weight again. As you know, losing weight isn't just about reducing your calorie intake. This person has made no systemic change to their lifestyle - they haven't taken more exercise, they haven't started walking to work, they haven't started evening classes to fill the time they would be tempted to snack in front of the television. Eventually, the system takes over and restores balance.

This example shows that balance does not necessarily mean happy emotional states for the people involved.

A human being is a balance of internal and external feedback. Internal feedback includes emotional state, mental attitude and current goals and worries, and external feedback includes what the person can see and hear around them. Your brain is a beautifully simple yet incredibly complex servo system which restores balance between these two feedback sources, and we could call the resulting balance a state of 'normal' and feeling normal means that we're right in our current perception of the world. The thing is, we would rather be right than be happy.

Any complex system has a constant – an element which will remain the same regardless of what else changes. You can think of this constant as being the point around which the system balances or revolves. It's the default setting for 'normal' which the system will always correct itself towards.

All the examples also show that maintaining the system requires action and energy. People spend time and energy maintaining the system that they believe themselves to be part of. People in an organisation will spend time maintaining the balance of that system so that they perceive nothing is changing. In fact, everything is changing.

Reorganise

All of this organisation and structure is part of the way that we notice patterns. We see shapes in clouds, faces in trees and hear music in the wind. It's all part of our human need to organise the world - to simplify it so that we can understand it. Of course, if you have a number of people all performing a similar task and working in parallel to increase output, you might as well have them all working for the same manager. Assuming, of course, that you think you need managers.

It's important to realise that there are some basic economies and efficiencies to be realised when you group people together by job function. For example, the members of a design team all need the same kind of basic information and support, so it makes sense to group them together for administrative purposes. My point is that you should group people together because it makes sense to do so - not because that's what companies do.

There are many times when it would not be useful to group people by job function. For example, if you give people responsibility to develop and deliver a product or project, you must also give them the ability to communicate effectively about its progress.

When you work on a practical problem you will tend to seek information which is directly relevant to the problem. For example, if your car breaks down you will tend not to want to hear stories about other cars breaking down when you speak to the mechanic. You may regard this information as irrelevant. In my experience teams who are organised to deliver a specific project tend to be pulled back into job function teams for regular meetings.

At some level, stories about other projects may be relevant if the meeting is called for the purpose of knowledge sharing, however meetings are often called so that the team's manager can keep hold of people who he perceives are moving out of his or her control.

If you're one of those managers, here's a surprise for you. They never were and never will be under your control. People are creative and self determined. When they follow someone else's instruction it is because they choose to do so and because they believe it to be in their best interests.

Here's a typical employee, represented as a system diagram:

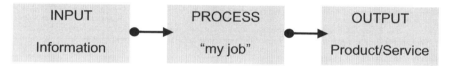

Often, reorganisations happen because middle managers in organisations don't know what else to do, or don't have any power to make the changes that will actually change anything. The only thing that middle managers can change is the apparent shape of the organisation beneath them, so they keep changing it.

By middle managers, I mean anyone with managers both above and below them – and that definition could include board directors, depending on the balance of power between the board and the CEO.

Here's what happens to the employee when a reorganisation takes place that has him or her doing the same basic job but somewhere else in the company:

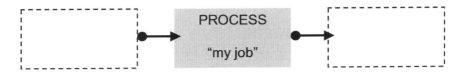

What has happened here is that the reorganisation has disrupted the employee's input. The employee is still performing his or her job but with no input or raw material, there will be no useful output. After a period of time, the employee will reorient himself and will learn the process by which he acquires new raw materials or information. At this point, output will resume.

How long does it take for an individual's output to resume after a reorganisation? As with everything in life, it depends.

Here are some of the contributing factors:

Extent of change

The more people who are affected, the more processes are disrupted and the longer it takes for information to flow from the first undisrupted link in the chain to the last. Perhaps more people being affected creates a wider social context for change.

Adaptability of the individual

Some people will naturally seek out new information or input following a change. Others will wait for it to be given to them. If someone who naturally waits for information from the outside world is put into an autonomous position, they will wait a very long time for the information they need.

Adaptability of the individual's manager or team

When people rely on someone else to give them work, a manager who acts decisively in implementing change will encourage normal processes to resume quickly. A manager who acts as if it's 'business as usual' will tend to generate more business, as usual. Note that acting this way is not the same as going to lots of steering group meetings and then saying, "it's business as usual".

The amount of autonomy that the individual has

If an individual has to wait for input to be re-established, it will take longer for the normal process to resume than where the individual normally seeks out information and input as part of his job. A process driven job such as sales order processing will therefore take longer to resume than a self driven job such as sales.

The frequency of change

Frequent changes lead to a "wait and see" approach, so more frequent change can lengthen the time it takes for people to recover from change. If change is initiated before an individual has fully recovered from the previous change, the individual may adopt a "never change" approach in which change is perceived as a constant, therefore the best choice is to do nothing.

Many management psychology books refer to people who actively embrace change and people who resist it. Are people born this way, or do organisations make them this way because of the way that change is handled?

Remember - people will adapt to their environment. They do not cope with it or put up with it, they learn to exploit it and thrive in it. Resistance to change is a learnt adaptation to change when the frequency or extent of change makes resistance a more effective choice than flexibility.

What I'm suggesting is that flexibility and resistance with respect to change are both strategies for adapting to a changing environment. When a public figure stands his or her ground to fight unwelcome change, he is regarded as a hero, or she is regarded as protecting our heritage. When an idea comes before its time, such as human cloning, the supporters are derided. Therefore, flexibility and resistance are neither good nor bad, they are both adaptive responses.

We could even say - and some people will hate this - that the people who resist change are actually the people who are changing. The people who move with the times are actually staying the same, when you consider the relationship between the individual and their environment.

When the leaders of an organisation want to make changes, the people who go along with it are called change agents, innovators and pioneers. When the leaders don't want to change, these same people are called malcontents, revolutionaries and activists.

Here are some new words that describe the people in your organisation who fear, resist or sabotage change:

- Reliable
- Consistent
- Loyal

This is all part of the change that you must make in your own thinking that allows you to gather information impartially and respond effectively, rather than simply judging right or wrong, good or bad, true or false as you may have done in the past. From now on, you only need to think about useful and not useful.

If anyone in your organisation wants to reorganise part of the company, here's a useful question to ask to test if reorganisation is the real answer or if it is just the only option available.

"If you had complete and total control and authority for everything in the company, would you still reorganise, or would you do something else?"

Many managers in large companies reorganise regularly because that is the only aspect of change that is under their control. They can't dictate product sales or profit margins, they can't set marketing strategy and they can't change the way the company operates in its market. In some of the biggest companies, even very senior managers have surprisingly little authority to make changes.

In one company I know very well, divisions of hundreds of people are reorganised at least every six months. Teams of fifty people find their jobs changing completely overnight. The topic of conversation at every coffee machine is the next reorganisation - who's going to replace who and when. Political affiliations drive change and the people who do the real job of working with customers are left to fend for themselves.

Of course, the end result is that the customer suffers because all the employees are too busy wondering what lies around the corner. The change culture absorbs time and energy that could be used to win business and satisfy customers. The managers want to succeed and they believe that if they make one more reorganisation, they'll get it right. They fail to recognise the simple fact that the organisational structure is irrelevant. It's stability that matters. Of course, in large organisations, change is often driven by political pressure and the need to promote your friends and isolate your enemies and this is a different subject altogether.

It seems a great pity that some people use the rich resources of an organisation to further their own short term interests.

You can help to stop them and make the world a better place to work in.

Balance

There is one very important thing to bear in mind about the idea of systems. In order for a system to exist, it must be in balance. If you change one part of a system, you will change the whole system. For example, if you try to stop the unwanted output of 'vibration' from the washing machine system, then an equal and opposite vibration will be required as a new input. If you encase the washing machine in concrete, the system will require more electricity to balance the load on the motor. Constraining the machine's vibration in such a way will destroy the machine as its internal components fail under the stresses imposed.

Some environmentalists say that this is a common misconception about ecosystems, that in fact they are not necessarily balanced. I would simply say that any system needs an equilibrium or balance, otherwise it will eventually spiral one way or the other, which seems to be the main concern with global warming – that it indicates a spiralling out of control rather than a small part of a much longer cycle.

Servo control systems will automatically change a system's output in order to achieve a goal, based on comparing feedback and adjusting outputs accordingly. When a servo control system's goal is too far away from its current state, it can swing wildly out of control as the system moves so fast to correct itself that it overshoots in the opposite direction.

In a complex system such as a company, change in one area will ripple through to affect every area. You may find that the change, however well intentioned, has side effects that you had not thought of as the system rebalances itself.

In fact, unplanned or unwanted side effects are really the best that you can hope for if you introduce change into one part of a company. Side effects are a strong indication that the system is rebalancing itself and is continuing to function. If there are no side effects, the system could be about to grind to a halt, so learn to think of side effects as useful, positive feedback rather than a sign of failure.

Remember the useful belief:

Problems and side effects are a sign of the system restoring its natural balance.

Simple Solutions

People are forever solving problems. You're hungry, so you get something to eat. You're thirsty, so you make a drink. There's no milk in the fridge, so you go and fetch some milk.

In order to restore 'normality' we can and will solve any problem.

People in companies solve problems too. The sales people don't sell enough, so we need some sales training. We spend too much money, so we need to cut costs. We have too many people, so we should get rid of some people.

This is a common side effect of the relationship between the world, our perception and our language. Language is a coding system for translating our perceptions into a communicable symbolic format, and the problem with language as a form of communication is that it restricts what can be communicated.

Think of the concept of 'colour'. How many colours are there? And remember, colour is not an intrinsic property of an object. You might say that your office is green, or these words are black, or the sky is blue, but these attributes exist in our perception, they are not an inherent property of the object.

Some of you will understand this right away and be familiar with the concept. Some of you will say it's rubbish, because the paper you are reading these words on is quite clearly white, and that is a universal property of the paper. In fact, the chemical make-up of the paper means that it scatters light across the visible spectrum, and when your eyes detect that light, you perceive what you have seen as 'white'. Our understanding and representation of the paper as 'white' is the result of an interaction between the paper, light and your eyes.

How is this relevant to organisational change?

Well, it is relevant in that it is important to understand the underlying process by which people perceive problems, half solve them and in doing so, create a bigger problem.

Think again of the concept of 'colour'. First of all, you are thinking about a range of electromagnetic frequencies in the range that we call 'visible light'. At one end, we have Red, and beyond that, Infra Red, which we can feel as heat but not see. At the other end, we have Violet, and beyond that, Ultra Violet, which we can feel as sunburn and the greenhouse effect but not see. In between, we have the infinite variety of frequencies which we label as 'colours'.

So the range of perceptions which we call 'colour' is infinite. There are no distinctions, no categories inherent in the field. By splitting it into Red, Blue, Yellow and Green, we impose categories. Imagine you are choosing a colour for your new kitchen, and you are only able to communicate your choice using those four labels. Do you think you'll get a colour you're happy with?

So to get round this problem, the paint manufacturers create arbitrary labels for the intermediate colours, so that you can get a colour card and test pot and decide on "Willow Green" or "Dark Lavender" or "Bumblebee" and know that your kitchen will end up roughly as the colour you intended.

So we can refer to colour as a 'unified field'. It has no inherent categories or distinctions. We impose categories upon it in order to communicate about it. It is a set of analogue data. Language codes that data into a digital form, imposing boundaries which are not really there.

Now let's take another unified field – money. When I look at my bank account online, whatever number I see I convert into one of only two values; 'enough' or 'not enough'. Therefore, I always have either enough money or not enough money. When I have enough, I spend it. When I have not enough, I stop spending it and worry about how to get more of it.

So what do you do when your bank account is running low? Cut down on shopping? Stay at home more? Maybe, if your income has fallen for a long time you might get rid of the cleaner, the gardener, the person who does your ironing.

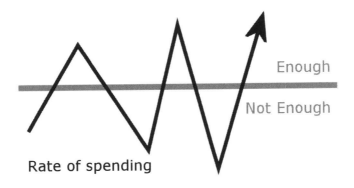

Enough

Not Enough

Rate of spending

Assuming that my income is reasonably constant, the only way to control my bank balance is to increase or decrease my rate of spending. Therefore, if I have enough money I can spend, and if I have not enough money I cut back. It's only one or the other.

This is the effect of a servo control system, controlling the output of money in order to maintain "just enough". Ten years ago, I had no debts, and 'just enough' money in the bank. Today, I have some credit card debts left over from the recession and still 'just enough' money. My system has become biased to accept debt as an aspect of 'normal' and, while I have a plan to pay off that debt, it's not a high priority.

By splitting the unified field of money in this way, you will always have either not enough or enough money. There are no other alternatives. A compulsive dieter is either overeating or starving themselves. This is the pattern of addiction.

And what do companies do when there is 'not enough'? Redundancies.

1

Look at the graduated shaded bar above.

Where would you say the following shade of grey appears in the graduated bar above?

2

Did you just say, "It's around here somewhere" whilst pointing at the middle of the shaded bar? Very good.

Now let's categorise the shaded bar into two parts; black and white.

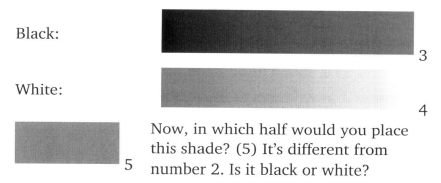

Black:

3

White:

4

Now, in which half would you place this shade? (5) It's different from number 2. Is it black or white?

5

If you think you know, then try this. Show a friend or colleague only the first complete shaded bar (1) and then describe the solid colour above (5) to them so that they can find where it is on the shaded bar. You are not allowed to describe it using any comparative references, so for example you are not allowed to say "it's about half way between black and white" or "it's a bit darker than my shirt". You can only describe it by reference to itself. Of course, you have a language for colours like Red and Yellow, and even Cyan and Magenta, and even Pantone 164 or HTML #CCFFFF if you are that way inclined. But a middling murky grey?

This may seem like an abstract example. I'm even confusing myself. By dividing the unified field of data into two sets, we create a problem that didn't exist before. The problem is one of coding and categorising data, not one of defining a colour.

To put you out of your misery, the box number 2 would be 'White' and the box number 5 would be 'Black' according to our arbitrary definitions.

Consider a person who says, "I'm disorganised". They have already perceived their problem and told you their solution – to be more organised. Now think about the way that a workplace might be organised. One piece of paper out of place? Ten? A small 'to do' pile? A big pile? How much or your desk has to be visible? So 'organisation' is a broad continuum, a unified field.

A sales team is not pulling in the volume of sales that someone in the organisation would like them to. They're either performing or they're not. Someone else, tasked with improving sales, goes to look for sales training. They look for sales training providers and then select a course based on very different criteria than the original problem. They end up with a sales training program that fails to address the original need, and, in doing so exacerbate the problem by spending more money, thereby reducing profits and increasing the need for sales.

So faced with the problem of not enough money, the managers of an organisation will look for either more income or less expenditure. Increase sales targets and make redundancies. But it is not that simple, because the problem is not that simple. In fact, it's trying to simplify the problem in this way which creates the problem.

So if you don't have enough money, the solution may not be as simple as spending less or earning more. When you watch life makeover programs on TV, you'll see that the solution is not that simple. It's usually simpler, because people get caught in the trap created by their own dilemma.

So, the moral of this chapter is to avoid the temptation to solve the obvious problems, because often the problem has been created by the need to define something as a problem. And in any case, the problem isn't even the problem, it's merely the end result of something else.

Defining colours as black or white creates a problem if you had a different colour in mind but now lack the language to communicate that. So be wary of people who tell you the solution to the problem as being the converse of the problem itself, because that is a solution defined only by an arbitrary symbolic language, it is not really a solution at all.

In the old days, you could only buy the colours that the paint manufacturers wanted you to buy. When 'off whites' were fashionable in the early 1980s, everyone wanted Daffodil White, or Bluebell White, or Apple White. But what if you wanted a colour that they didn't sell? Tough. Now, you can choose from thousands of colours, made to your exact specification.

So you expect to choose the colour of your kitchen to your exact requirements, you should expect the same of solutions offered to your business problems.

At a recent meeting, a client told me that her company needed customer awareness training because their staff are not sufficiently customer focused. So, the perceived problem is a lack of customer focus, and therefore the solution is customer focus training. Simple.

Except it isn't. The staff are perfectly capable of caring about customers. I bet that if you were to ask them individually, they would be quite upset at the though that someone believed them to be not customer focused. After all, that's their job.

By defining the problem as 'customer focus' there are only two options; there either isn't enough customer focus or there is. You might agree with that. You might think that customer focus is important, and that if you have enough then you have enough, and that's that. But here's the problem. The problem has nothing to do with the staff's ability to focus on the customer. Therefore, that solution will not fix it. The problem is a function of perception, it is not inherently a part of the way the business operates.

What can you do about it? If you need help to solve a problem, either internally or externally, you need to know who to ask, don't you? You need to know whether to call a plumber or an electrician.

Just be wary of anyone who offers to give you exactly what you ask for without backtracking to check the conclusions that you may have jumped to.

Why are there even blank pages?
Because a chapter always starts on
the left, and I'm not going to
right something just for the sake
of filling an empty page

Culture

What is culture?

Is it an ethereal feeling that you get in one working environment that is different to another?

Certainly, some people say that culture is something that cannot be created or changed, it's just an intangible quality of a particular environment. Well, you can change it, but only with a long drawn out culture change program that involves sending everyone in the company to focus group meetings and covering the walls with posters bearing the slogan of the change program, something like, "Embrace the future! (or else)".

Let's define culture, simply, as "language + rules".

By defining it in that way, we can see how to change it more easily. Traditional change programs certainly do focus on changing language, redefining problems as breakthroughs, and old habits as rackets. However, calling a problem a "challenge" or "opportunity" always works really well to motivate people, doesn't it?

Is that enough?

Changing rules might be harder, because it seems that for most organisations, changing rules in fact means relaxing rules. Instead of people sticking to rigid business processes, what is now required is for them to think outside of the box, be creative, work harder and take responsibility for their own development.

If you went into the zoo at night and unlocked the cages, I imagine that most of the animals would stay in there. And many would actually be more scared with the doors open. So relaxing rules isn't easy, because many people like those rules, because they're comfortable. We complain that rules constrain us, but they also keep us safe. It's a compromise.

Have you ever been for a walk in the countryside and seen a field full of rabbits? Have you noticed how, when they sense a predator such as you, they all dive for the nearest rabbit hole? And have you noticed that you have to stay still, and downwind, for quite a long time before they will come out again?

And they don't all just charge back out, they will tentatively have a peek and see if the coast is clear. A few will put their heads out first and look around.

Well, people are very much the same. After getting used to a culture and then being told that there is now no blame, ideas will be cultivated and anyone can challenge working practices, it takes a long time for people to want to test the rules.

There are many urban myths of experiments with monkeys where successive generations inherited the same fears, even though they hadn't experienced the original punishment.

You might remember, or you might find out later on (I forget when I've written these things) that I worked for a very lovely Canadian telecoms manufacturer once. The first time my mobile phone rang in the office, a number of people pounced on me and told me to turn it off. I asked why, and they said that the sales manager hated the sound of mobiles ringing in the office.

I was curious about how he could tell the difference between a mobile and a desk phone ringing. The sales manager used to sit in his office at the end of the building like a short tempered dragon, waiting in his lair. The main characteristics they shared were that you would imagine him to be a mythical creature as we hardly saw him, and when you did see him he would lunge out of office, breathing fire as he yelled at someone about something.

One day, in the kitchen, I bumped into him and asked him about his mobile phone phobia. He said, "I just think it's unprofessional to talk to customers on mobiles in the office, we should call them back from a landline. I also think that if you're on the phone to a customer, you shouldn't have your mobile ringing and disturbing you". Seemed like a reasonable explanation to me, it was just that no one had ever asked him before.

I wonder how many of the people in the office had actually witnessed, first hand, the incident where he shouted at a salesman to turn his mobile off. I suspect that the majority were like the rabbits, hiding in their holes because someone had said there might be a fox about.

I wonder if it takes a certain kind of person to ask obvious questions like this? In any case, it is something that managers in organisations often ask for – 'out of the box thinking'. You'll find out later that I think that out of the box thinking is another illusion.

Many years ago, during one corporate change program where the company I worked for built a huge tent on a car park at a national exhibition centre and sent all 10,000 employees on a 3 day training program, one of the facilitators drew this diagram on the flipchart:

He asked someone from the audience to come up and connect all nine dots with a single line, so that the pen didn't leave the paper. After an embarrassing silence, someone put him out of his misery and drew this:

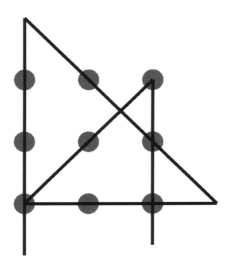

Do you see the point he was making? Well, he spelt it out for us anyway. To be successful, to make a real breakthrough, you have to think outside of the box.

I think that this was the point at which the engineers started doodling and playing hangman, drawing a little stick hanging man that looked oddly like the facilitator.

Now, you might be using this demonstration in your own workshops, in which case I am sure you handle it far more elegantly and with none of the patronising delivery of the person I saw.

Anyway, the point is this: telling people that the culture has changed and that they are now allowed to think outside of the box does not mean that they will. It doesn't even mean that they *can*.

At the same company, the next CEO scrapped the program and introduced his own, about a year later. He put suggestion boxes in all the offices. When you submitted a suggestion, it was reviewed by a committee who would write back to you after a few weeks and tell you why it would never work.

Are you beginning to see a pattern? And does any of this resonate with your own experience?

We're talking here about the components of culture; the behaviours that imply the presence of rules, a rule such as, "Do not make suggestions".

This particular company was fast growing and thriving. I think at one point, it was the fastest growing company in Europe. And people loved working there. It had a buzz. As a start up, it had attracted people who were frustrated in the incumbent, monopoly telecoms suppliers of the day. People with initiative and determination. And with such a promising start, the CEO decided we needed a culture change program. The result was that in every office, people were seconded from their day jobs into breakthrough teams who were tasked with coming up with wild ideas. One of the craziest was from a team who envisaged a device that would fit into the palm of your hand and give you wireless access to people, information and entertainment. You would be able to access databases, book theatre tickets, read emails, talk to people, watch TV and so on. Back in 1992, the technology to make this happen was barely emerging, so whilst this was a ground-breaking idea, the short term result was a huge number of key people no longer doing their day jobs. Guess what happened to the company?

So coming back to what I said at the beginning of the chapter, that culture could be defined as language + rules, this means that in order for someone to integrate with a culture, they must speak the language and comply with the rules.

Perhaps you have experienced this yourself? Perhaps on joining an organisation, you have found some unique language or jargon? Perhaps you started to get a sense of the unwritten, unspoken rules that people are expected to comply with?

For example, Friday is officially 'dress down' day, but actually we expect people to dress as usual in case a customer comes in. Or perhaps there is a work life balance policy, but actually we expect people to work late. Or perhaps we give people remote access to work from home, but we know that people who work from home are actually watching television.

There are two layers of rules within an organisation; explicit rules and tacit rules.

Explicit rules are spoken out loud and written in your employment contracts and procedures manuals.

Tacit rules are learned by observation and never stated directly.

For example, let's say that an employment contract defines the normal start time as 9:00. Does it really mean 9:00? What if someone comes in at 9:05? Will they be disciplined? Will they get a verbal warning? Will their manager even raise an eyebrow in their direction? What if it's 9:15? And what if they come in at 8:15?

Explicit rules create the baseline and tacit rules modify the explicit rules. Tacit rules tell you how closely you have to follow the explicit rules. As Morpheus said, "Some rules can be bent. Others, broken." From the conflict between these sets of rules, we also get the saying, "Do as I say, not as I do."

If you want to know more about cultural rules and how to decode them, my book Genius at Work has everything that you need.

These rules are all too often overlooked in culture change programs, and I think there are two reasons for that. Firstly, they're hard to measure and secondly, no one wants to admit to them.

Well, someone has to come out of the rabbit hole first, so it might as well be you.

When an organisation gets caught between two sets of operating rules or cultures, often as a result of an acquisition or change in leadership, there is a danger that the organisation fractures across the middle. The 'disconnect' in communication occurs because what is happening on the ground is not what managers want to hear, and the easiest way to resolve the conflict is by altering the information that is being reported.

The greatest threat to the organisation's survival is that senior managers believe that their decisions are being successfully implemented whilst junior managers and staff believe they are acting in the best interests of customers. These two forces act in opposite directions and pull the organisation apart.

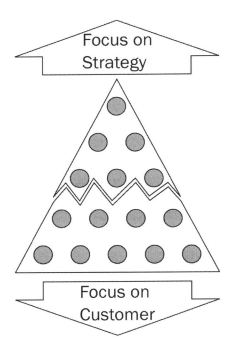

Customers are part of the culture of a business. Their expectations and relationships exert a pull on the organisation. When customer relationships span many years because of the nature of contracts, this pull can hold the organisation back and expose it to threats such as changes in the market place or increased competition. When the business direction changes even slightly, customers' inertia pulls in the opposite direction.

For example, when the focus shifts from technical excellence at any cost to cost control, some customers will have to get used to the fact that they no longer have unlimited access to technical experts. At first, customers will resist this and if the customer facing staff give into that resistance, they will find themselves torn between the needs of the business and the needs of the customer.

The result is another gap, running across the organisation, within which costs are hidden.

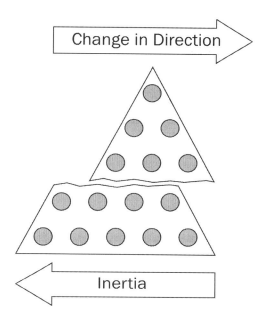

Essentially, what we see in these situations is the strength of individual relationships over corporate loyalty. Customer facing staff do what they feel is 'right' for customers, and the board do what they feel is 'right' for shareholders.

Unfortunately, customers and shareholders have rather different needs, and therefore a company cannot comfortably serve the complete needs of both. A company that tries to do this will tear across the middle.

When business strategies fail, it is generally not because they are 'wrong', it is because they are not implemented consistently across the organisation and so a critical mass of staff give in to this inertia to keep on doing what they're doing.

What is the answer? A company that is guided by its own internal needs will be more immune to this conflict, but it risks alienating customers and shareholders.

Recently, there is a movement towards customer led cultures, with the view that if customers are happy, shareholders will be happy too because happy customers means more spend means more profits. Wouldn't it be lovely if happy customers spent more with you?

Unfortunately, the reverse is often true.

In a retail or 'B2C' (Business to Consumer) environment, the customer is indeed a fickle beast. People have been known to switch allegiances for the sake of pennies off a loaf of bread or a free energy monitor.

Retailers understand that their products are far from unique. While they try to differentiate themselves from their competitors, the reality is that the majority of people shop at the supermarket that's closest to home, and if they have a choice, they'll select based on very narrow criteria.

Customers are driven through the door by marketing, loyalty schemes, advertising and, above all, price.

Regardless of what the retailers mission statements say, their advertisements and weekly newsletters all scream one message; 'Bargains!'

When retailers train us to demand lower prices, they back themselves into a corner. The happiest customers are the ones who save the most money, pushing down sales margins and playing one retailer off against another. Consumer websites allow bargain hunters to share their latest finds, diminishing the retailers' ability to 'switch sell', tempting us in with a low price on one product and stinging us with higher prices on others.

In a price driven environment, there is no loyalty and household names in all industries have disappeared as a result of price wars. One retailer drops prices in an attempt to quickly gain market share, hoping to increase prices once customers are 'locked in' by quality or service. Unfortunately, the lesson that CEOs keep on having to learn the hard way is that the customers who move for price don't care about quality and service. What actually happens is that another retailer steals the customers back, and more, with even lower prices. The only winner in a price war is the customer – and of course the retailer that buys up the assets of the losers in the inevitable 'fire sale'.

In a 'B2B' (Business to Business) environment, the customer is not buying a product or service for final consumption; it forms a part of a product or service that they then deliver on to another customer.

B2B sales often take place within some kind of contract, for example a contract to supply IT hardware and services or a contract to maintain equipment.

With or without a contract, a good supplier/customer relationship has many more dimensions than just price. A well balanced relationship has benefits to both sides, and an unbalanced, manipulative relationship often works in favour of the customer at the supplier's unwitting expense.

Customers exert pressure on a business' direction by demanding product changes, marketing partnerships and other concessions that appear to be in both parties' interests. However big the promised deal is, producing customised software, unique branding or sponsored advertising is often a cost not borne by the profits from the deal.

Countless books have been written on the subject of change, including the best selling business book of all time. 'Who Moved My Cheese?' has sold around 26 Million copies to date. What does this tell us? It tells us that coping with change is a big problem.

No-one is writing books on the subject of mass producing pins any more. Why? Because that problem was solved a hundred years ago.

The biggest problem in introducing change seems to be getting staff to 'buy in'. Methodologies exist that 'sell' the benefits of change to staff, that get staff 'engaged' and encourage them to take 'ownership' of change in their local areas.

Does that sound familiar? Asking staff to take ownership?

"OK children, we want you to take ownership of the sweet jar. You work out how to share the sweets fairly, and we'll trust you not to eat them all."

In a career coaching program that I delivered over two years at a global engineering company, I required participants to be honest about their current situation. Frequently, they reported on where they thought they should be, telling their coach what they thought sounded good. In fact, their coach could only support them if they knew the truth. We often had participants say that they had tried very hard to complete an agreed task but just couldn't find time, when in fact the honest answer was that they had no intention of doing so.

Until someone accepts full responsibility for their present situation, they cannot change it.

As soon as your organisation gets big enough to need to change, it's too big to allow individuals to accept full responsibility. The pressure of weekly reports and performance appraisals will tend to push staff towards telling managers what they think the managers want to hear.

Have you ever heard the question, in a job interview, "Where do you see yourself in five years' time?"

What's your answer? Is it, "I see myself working at a senior level having cemented my reputation within a performance led environment that rewards my dedication and commitment"?

Or would, "Who cares as long as I've still got a job?" be nearer the truth?

If your staff can't even be honest about where they are right now, how can you ever get them to embrace change?

Route Planning

Effectively managing change is one of the most important capabilities of any manager or leader. Many books have been written about change management, mostly about peoples' resistance to change. What you have to understand is that **people are not resistant to change**. What they react to is loss of control, which comes from the fear and uncertainty of not being able to see what is around the next corner, or over the edge of the cliff.

I say that people are not resistant to change because of the fact that they already are changing, every day. Every day, something is different in your life.

When people know that they will land safely, they will make huge leaps for you.

Here's a map of the location around my house:

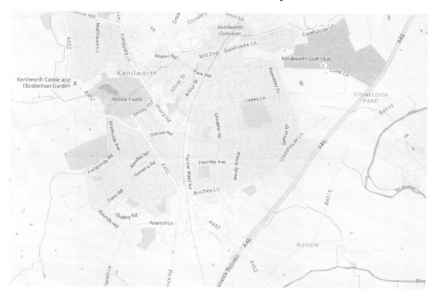

Your task is to plan a detailed, turn-by-turn route from your location to my house. There is no reward for doing this, but you may lose your job if you fail to arrive at the correct destination.

Is it too difficult? OK, let me help you by showing you the 'big picture' for the task:

OK, off you go...

How does that feel?

This is what happens during 'organisational change'.

As animals, we do not interact directly with the outside world, we interact with a 'map' that we create though our perceptions and experiences. We get confused when the world doesn't match our internal map, when things are not as we expect them to be.

Imagine getting home at the weekend to find that your house has moved, or your rooms have switched positions. It's not how you remember it, so what do you do? How do you feel?

How do you feel when the world is not how you expect it?

People who suffer from illnesses which affect their memory such as Alzheimer's or Dementia, or suffer brain injury, experience this every day. It's very difficult to care for someone who is constantly confused and angry, and doesn't even recognise their own children.

However, communicating change with a long list of turn-by-turn instructions isn't helpful either, because your map isn't accurate, and your instructions will not make sense to anyone else.

What you therefore need to do is ridiculously simple, once you think about it, and yet it's what very few people actually do.

In order to implement even the most complex change you need to:

1. Clearly define the end point

2. Clearly define the start point

3. Enable the people who are working within the environment to figure out the route from start to end

4. Write the route down for others to follow

I suggest to you that the biggest problem in change management today is that same problem that there has always been – that we have a tendency to jump into step 3 and assume that the end and start points are understood by everyone. The second biggest problem is that most people define the start first, and then the end. More on that later.

Here's an example of a typical end point as defined by a client of mine:

£50 million turnover by 2018

And their start point:

£35 million turnover in 2015

Is that enough information? If not, what else do you need? They're asking for a 50% increase in turnover within a 3 year period. Is that a lot? Is it conservative?

You might be wondering about a few things. What kind of business is it? That will dictate their overheads and therefore their margins, because we know that to increase turnover, they have to do more of something, and to do more of something generally costs more, so that increase in turnover has to be funded by profits, and if the profits on current turnover are low, that will limit growth.

All of these are good questions, and they are obvious questions. As soon as you look at the difference between end and start, the questions become obvious. From the answers to your questions, you might conclude that the state of the market, including the activity of competitors, means that there isn't enough profit to fund that level of growth. This doesn't mean that it isn't possible, it means that the company will need to borrow some money, which opens up the possibility of capital investment instead of funding growth activities on a month by month basis.

I'm no business funding expert, but all of this seems obvious, and it's obvious to most people because funding a company is really no different to funding a lifestyle. If you want to buy a new car or book a nice holiday, you either save up and pay for it or you take out finance and then pay the finance company back. However, weekends away and train fares can probably be paid for out of your monthly salary. Companies are collections of people, and are operated by people, and are subject to the same physical rules and constraints as people.

Here's another example, a company created a project to improve its customer complaint process. When the internal project team looked in detail at the process, they found that the process was actually fine, but the list of names of people who problems could be escalated to was two years old. When asked why the list wasn't up to date, the answer was, "Because we haven't been told by head office to update the list".

What's the problem here? If we tell them to update the contact list, all we're doing is creating the same problem for the future. How do we ensure the list is always up to date? Could we put some kind of connection into HR systems so that our customer care team are notified when certain people leave? Would that be the easiest, and therefore most reliable, approach?

What do you think?

I'll assume that you said, "Add a step into the process so that the person who finds that a contact is out of date is personally responsible for updating the contact list."

This real life example perfectly demonstrated an important principle: that where you're starting from isn't where you're starting from.

Imagine going to the doctor to get treatment for an embarrassing problem. You don't tell the doctor all of the facts, and then you blame the doctor when the treatment doesn't work.

When you plan a route using a map, you don't lie about your start point, do you? But sometimes you might do. Let's say you are late for a meeting because you decided to have a lie in or take a detour to the beach. You call and ask for directions. The client asks, "Where are you now?" and you lie, you say that you're coming from your office, which is where you were supposed to be. But you're nowhere near your office, so your client's helpful directions won't help you.

In the customer care example, the start point was that the customer care process is broken. In fact, the process was fine within itself, it just assumed that the raw data would always be up to date. Why did none of the customer service staff fix this? They did fix it. They fixed it by stopping using the process. People adapt, remember.

The current situation is therefore not a problem. If anything, the current situation is already a solution – to a different set of previous problems.

Think of this in a personal context. What problems do people often seek to solve? How about addictions? To 'cure' an addiction as a problem is a huge mistake, because the addiction is not a problem, it is a solution to a previous problem such as stress. Even stress isn't the problem, that is a solution to a previous problem, such as being unable to say no to conflicting demands. And even that isn't the problem! You get the idea.

When you try to define your current situation as a problem, you are instantly labelling it as broken in some way. This implies that there is a 'perfect' situation which is different to the current situation. We are talking about a configuration of a system, and you have to remember that, if the company is trading, it's not broken. In fact, there's nothing wrong with it at all – it's working perfectly under the current conditions.

What we do need to do is to be very honest about our start point. As I said, if you lie to the doctor about your symptoms, his diagnosis will be meaningless. Now, I'm not saying that you or anyone in your business will lie about the current situation, only that they will tell you what they think you want to hear.

A skilled management consultant will dig around and unearth other information which people don't think to mention but which is very important.

You can save yourself all of that trouble with a very simple philosophy, which is this:

No matter how you feel about your current situation, nothing is broken. Everything is working perfectly, and is exactly the way it's meant to be.

Imagine asking for directions, and that your start point is in Birmingham. There's nothing wrong with that. As my friend Gary says, "We are where we are".

I'll summarise this:

Everything is working perfectly. We are where we are.

This might sound simple, yet it's so very important.

A manager at a furniture factory told me that he had taken an interest in lean manufacturing principles and spent some time watching people in the factory. One guy had the job of cutting pieces of wood to make the frames for sofas. He would walk to the pile of wood, pick a piece up, walk to the cutting machine, cut the wood, walk to the pile of cut pieces and drop the cut piece, then walk back to the machine, pick up the waste pieces, walk to the bin and deposit the waste. Every day, he repeated this routine, over and over. The manager calculated that the guy was walking 12 miles a week.

Was that a problem? No, the situation was perfect. It was meant to be that way. If the man worked any faster, he would produce more wood than his colleague could cope with. The whole factory was organised around a certain level of productivity, and that level of productivity defined everything from the number of employees to, of course, the cost of production.

Remember, we can't change one part of a system. It doesn't feel right that someone is unnecessarily walking 12 miles a week, and we can see obvious ways to 'improve' the situation by moving the stock and the waste piles closer to the cutting machine. However, we then have to make 'improvements' in the whole production process. Production costs will plummet. Product quality will soar. People might even lose their jobs.

In order to plan our route, we need to know where we're going, and that means that we have to be able to measure something. This is the equivalent of your sat nav saying, "You have arrived at your destination". Your sat nav does not say, "It's around here somewhere". Within GPS' margin of error, your sat nav is certain that you're exactly where you're supposed to be. Your sat nav does this simply by comparing numbers.

You'll define your end point in numbers too. They might not be broad, financial numbers like £50 million turnover. Instead, they might be numbers such as:

- All staff to have a current Personal Development Plan

- All stock on shelves to be undamaged

- All sales activity to be recorded on the CRM system

A forerunner to today's business improvement models, Total Quality Management, used the phrase 'zero defects' as an aim. It didn't really mean that a production process would never produce a defect, it meant that zero defects was the standard that performance would be compared to. Any deviations would then be investigated to understand if a defect was due to a one-off glitch, human error or a systemic failure that could be eliminated.

As soon as we use absolute terms in our measurements, such as "all staff" or "all stock", we risk creating standards which are, in practice, unattainable. These kinds of standards cannot be used to punish staff for non-compliance because we cannot eliminate the risk of human failure. A retail assistant could check their aisle every ten minutes and still miss damage caused by a customer in between checks. And you know that, if you were that retail assistant, you could expect the area manager to do a surprise audit at that exact moment.

Therefore, we cannot reasonably hold staff accountable for measurements which are not entirely under their control.

What if we take a step back from these measurements?

- All line managers to create a Personal Development Plan for their team at least once per year (where the content of a PDP is clearly defined)

- Store assistants to perform aisle checks every hour (where the content of an aisle check is clearly defined)

- All active prospects to have current status and next step recorded on the CRM system

A bit more realistic, do you think? What we're aiming for is an activity which is entirely under the person's control and which we know will lead to the right end result.

Some years ago, I worked with a UK supermarket to identify the characteristics of their highest performers. The methodology, and the modelling report itself, can be found in my book Genius at Work.

The best store managers were those who achieved both their financial targets such as turnover and waste and also their 'soft' targets such as staff and customer satisfaction. One of the interesting characteristics of the best store managers was the way in which they checked for the completion of tasks.

One of the things that has to happen in any shop selling fresh food is that products have to be within their 'sell by' dates. Large retailers have systems and procedures to check on product freshness and quality, so that staff perform regular checks and complete a record to keep track of what checks have been performed.

How does a store manager know that stock has been checked?

The average store managers would ask an assistant if it had been done, and of course there were times when it hadn't been done, and of course there were times when the assistant would say, "yes", when they really meant, "no", meaning to do it later, and of course there were times that they forgot with the result that produce was on the shelves past its sell by date. Now, I know that no-one is going to die of food poisoning because a strawberry yoghurt is a few hours past its sell by date, but that's not the point. The point is that the company had a procedure, and some people followed it and some didn't.

Because the average managers checked procedures by asking staff, those procedures were followed inconsistently.

Yoghurts past their sell by date? Big deal. Let's make it an airline instead. Are you happy for aircraft maintenance engineers to follow procedures inconsistently?

Outside the manager's office in each store are a series of plastic trays which contain folders, and each folder contains checklists. Fire tests, toilet cleaning, customer complaints, product faults, maintenance reports, fresh produce and so on.

The best store managers checked to see if the procedures were being followed by simply stepping out of their offices and checking the paperwork. If the paperwork wasn't complete, the task wasn't complete. All of the ifs and buts associated with asking staff if they've done something that they should have done disappear when you focus on the end point of the task.

The average managers focused on activity, the best managers focused on results. They trusted the processes, and they didn't interrupt their staff constantly to ask if they were going to do something, they simply checked that it had been done.

It appeared that the best store managers cared about having their paperwork up to date, but this wasn't actually the case. What they actually cared about was delegating responsibility to their staff for complete tasks, from start to finish.

When we focus on these kinds of measures, we can create benchmarks, and when we have benchmarks, we can change things. When we measure the results of those changes, we can keep the changes that deliver the results we're looking for.

Our measures tell us what our end point will be, and they tell us where we are right now. Our route is only the difference between the two.

The Leadership Illusion

Every day on social media sites I see a post about leadership. The difference between leaders and managers. The sage advice of the latest leadership guru. How to be an awesome leader.

It is all rubbish. Rubbish. Nonsense.

All the money you've spent on leadership development?

Wasted.

Why? Because the focus of all of this nonsense is on how to be a leader. You cannot be, and here's why:

Leadership is not a behaviour.

Whoa! What does it mean? If leadership is not a behaviour then you cannot teach someone to behave like a leader.

Leadership is a relationship.

So leadership is not something that you do, it is something that others perceive in you, and it's the set of qualities that will mean that they believe you, trust in you, follow you.

The paradox is that you can't fake those qualities, you can't pretend to have them and you can't be trained to develop them. And yet, it also doesn't mean that you either have those qualities or you don't.

People have long asked if leaders are born or bred, and here's the conclusion I've finally reached. Leaders are born.

Do you see? Leaders are born, not bred.

The good news is this; we're all born with those qualities. We are all born leaders. That's not wherever need to focus.

What we really need to focus on is what we do with those qualities. Like it or not, people will choose to follow each of us at some time.

Where will you take them?

The People Cycle

There is a natural life cycle for the people in a business. They join, they do stuff, they leave.

What can we learn from this, and how can it help us to build aligned, purposeful organisations?

I'm going to suggest that there are three cycles within this, and each cycle has three parts to it. The three cycles are Attraction, Development and Retention.

Attraction

The right people for your business already know you exist before you place the job advert, because they are responding to your sales and marketing, thinking about what a great company you look like to work for. They are already sending speculative CVs and looking for companies like yours. This is the stage where some companies' marketing creates an impression of a culture which is different to what people experience after they have started working there.

Once you have attracted the right people, the next stage is to get them into a recruitment process, where you have specific roles that you need to find people for.

Traditionally, recruitment and selection focus on finding people with the right skills and experience for the role. Approaches such as competency based interviewing make it hard for managers in many large corporations to hire people who show promise but are unable to demonstrate a track record, and so these companies continue to hire people who keep the company the way that it is. Managers complain that the recruitment process actually stops them from following their instincts and hiring people who 'fit in', where the HR people usually say that following a process is a good thing because it prevents costly mistakes, or at least it means that you can show a fair process has been followed if an applicant ever takes a complaint to a tribunal.

Development

Once you have someone in the business, the next stage is to develop their individual skills and knowledge so that they can perform the job to the best of their ability.

This starts with the induction, which overlaps with selection in that it's important to portray an accurate impression of the culture and give people an opportunity to walk away if it's not right for them.

Managers in most large companies have a standardised performance management process to follow which includes setting objectives and an annual appraisal, perhaps with shorter term review meetings, and some managers complain that they are too busy to conduct all of those performance reviews. Some managers in a corporate bank recently told me that they didn't were expected to spend an hour with each person in their team per month, and they thought this was a ridiculous demand because it just took up too much time. The managers are so busy doing their own jobs that they don't have time to manage. The largest team that any of them had was eight people, so they were saying that they didn't have time to spend one hour with eight people in a month of typically 168 hours – roughly one twentieth of the working month.

And at the end of the year, they're probably the same managers who don't have time to do appraisals, and then don't have time to attend the interviews for the new staff to replace the ones who leave because they aren't being developed, and then they complain that HR don't find them the right people.

Traditional learning and development steps in next, with activities such as training and coaching. As I'm sure you know, the training market is hugely fragmented, with a few high volume corporate suppliers and thousands of independent trainers. This creates a problem of isolating learning and development from the rest of the cycle, and from the business. One of the UK's largest training suppliers says on their website that they offer a comprehensive service, covering Training Needs Analysis, design, delivery and evaluation. I don't call that comprehensive!

Retention

Is it enough to have individuals developed to the stage where they are performing to the best of their ability? This would presume that they can do everything themselves, without being part of a team.

If this is the case then there would be no need for managers, and no need for team meetings. Clearly, there is some benefit in being a part of a team. The ability to share work, to inspire each other, to have a sense of belonging are all important aspects of being a part of a team.

So we need a stage where we align individuals into teams and align those teams behind the vision or business plan. Each team has its objectives which contribute to the overall business plan, and each individual understands how they contribute to those.

Once we have high performing individuals aligned into high performing teams, what next? We need to give people career paths, and we need to make sure that the right people have an opportunity to take on more responsibility and grow into new roles.

If team alignment gives us a sense of purpose then succession planning gives us a sense of progression and growth. It also serves the very important purpose of knowing what the organisation is likely to look like in the future as it evolves.

Finally, people are going to move on. Some will retire, some will fulfil their lifelong dreams by moving to Australia and opening a diving shop, some will get married and have children and some will move to other companies. And of course, sadly, some people will leave unexpectedly as a result of accidents and illness.

Therefore, we can manage people's exit from the organisation as carefully as we managed their attraction to it. I don't mean conducting exit interviews, that is mostly pointless. The person leaving probably won't tell you the real reason and you'll probably do nothing with the information anyway. Think of the experience of waving off a grand steam ship on its maiden voyage. That's what the exit should be like.

Everyone I've spoken to does some of these things well, because they're the activities they focus on. Some people enjoy the recruitment process, so they're really good at that. Others enjoy organising and delivering training, so that bit's covered.

I haven't met anyone yet who puts as much effort into a person's exit from a business as they do their recruitment. You might wonder why you would bother? What I mean is this: the way that people leave the tribe says a lot about the tribe.

Imagine a floor of financial brokers. The boss comes out of the office, publicly calls out the sales figures, the lowest performer clears his desk and security march him to the door. What does that say to the others?

Now imagine that everyone who leaves has a leaving party or presentation, a card, hugs, "we'll miss you", "you've been a valuable member of the team" and so on. How does that make people feel? And how likely is that person to come back, or to recommend his or her friends to you? How does knowing that it's safe to leave influence your willingness to stay?

In the film Mission Impossible 3, the baddie says "You can tell a lot about a person's character by how they treat people they don't have to treat well"

I worked for a company once where we had a very good manager, except if he heard the slightest hint that someone was thinking of

leaving, he would cut them off completely. He would regard them as disloyal, stop inviting them to meetings, give them a beaten up old company car and so on. Well guess what? People have dreams, they want to get on and do stuff in their lives. And if I can't do that here, what choice do I have? And so, seeing this, other people would keep their career plans very much to themselves, and the first he ever knew about it was when he got the resignation letter.

Another thing to consider is that the team will look to the manager for reassurance that all will be OK after someone has left. The manager needs to show the team is still intact, even when members of the team change. It builds a sense of what it means to be a part of this tribe.

You can see from this that the attraction, development and retention of people in a business is fundamental to achieving your business objectives, for the reason that I keep on telling you – that your business does not depend on your people – your business **is** your people.

Don't be fooled into thinking that your business is an office or a supply chain or a product. None of that would exist without people.

Therefore, any business is a people business. Any business exists to organise the behaviour of a group of people in such a way that the product is made or the service delivered, cost is minimised, quality is maintained, customers are happy, profit is created and so on.

The basis of all of this is your ability to attract, develop and retain the right people.

Even the best product in the world doesn't make or sell itself, and the focus and energy of your people is what makes the difference.

What's the point of all this?

I would say that the majority of companies are used to buying people services as separate components. This is actually causing a number of problems.

If you work in a large company, you have a phone and a PC on your desk. How did they get there?

Some companies employ very large IT teams. They buy products from low cost distributors who dump boxes on your doorstep, and your very large IT team then spends a long time putting those boxes together and figuring out how to make them all connect to each other. And while they're doing that, they're not fixing problems that are cropping up on a daily basis, so their service quality is suffering.

Banks typically employ such large IT teams that this isn't a problem. They have so much work going on so much of the time that they can afford to keep these people busy.

However, for most businesses, you wouldn't dream of buying a new computer or telephone network and assembling it yourself. Certainly the average person sat at their desk wouldn't expect to.

What most companies do is but a new IT infrastructure from a systems integrator. Their job is do understand your business needs and turn that into a system design and then to make that design work, so what you get is a working PC and phone on your desk.

You wouldn't expect a courier to deliver just to the end of the street, would you?

Yet companies waste huge amounts of time and money buying people development services that do not integrate with each other. Recruitment is separate from induction, which is separate from the appraisal process, which is separate from training, and so on.

This causes a problem in that it separates these activities from the underlying business need. A HR manager spends money on a training program which doesn't deliver the expected results. The HR manager says that the trainers didn't do a good job, the trainers say that the HR manager didn't specify her requirements properly. Each blames the other. Worse than that, another year has gone by and the people in the business are still not getting the development they need, and in that time, your competitors are moving ahead.

Some HR managers buy coaching because everyone else is and so they think they should give it a try. They engage coaches to work with staff without clear targets and metrics, and then when they can't quantify the output of the coaching, they say it doesn't work.

Now don't worry. Just like the banks with their IT experts, there are many HR managers who do a very good job of understanding the needs of the business and supporting people with high quality, relevant training and coaching.

What we need to do is take the same approach as a systems integrator. We need to understand the business plan, and we need to understand what we need people to do in order to deliver against that plan.

Every single person in the organisation should be able to express their purpose in terms of that plan. Instead of thinking in terms of 'internal and external customers' or prioritising the people who deal directly with customers, or the people who are more 'senior' in the organisation, every person needs to understand how they, personally, help to deliver those business objectives. No one person can do it, so presumably, for everyone to have a job, everyone must be important.

The mass redundancies of the 1990s often led to layers of middle managers being stripped out, because the perception was that we didn't need managers managing managers. Does every person in your organisation know what their purpose is, what they are there to achieve? If not, at what point in the cycle do you need to tell them, or help them to work it out for themselves?

So the moral of this tale is that we need to integrate the full people cycle, just like you integrate other parts of your business such as your supply chain. If we all did that, we wouldn't need books like this.

People, Place, Program

A few years ago, a rather tall man squeezed into a rather small airline seat on an internal flight from Istanbul to Izmir and told me something that he had been told whilst at University, serving on a student council. He had built a global business upon this premise, and so I thought it worth mentioning.

He said that there are three components to a business; people, place and program.

People means specific people; people who you like, or people who have specific skills that you need for the business.

Place means the working environment.

Program means what it is that you actually do and how you do it.

He asked a simple question: In starting a business, would you focus first on people, place or program?

Stop reading. Think about this question. Where would you start?

Seriously, put the book down for a moment and consider the question; if you were starting your own business, would you start with the people you wanted to work with, would you start with the place you wanted to put those people, or would you start with the program, what it is that you wanted those people to do?

I said 'program'. It seemed to me that first we have to know what we're doing, what the product or service is and how we deliver it. He said no. Starting with the program means that you become too closely attached to one way of doing business. This makes you inflexible and unable to respond to changes in the market and customer demand. You become restrained by your own products. You become tied to what you do, so you have to do more of it to make more money and it becomes difficult to step back from the 'doing' as the business grows.

I could see some truth in what he said about this. I have certainly seen a lot of people start businesses and then fail because they were too tied up in a certain way of doing things, irrespective of what the market demanded. They were unable to respond to new opportunities because they had too much invested in their own ideas and products. Or they were too close to the day to day activities, and too detached from the generalities of running a successful business.

Well, what about people? He said that if you start a business with people and those people leave, you don't have a business any more. Again, I know many people who have started businesses with specific people, relying on their skills or contacts. One friend, an amazing salesman, started a marketing consultancy with a friend of his who was a marketing expert. After my friend had already left his job and set up the new business, his friend decided he would be better off with a nice safe office job, and suddenly, my friend didn't have a business. So I could see the merit in not depending on specific people. Of course, you need people. Just avoid setting up a business that depends on irreplaceable people. Create systems that many people can follow so that you're not dependent on the knowledge of specific people.

So that leaves place. Why would the working environment be the place to start? Surely, you just need a place to put people when you have enough people who need putting somewhere? John said this:

"If you build the right place, it will attract the right people who will run the right program"

Interesting, isn't it?

He interpreted 'place' literally, so if you go to his offices in Hong Kong or London, they look the same. They have the same furniture. They feel the same. There is a sense of global belonging to his business.

When I first heard this, it really made me think, and for the next three years I tried to figure out how to make it work. My business doesn't have an office because my occasional team is spread across the UK and works almost exclusively at our clients' premises. I tried to apply 'place' in a more cultural way, defining what it feels like to work here.

What I found by doing this is that people would call me and say, "Your company looks like a really great place to work, can I come and work there?"

It's a typical situation. A company hires someone who they feel is the best in the market, and then they squeeze that person into a job specification. All of the qualities that make that person who they are become lost or subdued because they're not part of the job description. The person doing the hiring doesn't realise that the creativity, or the family time, or the charity work are an integral part of that person's expertise. Therefore, traditionally organised companies hire fantastic people and then turn them into average people, because they either have to fit into the system or get out.

On the other hand, an organisation has roles which are designed in order to deliver something to that organisation's customers. Whether it's mobile phones or famine relief, people do actually need to do what is required of them, and they do actually need to fulfil the function of the role which was designed long before they came on the scene. We have to distinguish very carefully between roles which are too restrictive and people who just don't like being told what to do.

I realised that culture couldn't be analogous to place, not entirely, because there is nothing to hold people together. Imagine you have a group of friends and you go out together for the night. You end up talking about all kinds of things that you wouldn't have talked about if you weren't in the same place. You wouldn't have picked up the phone or emailed them to have those conversations. The fact that you were all together did two things; it shortened the communication lines, and it created an expectation of conversation, laughter or whatever you do with your friends. Of course, take a group of strangers and the same conversations might not happen, or they might take a long time to get started. I don't necessarily subscribe to Bruce Tuckman's 1965 model of team formation (forming, norming, storming, performing) yet certainly there is an evolutionary aspect of team development, as a common mind emerges, a collective consciousness that we might call a culture.

I certainly agree that the physical environment in the 'place' plays a huge role in culture. I occasionally use a local printer where the design team are packed four into a small room with bars at the windows and a barbed wire topped wall just visible outside. What does that environment remind you of?

Environment is important perhaps because we are a product of our environment. Our environment is what shaped our evolution and that continues to happen within our own day to day lives. As adaptable organisms, we fit ourselves to our environment in order to survive. Our environment is holding all the cards, calling the shots. The environment, the outside world, decides when the sun comes up, when the rain falls, when spring arrives, so while we scratch at the surface of the earth with houses and roads, on a bigger scale we're wired up to adapt.

If you already have a place of your own, how is the environment supporting the culture that you want? I met a Director of a small financial services company a few years ago. They ran adverts in newspapers which sent the message that they would take good care of their customer's finances, so each advert was connected with the theme of relaxation, and had the word "Relax...." in large letters across the top.

The Director thought that the sales and service people were too laid back, that there wasn't enough of a buzz in the office, that there wasn't enough activity, enough motivation, enough energy. He thought that training would be the solution. I suggested there were some other, much more effective things to do first.

All around the walls were the company's advertising posters, and a big one was placed on the wall facing the main door into the open plan office.

Imagine what it would be like, every day, to walk into a large, dimly lit, beige room and be hit with the word "Relax..." Consciously, you would stop seeing the posters after a while. And that's when they become most powerful.

Water creates fish. Air creates birds. Open plains create Cheetah. Trees create monkeys. The environment shapes the organism. So stop reading and look around you. What is your environment shaping in you, right now? What kind of organism would adapt and thrive in an environment like that? Because remember, life doesn't survive, it flourishes. It doesn't just hang on, it exploits. And we are an undeniable part of that system.

In his excellent book 'Surely you're joking, Mr Feynman', the Nobel prize winning physicist Richard Feynman reproduces a transcript of a lecture he gave on the spirit of good science. For bad science, he uses the phrase 'cargo cult science'. The idea is that, during the Second World War, the American military used islands in the South Seas as temporary air bases. The natives enjoyed having the planes land, bringing clothing, food and other supplies, but after the war ended, the planes stopped coming. They built runways in the sand, lit fires along them, built bamboo control towers and had someone sit in there with half coconut shells on his ears. They reproduced the conditions for the planes to come, but they never did.

They reproduced all the external factors, thinking they were what caused the planes to arrive, yet they didn't understand what were the real underlying causes. They didn't understand what would make the planes come back.

I see lots of people start up businesses as coaches and consultants. They get business cards, compliment slips and headed paper printed. They have logos designed, websites created and brochures printed. Some even rent offices. And then they sit and wait for the phone to ring. In a way, they reproduce the effects of a business but none of the causes.

I heard of a survey that found that only around 2% of people who are 'qualified' as life coaches ever make a living from it. Let's be generous and say that only half of the people who take those courses ever want to do it for a living. That's still a very small number of people who succeed, commercially.

And this doesn't only apply to sole traders and small businesses. Big companies also sometimes seek the appearance, the signs of success or high performance. Personal image experts advise you to dress for the job you want rather than the job you have. I suspect you have to have some of the right skills too!

I know that this isn't rocket science, so you're probably thinking that this is all well and good, but how would you tell the difference between understanding the cause of something rather than just reproducing its effect?

This applies to those high performing store managers too. Just replicating their 'competencies' would be cargo cult science. Store managers pretending to do the things that high performers do, such as wearing expensive suits and swanning around like they own the place. We need to get at the underlying mental processes, which fortunately is very easy to do, once you know how.

I think a useful analogy would be watching cookery programs on TV. When you watch your favourite chef, are you aiming to remember the recipe so that you can reproduce what they cooked, or are you aiming to work out how they're thinking so that you can produce something slightly different? If you're aiming to reproduce their recipe, it won't work for you. It won't turn out as you expected. If you're understanding how a professional chef combines flavours and textures, how they think about colour, how they think about presentation and visual appeal at least as much as flavour, then you'll create something that is your own, that is generated from the underlying rules rather than the superficial results of those rules.

The place, people, program idea is relevant to organisational change too. I have a client, an alternative energy startup, who wants to develop a sales team. Essentially, they have grown through investment funding and now it's time for them to be self sustaining, and the only way to do that is to sell some products. Until now, they have developed a technology which has found its way into other peoples' products through joint ventures. What they need to do is productise that technology so that they can mass produce it (reducing cost of production) and sell it in high volumes (reducing cost of sale).

The have a group of what we could very loosely call sales people. They understand the technology and what it can do, but they're not really driven by the commercial process. So their sales cycles are long, their solutions are bespoke and their margins are low. Dangerously low.

So, their sales people currently enjoy long technical conversations about what is possible, and since they aren't driven by sales revenue, they have no incentive to accelerate sales cycles. They don't qualify sales leads, because they're happy to talk to anyone.

The solution? Sales training of course! Sit them in a room for a couple of days with a spiky haired, pointy shoed over-enthusiastic sales trainer who calls everyone "guys" regardless of their sex and all will be well. Yes? No. Because until they actually go and talk to a potential customer, they have no need to qualify, or uncover needs, create a value proposition, negotiate or do any of the things that sales people have to do. So the training will go in one ear and out the other. More than that, they'll probably look down their noses at the trainer, because he doesn't understand their business and he doesn't understand how different and special they are. Because what they're actually doing is hiding their fear of rejection beneath a veneer of disdain.

In order to migrate to a commercially focused, direct sales approach, they need the following:

- A performance management environment that incentivises short cycle product sales
- Skills development in how to drive product sales
- Products for the sales people to sell

If any of these elements are missing, the consequences will be as follows:

- Environment: sales people will stay in their comfort zone, sales will stagnate
- Skills: sales people will have poor conversion rates and cost of sale will be high
- Products: sales people will be unable to fulfil customer needs, company reputation will decline

So they could train the sales people, but without standardised products they'll have nothing to sell so they'll slip back into their comfort zone of long, expensive technical discussions.

Yet look closer - Environment, Skills, Products. That's Place, People, Program.

So not only is this the way to think of a new venture, it's also a valuable way of thinking about organisational change.

So bear in mind the wise words of John Wright:

If you build the right place, it will attract the right people who will run the right program.

Alignment

One of the key principles behind Change Magic is that we can use systemic personal change tools to change organisations if we imagine that an organisation is a community of parts, just like a human being. We can use tools and approaches that deal with the issue of Identity to work on a company's brand image, in just the same way that we could work on a person's self image.

Humans understand the world through reflecting themselves onto it. We anthropomorphise – seeing human traits in animals, places, objects and so on. Aesop's fables reflected human stories through the characteristics of animals; the sly fox, the stubborn donkey, the wise owl. So we project aspects of ourselves onto the outside world, and onto other people, in order to understand ourselves.

Star Trek did the same thing, using fictional aliens to explore human traits such as aggression, love, avarice and logic.

We do the same thing with brands, which we could regard as the identity of a company or organisation. Companies like Disney, Virgin, Coca Cola and IBM spend lots of money developing a brand image – a corporate identity. And yet, we don't interpret and interact with this identity in an abstract way - we treat the company as if it were a person. We love it, hate it, blame it, trust it and fear it just like we would a person with those characteristics.

And here's the important part for us: We create that personification, not based on what the branding consultants want us to see, but on our real, personal experiences. We respond to the sexy advert and then the reality of the call centre creates a huge sense of disappointment. We fall in love with the salesman but fall out of love with the service engineer. It's the same sense you had as a teenager when you realised that person you had a crush on was not all they seemed.

Think about your mobile phone service provider. Their branding consultants created a logo, a colour scheme, a font style, even a style of writing for their adverts. They write guidelines such as "The minimum space around the logo should be no less than 5 pixels. Use this exact gif logo file in all cases. Do not resize the logo or place it on any background colour except White".

The one thing they did not create was an identity. When you think of your mobile phone provider, your natural human processes create a person. For some time now, computer games and online chat rooms have used images called Avatars to represent the user's identity. Rather than have a photo of yourself, you have an image of a warrior, princess, alien, king or whatever represents the way you feel on the inside rather than the way you look on the outside.

So going back to your mobile phone supplier, do you see a man or a woman, or even a child? What colour hair? How tall? How do they dress? How do they speak to you? What is their relationship to you? What are their hobbies?

Branding consultants will describe their target market in these terms, but not the brand itself. Well, let's take this natural human process and use it to create a personality. Let's take a company's target market and ask, "what kind of person would they fall in love with?"

Many products create such feelings in their customers; VW Beetles, Converse shoes and iPods create more than a market, they create a following. We might call them brand leaders, but they are more than that. If they have followers then they are leaders in the same way that Ghandi, Martin

Luther King and Adolph Hitler were created by their followers, not by their image consultants.

Leaders have a vision, and they communicate this vision through their actions and commitment.

So think about your own company now. Man or woman? Age? Personality? And are those aspects reflected in the projected brand image? If not, we have a conflict. In people, this conflict manifests itself as balding middle aged men looking in the mirror and seeing a virile young hunk, and beautiful, average teenagers looking in the mirror and seeing someone who is ugly and overweight. In extreme cases, theses conflicts become diagnosable illnesses such as anorexia. In less extreme cases, these conflicts are laughed at. "Mutton dressed as lamb" or "Doesn't he know we can see it's a wig?" are the unkind observations you might hear. And if your company's projected image isn't supported by your behaviour then people will say the same things about you. And when those people are competitors and potential customers, you're in trouble.

So how can we use this information to our advantage? What if we start with the current personification and give it a TV makeover? Give it a personal shopper and some cosmetic surgery? Have its teeth whitened? If you watch those programs you'll see that the people who have a successful makeover are the people who have 'let themselves go', and the makeover is really just revealing what was already within them. In a way, the makeover reveals their inner beauty. If they don't have that to start with, they end up looking a bit silly.

God created man in his own image, or perhaps man created God in his own image? Either way, what if we personify our target customer? We do tend to like people who are like us, so what if we become what we seek?

Marks and Spencer personified their target customer perfectly, and then they found that their target customers were dying off, and younger generations were not taking their place.

Do you believe that people can change? I mean, really, fundamentally change? Sure, they can change their looks, learn new ideas, change their behaviours, but can they change who they really are inside?

A well known IT company has a reputation in the industry for being arrogant. At a job interview, a manager there told me that they're not arrogant, they're paranoid. I believed him until the second person interviewed me, a technical consultant. I didn't see any evidence of paranoia as he asked me a question and then read his emails or looked out of the window while I answered.

Let's take this approach for a while. What is your company afraid of? Let's say it's 'not being credible, being ignored'. What behaviour would you see in someone who had this fear? Perhaps overcompensating, making too much noise, too many bold claims. Perhaps trying to prove credibility, almost shouting, "We're credible, honest!", yet in doing so making potential customers question that credibility. If you're credible, you don't have to say so, people just know it. In many years time, the company will have earned its reputation, and enough people will have been through the organisation to accept that reputation as a constant. The people who work for Hewlett Packard now don't question its reliability in the way that the first employee may have done. The reputation has been earned, and now the employees only have to live up to it.

What reputation has your company earned? You cannot develop a reputation by talking about it, people will only take heed of your actions. My driving instructor used to say, "Do as I say, not as I do". Did that make him a good role model?

Another way to look at it is that their conscious minds will try to respond to your words whilst their unconscious minds will respond to your behaviour, so any conflict on your part will lead to confusion and conflict on theirs, and since they won't like those feelings, they will decide that they don't feel good about your company. We're talking about congruence, about alignment. When a person is congruent, we regard them as being honest, trustworthy, reliable. When they are incongruent, we interpret their mixed messages as confusion or dishonesty.

So what to do? Firstly, don't bother asking your customers about their brand impressions, service, quality and so on using standard questionnaires. Ask them to describe the person they see your company as, and what feelings that identity elicits in them.

Secondly, find out what the projected personality is, and if it's different from the true personality. If this is the case, the projected personality is operating out of fear, and since that's the case for most humans, we can presume it's also the case for companies. Fear of going out of business, fear of being ignored, fear of failure and so on.

Thirdly, what makes a credible makeover? What can you do to release that true spirit? What can you do to let the inner beauty shine through? The simplest way is to let go of the fear. It's simple, yet simple things can be difficult. When you let go of fear, there is no stopping you.

We all carry insecurities around with us. We fear criticism, rejection, physical harm. However, we don't want other people to exploit our weaknesses so we hide our fears behind a pretence. When we say, "I'm not afraid", what we're really saying is, "Please don't find out that I'm afraid". By hiding our insecurities, we scream them out more loudly.

Sometimes, the insecurities of a company's founder or CEO are broadcast through the brand. "Look how cool we are!" might reveal a fear of not being accepted. "Look how big we are!" reveals a competitive streak, a need to be the biggest and best for fear of somehow not being enough, no matter how hard you try.

So thinking at the organisational level, what does your company behave as if it's afraid of? Competitors? Not being big enough? Not being fast enough? Not being fashionable enough?

At a human level, there are some basic fears such as rejection, failure, ridicule and worthlessness that drive higher level behaviours. Drivers such as a need for recognition, love, acceptance, safety or belonging also drive behaviours. We can see these needs manifested in the behaviour of teams and companies, where the leader projects her or his needs onto the team. A manager who needs to belong builds a team around this need, where other people in the team just want success or recognition.

Let's look back at the organisational level and see what we have so far.

The reason that we become afraid of ourselves is that, as children, we are told that there is something wrong with being who we are. We hear "no" or "don't" when we do the things we are naturally drawn to, for example laughter or play. We learn that when we try our best, it's not good enough. We learn that we're not as nice or polite or well mannered as other peoples' children. We know there's something wrong with us but we don't know what it is, we can't find out what it is, and we don't know what to do to fix it.

Just this morning I spoke to a client who takes on more and more work whenever he's asked to do something, or even when he's not asked but he's sees something that needs doing. He's working at least 12 hours a day, 6 or 7 days per week, every week. It's completely unsustainable. Yet he can't stop himself. He asked me, "Why can't I say no?"

The answer is that he is addicted to the feeling of validation that he gets when he takes on more responsibility. Sadly, that feeling is short lived, and he doesn't get the same feelings from actually doing the extra work that he's taken on. In fact, he feels angry at himself for not saying no. It's absolutely the typical pattern of addiction, and he keeps going back for another hit.

Why would he need that feeling of validation? Because, somewhere inside, he suspects that he might not be good enough. He might not be important. He might not be valuable. These fears create a need, and that need drives his behaviour.

The problem actually isn't the extra work, and it's not even his pattern of behaviour. The problem is that some feedback has gone missing, the feedback that tells him that he really is important and valuable and that he is accepted and appreciated. He doesn't hear the feedback, so he keeps on looking for opportunities to create it. Just like with any other addict, nothing will ever come close to the first high, and as he chases a spiral of diminishing returns, he takes on more, and more, and more. Something has to give.

What do you think will happen when he's forced to take time away from work? Do you think that he'll be sorely missed? Do you think that his managers and colleagues will say, "Oh no! Who will do all of this important work now?"

Probably not. They probably won't even notice. Because his habit has created a habit in his colleagues. They know that he'll readily take on more work so, even though they know it's harmful to him, they continue to feed his habit because it's easy for them.

In other words, the system is working perfectly. He can continue to prioritise work over his personal life, and his many bosses can get more done without having to hire more people. My client is doing the work of two people, and that creates a problem because one of those people has a contract of employment with clearly defined responsibilities, and the other is a casual labourer who works when he can and therefore cannot be relied upon.

In my first job, back in 1985, I had a colleague named Sid. Sid was the most talked about man in the whole of the company. Ironically, he was the most talked about man because he was the most paranoid man. His constant worry that other people were talking about him was what made other people talk about him.

Our pompous local manager, Alan, and his boss used to come out and visit Sid regularly and spend half an hour, drinking tea and telling Sid about how lazy all the other engineers were, what problems they created and how poor their workmanship was.

Once they left, Sid was so wound up that he would work twice as hard to make sure they weren't talking about him in the same way. "No-one's accusing me of doing a bad job, mate", he would say while running down a slippery factory floor carrying an 18 foot oak ladder on one shoulder and a huge coil of cable on the other.

Sid even had me dodging buckets of red hot aluminium to fix a cable outside of a foundry because it looked untidy on the inside. A foundry. The dirtiest, noisiest, most horrible place on earth, and Sid was worried about how nice it looked.

After Alan and his boss had left, and Sid had spent the afternoon working at 200 mph, Sid would get a phone call. "Sid, we're moving you to another job".

Alan and his boss knew Sid inside out, you see. They knew that if they wound him up by talking ill of his colleagues and then sent him to a job that was running way behind schedule, Sid would charge in like a one man hit squad and bring the job back on time. He was so obsessed with what other people thought of him that he would work Saturdays and Sundays and not book the overtime. Even when other engineers were working overtime on the same job.

On one particular job, the assigned engineer had spent two weeks drinking coffee and chatting up the receptionist, so Alan and his boss did their number on Sid and moved him to the job. Sid and I had to run a cable through the warehouse back to the main electrical connection in the building. On the back of 30 foot high concertina doors was a criss-cross of metal links. Sid said that we didn't have time to do the job properly with a ladder so he put the cable in his teeth and climbed up the back of the doors like Spiderman. In burgundy overalls. I stood in absolute amazement, an impressionable 18 year old apprentice, wondering what the hell I had gotten myself into.

Sid was absolutely certain that he was personally responsible for keeping the company in profit, for being the only engineer who ever did a decent day's work.

One day, Sid was working in a factory. He was expecting a visit from the big boss and was rushing around as usual. He realised that he'd left his hammer up on a girder in a factory and ran back to get it. He put his ladder up at the girder and ran up it - alone, because he didn't have time to get anyone to help him, to 'foot' the ladder. Inevitably, on the oily factory floor, the feet of the ladder slipped.

Sid fell. He fell all the way down onto the factory floor. He broke his back, and never worked again.

As my colleague Tony would tell me on a weekly basis, "There's no medals, mate."

It didn't matter how hard Sid worked, he would never get the appreciation that he needed. He was addicted.

All of these strange behaviours are pretences, fears. The fear of rejection forces people to conform and do things that they would never normally do. In a recent one-off TV show[1], the British psychological magician Derren Brown convinced three out of four 'volunteers' to push a man to his death. Of course, the man didn't really die, but if he hadn't been tethered to a safety harness, he certainly would have done. Their conformity began many weeks before they arrived at the fictitious charity event where they complied with requests such as marking sausage rolls as 'vegetarian' and dragging what they thought was a dead body into another room to hide it in a box.

---

1   Derren Brown: Pushed to the Edge

An organisation faces rejection from its potential customers, the public and the press every day, so it is not hard to imagine that an organisation also learns to deny its true self, to hide its fears behind a veneer of perfection.

A typical example of this is where sales people, tasked with introducing a new product, report back that customers don't want it, that competition is too fierce, that the price is too high, that the market isn't ready, that marketing have got it wrong. If the organisation believes those lies, it will learn to be cautious rather than innovative. I say 'lies' because they're not true, they are rationalisations for the fear of rejection. And I say 'organisation' when of course I mean individual people.

This fear of rejection creates conflict, and the conflict leads to one of two outcomes. Either the marketing people give up trying to innovate, or the sales people go back out and face their fears. When I say marketing people or sales people, what happens is that the people who personally don't like the pressure will leave, and the people who succeed are the ones who support the cultural role of their department. If the marketing department exists to serve the sales people, it will tend to attract less innovative people. If the sales department exists to realise the dreams of the marketing department, the sales people will tend to be more tenacious in opening up new prospects.

These are two extremes of course. Many companies operate with a cool distance between sales and marketing, and engineering, and admin, and senior management. Others have more cohesive teams where everyone knows they are on the same side.

The problem for our purposes is a conflict of intentions. The sales people, generally, want to sell more because that's what they're paid for. The marketing people, generally, want to innovate because it's hard to write a press release for old news. These two intentions may be in conflict. The engineers, generally, want to maintain quality. This is often in conflict with the need to innovate and sell more.

Some people see sales as an enabler for people's lives. As a salesman, I let you know about products that really enhance your quality of life, therefore I am doing you a service by ringing your doorbell.. Other people see sales as a nuisance. I have to force stuff on you that you don't really need, because if you needed it, I wouldn't have to sell it to you.

The second example is operating out of a fear of rejection, and rationalising it by saying that people don't want to buy stuff, which means I ring fewer doorbells, which means that I avoid rejection. If I am employed as a sales person, I eventually get fired for not selling anything – so I didn't avoid rejection after all, but at least I confirmed the fear that sales is tough and I'm no good at it.

In practice, people in your organisation will avoid certain activities because of fear. They don't know that they're motivated by fear because their fear is so strong, so powerful, that they never get close enough to feel it. Instead, their fear gives them a gentle nudge away whenever they get too close. They'll set out to do something and then find themselves doing something other than what they intended and make up a plausible story to explain their distraction.

Change Magic
258

These distractions mean that people do things other than what they intended to do, were asked to do and are expected to do. When you ask why, the reasons will always be rational, plausible and indisputable. Yes, people are busy and times are tough. But that's not the reason.

Whilst you could tackle these fears directly, there is a risk that you can provoke people and make them more uncomfortable. If they have willingly entered a coaching relationship then you have their permission to push and prod them, however in the workplace you'll rarely have that degree of trust. Even your line manager isn't close enough to you to provoke your fears and get away with it.

What we need is a tool that more gently creates alignment, or at least highlights misalignment within a system. We'll use a model called Logical Levels. There is some debate over who created this, and what it was created for. Whatever its history is, we can say that it's useful now, and we can certainly relate to the hierarchical nature of change using this simple model.

If you listen to comments that people make about themselves, you'll often be able to categorise them into levels, for example:

I'm not a salesman	Identity
I'll **never be** a good salesman	Belief
I **can't** sell	Capability
I **don't** sell	Behaviour
I'm not selling **this**	Environment

Can you tell the difference? (capability). So that you can get the hang of this, I'll categorise each level that I use (behaviour). I know you'll understand the relevance of this, once I explain it (belief) and that by the end of this book you will be a fabulous communicator (identity).

Note that we don't care why someone makes these statements, we just accept that the statement is a representation of that person's internal experience.

A person's choice of language, while unconscious, is very precise and very meaningful. If I say 'I can't sell', then my language includes certain information and excludes other information. I'm saying, by inference, that I *can* do other things, just not 'sell'. If I say 'I can't sell this' then I am inferring that I can sell other things, therefore I can sell, just not this.

Sometimes, people will give you 'sentence fragments', where they either stop speaking half way through a sentence, or they abruptly change the subject. If you're listening in order to understand or reply, the chances are that you'll miss these deviations. However, if you are listening more analytically, you'll hear interesting patterns.

For example, let's say you ask someone to write a report for you and he replies, "I can't". Normally, you would take that at face value. There's no need for him to finish the sentence, because he's referring to the specific request that you made.

"Can you write a report for me?"

"I can't (write a report for you)."

However, that isn't what he said at all. What he gave you was a sentence fragment, a deletion which hides something which he chose not to put into words. What possibilities could there be?

The clue is that our language is always grammatically correct within the constraints of our command of a language. When you hear something which isn't correct, it's a clue that something has happened inside that person's head, at the unconscious level.

Here are some possible statements that were hidden:

"I can't (give you a yes or no right now)."

"I can't (write a report for *you* because I've heard you're being fired)."

"I can't (bring myself to do any work today)."

"I can't (stay late today)."

"I can't (say no to you)."

The last option is very interesting. The person can't say no, but he can't say yes either. He resolves the dilemma by saying nothing, and you fill in the gap by assuming that he declined to help you. The overall effect is as if he said no, however he didn't actually say no, so he avoided the conflict of saying no. The pattern is a hallmark of a person who fears confrontation.

In responding to these statements, if someone says "I can't do this" then you can choose to stay at the same level (Yes you can, what *can* you do?) or you can move up a level (I know you will be able to do it, How can I make it possible?, You're the only person who can do it) or down a level (What are you doing now?, What will you do instead?). The reason for this? To apply some structure to the way that you explore information.

If we think about this as a verbal problem solving approach, then we could regard the example statements above as 'problem statements'. They may or may not be true, however they are a true and accurate representation of the speaker's internal experience. What I mean is that, if someone says, "I can't do that" then that may be factually incorrect, however their choice of words have a direct relationship to what's going on inside their heads, and if we can influence that then we can influence their behaviour.

If you choose to remain at the same level, you will constrain your thoughts within the problem. You will probably not generate any new ideas at this level, as the problem itself sets the boundaries for the solution. However, you may want this to happen, so it may not be a bad thing.

If you move up a level, you are able to think about other examples of this problem, and you will have better access to similar experiences to draw from. You will have better access to your experience by moving to a higher level than the problem. You will lead people to be more abstract in their thoughts and they will be able to think about structures, theories and concepts more easily.

If you move down a level, you are becoming more specific. You are requesting or giving more detail and you are converting possibilities into certainties. By moving down through the levels, you will force decisions and create motivation. By moving up, you are encouraging creativity and the generation of options.

The ability to move your level of thinking up, down and sideways in this way is amazingly powerful and it's something that the best facilitators and negotiators do intuitively. The concept of Logical Levels gives you a simple linguistic framework to influence the way that people think

- including yourself. If you want to finish something and the voice in your head says, "I should finish that" then this is unlikely to motivate you to take action. If the voice says, "I will finish that" or, "By the end of today I will have finished that" then you will generate genuine motivation. Remember - the voice in your head is your voice. It can say anything you want it to.

So, the Logical Levels model is just one application of your ability to change your level of thinking, and it's a very powerful model in the context of communication and change. Just bear in mind what I said earlier about models.

If you jump levels, you will create confusion. I'm not saying "don't jump levels", only that you should be aware of the results so that you can use this knowledge wisely. If I said, "I'm a plumber, I can't live here" then you will start to imagine all kinds of things in order to add the missing information that you need to make sense of the statement. Perhaps this place is too good for me, or not good enough? In fact, the answer is that there is nowhere to park my van, but you had no way of knowing that. We can call this a 'leap of logic'.

Whether we use the logical levels model or not, the important point to bear in mind is this: if we think in logical sequences and then simplify those sequences in language then we can misinterpret thought processes and intentions.

For example, I need to go to the bank today, but it's raining so I'll take an umbrella, but then I got delayed so I'll take the car instead of walking by which time it has stopped raining.

If you only observe my actions, it wouldn't make any sense that I took an umbrella to the bank in the car when it wasn't raining. Yet, as a logical thought process, it makes perfect sense. If we only look at the parts of the thought process that someone gives you in their language or behaviour then you will be missing all of the important information. It's not surprising, then, that we can so easily jump to conclusions about what people thought or intended, based only on the observable result.

If you want people to make up missing information, jump levels. For example, you can say, "Only leaders do this" and people will start to imagine all sorts of things about leaders in order to make sense of the statement. Alternatively, you could try, "Moving offices is easy for professionals". The effect is the same - the listener will unconsciously insert the word "because" and create reasons that support the statement.

Notice that the statement is accepted automatically as true, leaving the listener to create a connection that is true and meaningful for them. Each listener may create a completely different connection and so it is very important that, if this is your goal, you do not spell out the connection for them but instead leave it for them to create their own. The statement is accepted as true because you haven't said anything that anyone can explicitly disagree with. Their focus of attention isn't on the part of the sentence where the change takes place, so they have to accept it in order to understand the language.

This is very powerful, so you need to be careful with it. Let's take the statement, "moving offices is easy for professionals" and accept this as true for a moment. The problem is that this is not one statement but two joined together. Based on our expectations and state of mind, we might infer one of two meanings from this; either we're professionals so this must be easy, or this isn't easy so you're saying we're not professionals.

You can see how using this without care could get you into more trouble than when you started! You might wonder why I mention this, as it seems to suggest that these ideas are dangerous. I'm telling you this because people say things like this naturally without thinking about it. They cause harm and influence the outcome of a situation with the language they use – accidentally. You have the choice to take what you are learning here and use it purposefully.

Here's another example. In order for you to understand the sentence "When did you decide to change your mind?" you must accept certain ideas as true, namely that you changed your mind at a specific moment and that it was your choice. If you make the statement too far removed from the person's own experience, the result will be confusion followed by disagreement. This moment of confusion can be useful too, but hypnosis is not a subject I'm planning to cover in this book.

If we put the statement inside the boundaries of direct experience, there is no real impact, so "when did you decide to read these words?" is only a question about an experience that can be directly inferred. By stretching the structure slightly you will start to bring about gradual change, so the question "When did you realise that these words are changing you?" will achieve something different.

If your goal is common understanding, lead your listeners through the levels smoothly and slowly. For example, "Moving offices is something that is done by people who can easily adapt to new situations. We are all naturally adaptable and I know that this is what makes you the professionals that you are."

Health warning: The words I am giving you here are designed to demonstrate concepts. They are not a script. If you said exactly those words to a team on your organisation, they would probably think you were winding them up. Look through the words to the underlying structure, and use that structure to create your own communication.

When you come up against a problem that you think may be down to conflicting maps of the world, it may be useful to think in terms of scale. If you open up a street map of your home town, you'll see a level of detail that helps you find your way to a specific street - such as Acacia Avenue. The map doesn't show you where number 27 is, though. Now open up a road map of your country and see if you can find Acacia Avenue. Finally, have a look at a world atlas or globe.

An argument over conflicting maps is a bit like two people arguing over the best way to get to 27 Acacia Avenue, Birmingham. They can argue and argue until they're blue in their faces until you consult your world atlas and see that one of them has a map of the West Midlands, UK, the other has a map of Alabama, US. There's no way either of them could have known that, because they each thought they knew what the other was talking about. They thought they had a common frame of reference, but they didn't. You helped them - and resolved the situation - by moving up to a higher level frame of reference where the disagreement lost its meaning.

Of course, this raises another important point. We can only agree over the best way to get to 27 Acacia Avenue if we're both starting in the same place. With different maps, we can't be. I know that you understand the significance of that point, so I'll get back to the idea of scale, or levels of hierarchy.

If, when you are explaining something, you jump over levels, you are demanding that your audience makes a leap of logic to fill in the missing levels. A nice, smooth progression through levels guides the listener's brain on a journey. They will pay more attention to you because they are not 'inside' creating missing information and they will find information easier to absorb.

When explaining a new idea or concept, the name that you give this idea is expressed as an Identity level statement. A smooth progression through levels would then sound something like this:

- The name of the concept
- What it is good for
- What it can do
- An example of how you might use it
- When and where you would use it

If you are the kind of person who likes to build knowledge up rather than start with abstract theories and work down, then try this:

- A situation you might find yourself in
- What you would normally do in that situation
- All the things that you could do in that situation
- What is true to say about that situation
- A name for the concept or idea

Of course, in order to fully communicate with your audience, you would use both approaches.

In order for a person's natural language to shift from one level to another - from "I know how to drive" to "I'm a good driver", for example - specific internal processes take place. We have names for most of these processes, for example, if someone shifts from talking about what she can do to what she is doing then we might call that either motivation, or making a decision, depending on the context. If someone shifts from talking about what they are doing to what they can do, then we might call that process 'learning'.

You can hear these shifts in language as you take people through a change experience. They are a very important indicator to you that your audience members are rearranging their internal organisation to integrate whatever you are helping them to learn.

It's not only your audience's language that can shift during a change experience - yours can too. You can intentionally shift language patterns at specific points in time to effect change in your audience.

By listening to how people talk, you can understand how they think. The reverse is also true, so people will switch thinking modes depending on how you talk.

Think of motivation as being the mental process that takes place when a person naturally moves from thinking at the Capability level to thinking at the Behaviour level. Therefore, by changing the structure of your language you can directly influence people to take action.

I'll give you some examples.

What you hear	Example responses
I don't like the new office (Environment)	What improvements can be made? What happens in the new office?
I'm not doing that (Behaviour)	What do you want to do instead? Is there somewhere that you will do it? What else can you do?
I can't do that (Capability)	What can you do? How is it different to what you are doing now? What would it take for you to be able to do that?
This won't work (Belief)	What will be needed for this to work? What can be achieved with this? Who can make it work?
I'm not the right person for this (Identity)	How can you become the right person for this? What makes someone 'the right person'?

In asking questions to change minds, you can avoid asking "Why not?" Typically, you will hear a list of very logical reasons to support the initial statement which will make change harder.

"Why?" gets people to search for, or create, reasons where there are no reasons. The original objections are emotional, not rational and when you ask people "why?" they will defend their position – not useful if your aim is to help them change it!

When people change easily, the change moves through the levels quickly. When people resist change, it gets stuck at one of the levels, and eventually the change is undone.

In helping people make changes more easily, it's important to find out what level the change is stuck at. By asking the right question at the right level, you can free up change so that it moves easily through the remaining level and becomes permanent.

It is vital that you ask questions which focus attention on positive outcomes – what you want, rather than what you don't want.

So having talked for a while about maps and how they relate to these logical levels, let's get back to the issue of alignment, remembering always that the idea of logical levels is just a model, a concept. It isn't true, but it can be a useful means for exploring certain types of problem.

We can say that a person shows a high degree of congruence – of relaxed confidence, natural strength, health or however else you define it – when we see alignment through the levels. This includes a higher level that we haven't talked about yet, which is the system that the individual is a part of. For a person, that system may be a family, a culture, a society or a set of religious or spiritual beliefs. For a company, that system might be a market, an economy, a culture, a society or a different set of religious or spiritual beliefs. There really are companies that give their marketing people the job title of Product Evangelist.

So for us to help a person or company become congruent, healthy and fully effective, we must create alignment through these levels.

Think about it, if you're doing the right job but the working environment is terrible, how can you be at your best? When your natural talents are stifled by a restrictive job, or when you are good at your job but it doesn't really represent who you are, or when you're just in the wrong place with the wrong people, how can you perform at your best?

If you have every been in a situation like this, you'll know that the misalignment of levels just saps your energy. There's nothing intrinsically wrong with the environment or job, it's just not right for you. You know it, you feel it, and the more you ignore it, the worse it gets.

Market

Brand Identity

Culture

Skills & Ideas

Behaviour

Workplace

The greater the misalignment, the more of your energy gets absorbed by friction. Your ability to act is diminished, sometimes by so much that you feel totally ineffective and just give up.

Have you ever experienced this?

When there is alignment, when you feel that you are 'on purpose', doing the right thing, working in an atmosphere where there is a real buzz and a sense of shared purpose, your energy is directly connected to the world. You can see the results of your actions, you feel more motivated and you can overcome any barriers the world places in front of you.

Have you ever experienced a time like this? Perhaps on holiday, perhaps with your family, a sense that you were exactly where you needed to be?

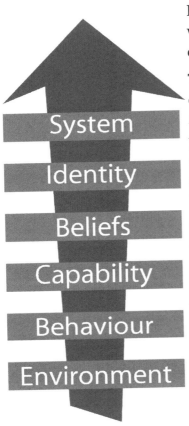

Imagine, if a team or company were aligned like this, what could it achieve?

The $64,000 question is, of course, how to achieve this alignment. Is it something that you can create purposefully, or do some situations just have that spark, that magic that can never be recreated?

The fact that we can produce a model of alignment suggests that we understand something about it, and we can therefore create some tools to achieve it.

You could think of this book as one of those tools.

If you can't hear me at the back, let me know

Understanding Personality

It's important to admit that, in the real world, people will conspire against you. Doubters and saboteurs will place obstacles in front of you, whilst zealots and activists will come up with so many wild ideas that's impossible to get anything done. It's useful to understand how this happens, and that it's not personal. After all, how can it be? They don't know you.

Since your saboteurs and supporters don't know you, their reactions can't be personal, or at least not personal to you. Their reactions are, however, personal to them.

For as long as the field of industrial psychology has existed, which is since the late 19th century, managers have tried to understand the mind of the worker in order to increase productivity. If we can predict what will motivate both groups and individuals, we can do more of that in order to get people to work harder. Since the widespread adoption of these methods, particularly since the 1950s, industrial productivity has increased dramatically, with systems such as TQM, Lean and Six Sigma emerging in more recent years.

Quantifying the personalities of large numbers of workers means that we need large scale tests that are easy to administer, and so the field of psychometric testing has evolved to give managers a simple way of understanding an individual's personality, what motivates them, how they prefer to communicate and so on.

However, using psychometric profiling tools to pigeon-hole people is not useful, because they're not like that all the time. Remember the marketing manager who would sit down in a supplier meeting and say, "I'm an ESTJ, so I'm very judgemental"? He could use that as an excuse to be rude to people, because it wasn't his fault - he was just born that way.

Sometimes, I'm very judgemental too, and I'm an ENTP. Some days I'm an ENFP, depending on what mood I'm in. How can this be possible if the profile is absolute? How can it be possible to change?

You may have heard of the Hawthorne effect, which is basically the idea that people work harder when you're watching them. Since any test of productivity requires measurement, anything that you do to increase productivity will work, for a while. After you've stopped watching, or after people have forgotten that they're being watched, their behaviour will return to 'normal'.

A very typical example can be found in sales training. Sales trainers have an easy job, because they know that sales performance will indeed increase in the period after the training, so they can say, "Look! My training was very effective". However, after some period of time, sales performance will decrease again to its normal level. So sales managers procure training for their teams every year, hoping that this time the trainer will have the magic formula for success that they promise.

If you run, or have access to, a sales team then you can run an experiment. Tell them they're going to receive some radical new sales training and that you're going to measure the impact of the training in terms of sales behaviours and results. Then deliver something that has nothing at all to do with sales and see what happens to their results.

Of course, no-one ever runs an experiment like this. It's easier to believe that more knowledge about sales is what makes performance improve. And that sacrificing a goat is what makes the sun come up. And that wearing your lucky tie is what closes the deal. The problem with superstition is that people rarely want to take the chance of walking under the ladder to prove their friends wrong. Just in case.

Actually, I'd say that most sales managers don't expect the trainer to say anything new, they're just tired of telling their sales people to do the basic, obvious things like actually get on the phone and call some prospects, so they want someone else to tell the team the same thing. They're like a frustrated parent turning to their partner and saying, "I just can't get through to them – you have a go!"

If you do want to use psychometric profiling, there are countless tools to choose from. They fall into two broad categories, type indicators and trait indicators.

One of the most popular psychometric tests is the Myers Briggs Type Indicator, or MBTI. Type indicators propose that there are a fixed number of types of person, and the test reveals which type a person fits into. I, for example, fit into the ENFP type, although at other times I've fitted into ENTP.

Academic psychologists are not very fond of type indicators, because the types themselves are arbitrary categories. Anyone can imagine a certain number of types of people and then find evidence for that. As they say, there are two types of people in the world; people who think there are two types of people, and people who don't.

According to the font of all knowledge, Wikipedia, "One study that directly compared a "type" instrument (the MBTI) to a "trait" instrument (the NEO PI) found that the trait measure was a better predictor of personality disorders. Because of these problems, personality type theories have fallen out of favor in psychology. Most researchers now believe that it is impossible to explain the diversity of human personality with a small number of discrete types. They recommend trait models instead, such as the five-factor model."

The 'Big Five' is generally the tool most favoured by serious psychologists, its five factors of personality being

- Openness to experience

- Conscientiousness

- Extraversion

- Agreeableness

- Neuroticism

So let's say you're hiring a new salesperson. You administer the test and find that she is high on neuroticism and low on conscientiousness. But she has hit target every year for the past five years. So what? What does it mean? How does it affect your hiring decision?

In short, it doesn't. Hiring managers will generally make a decision and then look for evidence to confirm the decision. A neurotic salesperson with no appetite for finishing tasks fits right into many sales cultures. As long as they look good and hit target, that's all that matters.

You have to remember that psychometric tools are commercial products, designed to make money. The business model is to charge a fairly low fee for each test but to charge people quite a high fee to become licensed to sell and administer the test. Once you're a licensed user, you then make a small percentage on each test you administer, and if you're lucky enough to sell the test to an entire team or even an entire company then you actually make some money out of it.

The psychology behind the test might be valid, it might not be. But it's the way that the psychology gets packaged into the tool that is the problem. Of course, the owners of the tools don't want you to think about that.

The biggest problem with psychometrics is that companies, typically HR departments, will deploy a tool on a large scale, give individuals and managers a briefing on how to interpret the results and then everyone sits around, wondering the most important question of all. "So what?"

A popular use of psychometrics is in understanding team dynamics. A particular tool gives participants a language for communicating their differences. I'm an onion and you're a potato, and that's why you're an idiot.

One of the greatest problems with all psychometric tools is the degree to which behaviour is learned. As a social species, we are adept at fitting in, so we will acquire new languages, appearances, habits, preferences, diets and more in order to be accepted into a particular social circle.

If you work in a large office, just keep track of how long it takes for the new starters to look, sound, act and even eat like their colleagues.

How is this relevant to change? Because managers often try to use psychometrics to predict the acceptance of organisational change. However, since in reality they cannot individualise the communication of change, any predictions are pretty much useless. Also, trying to predict the acceptance of change has one major drawback – it means that you are trying to control the outcome.

Trying to control an outcome through another person is generally called 'manipulation', and it is definitely not a good way to implement organisational change.

For example, some self help experts will tell you that some people are motivated towards goals, and others away from problems. Therefore, you should use language which appeals to these people:

"You should accept your new contract terms because it will allow you to keep your job"

"You should accept your new contract terms because it will prevent you from being made redundant"

You are not stupid, and neither are the people around you. We all know when we're being buttered-up or coerced into something. Any conversation which starts with, "Hi! How are you doing! What have you been up to?" raises suspicion. I'm fine thank you. Why do you want to know? Equally, when someone asks, "Can you do me a favour", your natural inclination is to want to know what the favour is first. And in response to, "Have you got a minute", well, you get the idea. You know when you're being set up. So any communication which promises to adapt to the listener is a deviation from the speaker's normal style, and is therefore odd, and therefore raises suspicion.

Resistance to change is not caused by change, it is caused by devious and manipulative communication.

"Now, I don't want you to worry, but…"

This opening statement serves as an alarm call, focusing the listener's attention on something that the speaker is worried about. Why would you be worried about worrying me?

Perhaps you've been in the situation yourself, where your manager or your HR business partner suddenly wants to 'get to know you'. Why? They didn't want to know you before, so what's changed?

If you're still thinking that there must be some mileage in psychometrics then allow me to introduce you to perhaps the simplest of them all.

One of the factors within the 'Big Five' psychometric is 'extraversion'. Does being an extravert mean that you're the life and soul of the party? Not at all. What it means is that extraverts like to connect with other people, whereas introverts prefer to detach from other people.

When you're born, you have broadly one of two types of experience within the first few weeks of your life. You either find that when you express a need, that need is met by your parents, or you learn that when you express a need, that need is not immediately met and you learn to take care of yourself.

The main way that babies express their needs is through crying, and the main way that babies meet their own needs is through thumb sucking or other 'Primary circular reactions', as they are called by child psychologists. In other words, babies learn very quickly how to alert others to their predicament, or how to comfort themselves in the absence of external help.

In extreme cases, children suffer from neglect, but that's not what we're talking about here. We're talking about normal, healthy, well adjusted people like you and me.

As a child gets older, the nurturing, supporting parent can of course be over-supportive and the child ends up 'spoilt', unable or unwilling to do anything for itself.

We very quickly learn that either the world is an abundant place that meets our needs or that the world is a scarce place where we have to sort ourselves out. Of course, both are true depending on how you look at it, and that's the point – it is a matter of perception. However, we acquire the perception so early in life that it simply becomes a universal truth that our successive experiences are built upon. We never go back and question what we learned in the first few weeks of life, we just blame other people for not living up to our expectations.

If, as a child, your needs were mostly met by	Yourself	Others
Your dominant tendency is to	Compete	Accommodate
You tend to trust others	Less	More
You tend to rely on others	Less	More
Under pressure, you tend to	Blame others	Blame yourself
Under extreme pressure, you might even become	Isolated	Needy
You tend to see resources as	Limited	Abundant
You tend to believe	Yourself	Others
You tend to value	Initiative and drive	Teamwork and harmony

Whilst we start life at either end of the spectrum, we quickly learn to adapt in order to survive in a world that is neither abundant nor scarce.

Most importantly, we learn that there are times when other people don't meet our needs, and we learn that there are times when we have to rely on other people.

And in learning how to interact with other people, we learn how to manage conflict.

Managing Conflict

Conflict is part of daily life, and for the most part we manage it well, for example when two people want to take the same day off, or when two people in a supermarket want to get their trolleys down the same aisle.

Some people see conflict as a battle which can only be won or lost, others see the potential for compromise.

Some people believe that there's enough of everything for everyone, and all that's needed in life is a little patience.

Other people believe that there's not enough of everything to go round, so if you don't fight for what you need, you might lose out.

Psychologists believe that this difference in how people deal with conflict arises from an underlying difference in their view of the world, which began very early on in their lives.

The basic difference is that people who had every need attended to as a baby grow up knowing that the world, and other people, will satisfy their needs, so it's safe to rely on other people. On the other hand, people who didn't have every need satisfied as a baby grow up knowing that if you want something, you have to get it for yourself and you can't rely totally on other people, especially where your livelihood or safety are concerned.

It's not a matter of which is best, as there are pros and cons to each type. As with most things, flexibility always wins.

Which type you fall into affects not only how you get involved in conflict, but also how you deal with conflict between other people. For example, how you deal with an angry customer is influenced by how you feel about conflict, even though you're not directly involved in it.

Conflict Styles

One theory of conflict resolution shows two competing needs; a need to look after your own interests, and a need to serve the interests of others. How strongly you feel these needs is reflected in how you deal with conflict.

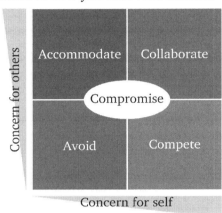

Avoid	Runs away at the first sign of conflict and hopes someone else will deal with it.
Accommodate	Gives in to the other person and may rationalise that as kindness.
Compete	Fights to win. May create conflict in order to win, or may feel that they haven't really won if they haven't had to fight for it.
Collaborate	Looks for 'win/win' opportunities. Makes the discussion bigger so that everyone can achieve a good outcome.

I've seen a fifth style added in the middle of the chart; Compromise. However, I personally ignore this one. A compromise is an outcome where no-one gets what they want. If that's because harmony is more important than getting what you want then your response is Accommodate, and if it's because you and the other person just can't find a way to reach an agreement then your response is Compete.

The ideal situation is that you care about what you want, and you care about what the other person wants, so you look for opportunities to Collaborate in order to resolve conflict.

The worst situation is to Avoid conflict, because you know it will only get worse if you leave it.

At least with Compete and Accommodate, someone gets what they want...

The natural introvert who believes that the world is a scarce, competitive place will of course naturally Compete in a conflict situation. The natural extravert who believes that the world is a supportive, giving place will naturally Accommodate. These two conflict responses are innate.

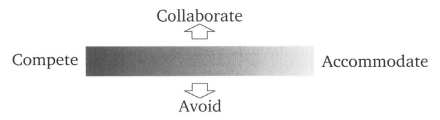

The Avoid response is driven by a fear of confrontation, and can be demonstrated by both introverts and extraverts for different reasons. Typically, the introvert will Avoid as a response to not getting his own way and will take his ball and go home, whereas the extravert will Avoid as a response to the discomfort of Conflict, hiding in their bedroom until the arguing stops.

Avoid is therefore a learned response.

Collaborate is a learned response too, more typically learned as an adult. Again, both introverts and extraverts can learn to Collaborate.

What causes conflict?

Beliefs - Conflict can arise because two or more people have different beliefs about the world. Whilst beliefs aren't true, people act as if they are and will go to great lengths to defend them.

Intention - Even in the same situation, different people can have very different intentions or agendas. Sometimes, one or more people will have a 'hidden agenda', which leads to conflict because, while both people say they want the same thing, in fact they don't.

Goal - People can experience conflict because they have very different goals. Normally, this wouldn't cause a problem, but when something connects those people, such as a sense of competition, those different goals create conflict.

Resources - Conflict can arise because two or more people have to compete for limited resources. Both have a goal to achieve, but for one to achieve their goal would be at the other's expense.

Conflict Cultures

Can you see the ways in which organisational cultures reflect these conflict styles?

"The customer is always right" = Accommodate?

"You made a mistake, but we'll give you a refund as a gesture of goodwill" = Compete?

"We'd never have done that, it's not our policy" = Avoid?

"We can see there's been a problem, let's work together to resolve it" = Collaborate?

The bottom line is that your customers don't notice when you do everything right, because that's what they expect.

Your customers only notice when something goes wrong, and by going out of your way to handle that as well as you can, you'll turn customers into fans.

~

If we look for categories to put people in, we will surely find that people fit those categories. On the other hand, it's impractical to adapt your communication or your methods to each individual. Instead, I suggest that you adopt a simpler approach – treat everyone the same. After all, what we really want in a team is to be treated equally and fairly.

Office Politics

Do you know what these are costing your business right now?

You might think, "It doesn't happen in my company". Well, that's why they're called 'hidden' agendas. You're not supposed to know what's going on. If you did, you'd try to put a stop to it.

You might think, "But this kind of thing is a way of life in companies, it happens everywhere". Just because this happens everywhere, is that a good enough reason to let it happen to you?

You might think, "But these problems don't really cost us anything". I know a major engineering company that loses around £16 Million per year because of problems like this, and their annual turnover is only £65 Million. People aren't doing what they are supposed to do, and they aren't doing what they commit to.

Office politics, manipulation and personal empires are powerful influences in any change project, because you think you're changing one business structure, when there's another structure working to stop you. It's like trying to keep a house tidy when there's a resident poltergeist that comes in at night and messes the place up again.

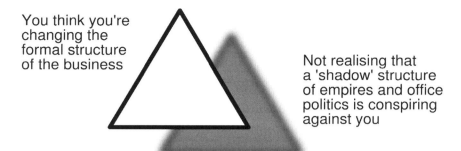

You think you're changing the formal structure of the business

Not realising that a 'shadow' structure of empires and office politics is conspiring against you

What are the symptoms that hidden agendas and politics are harming your business? You may see low staff morale or high staff turnover. You may see a cause for concern in sales performance, costs or financial reports. It may be that customer complaints increase, or you discover one day that customer complaints or production problems are not being communicated to you. Decisions are hard to reach, time scales and deadlines slip, hidden costs escalate and managers are losing control.

All of these symptoms add up to poor performance of the business, and what makes them important is that there is no consistent and satisfactory explanation. In fact, when you ask questions, you get so confused with the answers that you feel uncomfortable about asking. Your questions are met with excuses, blame and promises. At first, some of the excuses seem plausible until you start to dig deeper.

There is a fundamental, underlying problem in every case – managers do not have control of the business.

Weak management control means that people are not held accountable for their actions, which means that they can under perform or manipulate situations and resources to their benefit with no consequences. The company and everyone in it suffers the consequences on their behalf.

Weak management allows control to be pulled down the organisation, pushing accountability up. Managers work later the higher up they are, senior managers have to deal with customer dissatisfaction and staff get to go home early with no stress.

Some modern parenting and leadership philosophies propose that control, power and boundaries are bad things. Children should be allowed free expression. Staff should be allowed to define their own working environment. Leaders should lead through authenticity and shared vision and values.

Equally, taxes should be banned, chocolate should have no calories and small animals should climb in through our windows and clean up our houses at night.

A modern business can be a hostile environment. People live with the threat of losing their jobs, of feeling over-worked and under-paid, of seeing their colleagues promoted over them, of seeing pay rises pass them by and people respond to this perceived hostility in many different ways.

In one company alone, I found the following problems.

A project accountant has been making excuses for not completing a professional qualification for 5 years. His focus is on promoting himself by building an empire rather than through hard work. He has hired two assistants to do his work for him, based on a business case of how busy he is, when the reality is that he actively kills time during the day and then completes his work when everyone else has gone home so that he can earn time off in lieu and also miss family chores, getting home just in time to read the bedtime story after all the hard work has been done.

An engineer didn't want to put the hard work into getting a promotion so she developed a 'friendship' with her manager and then threatened to leave for a competitor. Her manager recommended her for promotion, which she received. Other engineers now know that they don't have to work for a promotion, they just have to threaten the right person.

An engineer has been making excuses for not completing professional qualification for 2 years. His focus is on building a niche position where he can avoid work. He costs the business in time, avoiding work and duplication of resources.

An engineer takes on secondments to promote herself and get noticed by senior managers. Her promotion strategy in the past has been to manipulate men into offering her promotions, but the business is now changing so rapidly that she is being sidelined by new recruits with the proper qualifications. She costs the business in tying up senior managers' time and not performing any of the roles properly.

The Operations Director is mainly concerned with promoting himself and covering up his poor performance. He creates graphs and monthly results which superficially hide the serious problems in the business. He has been asked to look at the delivery problems and has been thinking about it for over 4 months so far, because in reality he doesn't want to address the problems. He creates fictional milestones to make projects appear to perform better than they actually are, and has drawn his colleagues into this. He obstructs anyone who tries to delve into the causes of the problems. He is therefore responsible for anything up to £16 Million in lost profit.

Inventing project statistics probably doesn't seem so bad, until you consider that at some point, those project reports become financial reports, and those financial reports make it all the way up the reporting line into the company's official accounts.

Manipulating reports today becomes a corporate governance issue and a financial reporting scandal tomorrow. Global businesses have collapsed as a result of such activities.

When the problem gets to a high enough level, someone else will solve it for you, and you will like that a lot less than facing the discomfort of solving it for yourself today.

Office politics is the common term for systematic manipulation within the workplace. Some people say that they leave the 'corporate world' to escape office politics, although I doubt if they would be saying that if the politics had worked in their favour.

Office politics is the means by which subversive goals such as 'empire building' are achieved. A person doesn't want to achieve power and status through a legitimate route so, instead, they manipulate relationships to build an unofficial 'power base'. Their perceived status is far in excess of their official rank.'

You might call to mind images of corrupt politicians, living in luxury in return for providing political concessions to organised crime leaders. The reality is that they live not in luxury but in fear, because they understand the fragile life that they lead. However, in an average business, these people aren't so easy to spot.

Office politicians don't necessarily make a big show of their illegitimate gains, because that would be too obvious. It would give the game away. What they seek is often the power to influence other people. They seek authority for the rumours that they spread. They seek a strange form of respect from the people who need the information that they guard so closely

The basis of office politics is insecurity, and insecurity gives rise to manipulation and bullying too, so you'll see all of these behaviours together. You'll see people alienated within their own teams, managers regularly changing their 'favourites' and people driven to frustration every day by events which are, in themselves, too insignificant to complain about.

To the individual, a culture of manipulation, politics and bullying is demoralising and harmful, and it means that staff turnover can be high and that it's difficult to hang on to the people who will really support a business and make it successful

Hidden agendas build a business culture where the business is driven by power, manipulation, coercion and control rather than customer focus, sound financial decisions and a strong business plan and strategy.

Dealing with manipulation can be difficult because it happens indirectly and mostly out in the open, so traditional methods of management or HR policies are mostly ineffective. The manipulator will always have an excuse, or will have set up a scapegoat, like a child who gets his friend to throw the stone at the window.

When individuals pursue their own hidden agendas at the cost of the team or the business, quite simply their focus moves away from whatever their job is and they create more and more opportunities to serve their own needs. There are lots of high profile cases in the press where directors or managers covered up a company's financial performance in order to increase the value of their share options or the value of the company in preparation for selling it, and whilst these cases may seem very distant for someone listening to this today, they are the tip of the iceberg, because they represent cases that can be audited, that are big enough to go to court and appear in the press. These cases will start with activities that aren't illegal and where there is no trail of email evidence for the investigators to find.

At the corporate level, company directors make millions of pounds from their stock options (Fisons, Enron, WorldCom, Tyco, AOL) whilst at the SME level, individuals are allowed to build their own careers, run competing businesses during working hours, come and go as they please and use company resources for their own ends. Whilst these might seem trivial, the point is that they are doing this for their own gain and at the expense of the company, and ultimately that has an adverse impact on the other people in the company. Ultimately, the company can go out of business and the manipulator moves on, leaving everyone else to pick up the pieces.

Since an expert manipulator is highly skilled in covering up their behaviour, the best place to look for clues is in the business performance, sales figures, customer retention, turnover, expenses, promotions and so on. What's important is that you realise that a decline in performance is the result of an individual pulling the strings rather than an overall shift in the market or economy that is outside of anyone's control. The manipulator will always have an excuse, and it will rarely be their fault. They will change sides as often as they need to and they are therefore hard to pin down because they always seem to be on your side with a good explanation of what's going on.

I met a Managing Director who was manipulating the business strategy so that she could orchestrate a merger and move outside of the company. The problem was that the extent to which she was manipulating the people and the strategy meant that in the short term the business would fail against its performance targets before she could complete the merger. She had set up three directors as scapegoats and fired them to make sure that she couldn't be replaced, but the company was in danger of collapsing and taking her career aspirations with it.

In another company, a project manager's career depended on her establishing long term relationships where she could manipulate someone into favouring her for internal promotions. The problem for her was that the business was changing faster than her approach allowed for, because of the changes in the economy and the growth of the business.

Neither of them could see that their approach was destructive for them and for the businesses because of the time taken to manipulate the situation. Whilst their approach had gotten them this far, they were running out of time. Fundamentally, the manipulative approach may have worked in the past because the business culture allowed it to, but in today's market environment, businesses no longer have the luxury of time or resources to support people like this.

When the situation gets really bad, you might go as far as to use the word 'bullying', which is becoming a high profile business problem, with cases appearing in the media on a regular basis. The root of bullying is a person's insecurity which makes them alienate others in order to feel accepted.

A $325,000 compensation payout to a man subjected to months of workplace bullying has been applauded by anti-bullying experts. Pasquale De Petro, 53, won the payout in Victoria's County Court last week after months of harassment and abuse when he worked as an aeroplane cleaner.

Herald Sun, April 8, 2011

On April 6, 2011, at the Superior court of New Jersey, a jury of five women and three men issued a verdict awarding $804,214 in compensatory damages to Hope Bailey-Rhodeman in a race discrimination and retaliation case against Xerox Corp., a global leader in business processes and document management with more than 130,000 employees.

Business Week, April 8, 2011

A 56-year-old Irish teacher was yesterday awarded €88,000 (£77,000) in damages after a court heard how [her headmaster] subjected her to 'oppressive bullying', had 'marginalised' her and treated her with 'unrelenting hostility'.

Daily Mail, March 25, 2011

AXA PPP Healthcare has been ordered to pay £142,000 in compensation to a worker who was nicknamed SpongeBob SquarePants by colleagues and mocked for her accent.

Daily Telegraph, March 22, 2011

A woman banker in the London office of a Russian bank has been awarded £3.1 million after being driven to mental collapse by a campaign of harassment and unfounded drug slurs.
The tribunal last October ruled in her favour after hearing that colleagues at Sberbank CIB had referred to her as "Ms Bonkers" and that she had been falsely accused of being a cocaine addict.

London Evening Standard, April 7, 2015

Bullying is a high profile problem because employment law now offers protection, which means that cases hit the headlines and victims can seek compensation. However, these represent one-off costs and are a drop in the ocean compared to the money that leaks out of a business on a daily basis.

Consider the example of a finance manager in an engineering company. It's a long story, but for now suffice to say that the sum total of a day's work for him was two emails, a letter and two phone calls. One of his main activities was creating the illusion of work so that he always looked busy. This meant that he could work late every evening and earn time off in lieu whilst not actually doing anything productive. He frequently had people come into his office and ask him what he was doing with their projects, which was often embarrassing as the answer was usually 'nothing'. He bought a whiteboard so that he could write what was happening with each project for all to see how busy he was.

You might be thinking that writing project activity on a whiteboard on your office wall is a good thing. You might also be thinking that I'm clearly paranoid for thinking that he had any ulterior motive.

But here's the key. When he told me about the whiteboard, he didn't say that he'd bought a whiteboard, he said that he had 'invested' in a whiteboard. What a strange word to use.

Here's an exercise for you. Walk around your office and look at what people have on their walls. Look for posters, notices, to do lists, flip chart paper and so on.

Now, ask yourself this question: who are those posters for?

Are those posters an advertisement?

Are they there to tell you something? To impress you?

What about the books on their shelf? There to be read or to impress visitors to their office?

Presuming that you saw some offices with posters and books for the occupant's benefit, and some where they were for your benefit, how did you tell the difference?

And now that you have begun to notice, how does it change your opinion of that person?

You might still be wondering why a whiteboard is such a big deal. The person in question hired an assistant and was in the process of hiring his assistant an assistant. Three people to do the work of one person, who was working for a sum total of perhaps two hours per day. Luckily, the company made some redundancies and his assistant never got the assistant.

Why did the company make redundancies, do you think? Because profits were significantly lower than predicted.

Why would profits be lower than predicted?

Firstly, loose change falls down the cracks between the floorboards. Every whiteboard, every lazy day has a cost associated with it. These costs are only difficult to measure because managers generally don't question costs that are covered by business cases and purchase orders and which fall within their budgets. Some managers especially enjoy signing purchase orders because it's one of only a few ways in which they can exert what they feel is genuine power.

Secondly, management reports are inaccurate so future forecasts are inaccurate. In fact, because people aren't doing what they should be doing, they tend to report on what they should be doing rather than what they are doing.

Management reports are deliberately inaccurate, and therefore profit forecasts cannot be reliable.

Profits are lower than predicted because hidden costs are rising, so profit predictions are higher than they should be.

Hidden agendas are hidden for a good reason. The person with the hidden agenda isn't open because they think that other people will prevent them from achieving their goal, which is often status, power or the simple avoidance of work. All of these have a cost to the business.

Any business exists solely for the purpose of making money – it is what distinguishes a business from a voluntary operation. Every business has a set of core activities which must be performed, and since those activities result in income for the business, they have a monetary value. That, in a nutshell, is the value of someone's job and hence their value as an employee.

Hidden agendas and office politics have the potential to derail your change program before you've started. When you're mapping out the current organisational structure and status, don't look at organisational charts, get out there and see who's really in charge. Only then can you hope to have any influence on the future.

Changing Minds

During the course of any change, the most important thing you have to change is people's minds. Their beliefs, opinions, rules and attitude are all elements that can hold back the tide of change.

In traditional change management approaches, this is often glossed over, or approached in a rational, logical way. If you make enough posters and mugs, and if you tell people all the reasons why there is change, they'll come round to the idea eventually. I think the reality is far simpler than this, and remember, the reason I say that is from my own personal experience of working in companies in 'core business' roles such as being a service engineer and a sales person. I worked in the telecoms industry during the time when it changed probably more than any other industry at any other time in history, and some of the companies I worked for responded to this with a different culture change program every year.

What I think is far simpler than most people believe is that companies often aim for a lofty culture change when what they really want is people to do things differently or work harder. If you tell someone that a manufacturing process is changing, I'm pretty sure their reaction will be, "OK then. Show me what to do". They only become resistant to change when they think it's about them, because someone who has seconded themselves to the change project tells them that they are running a racket and need to have a breakthrough because they don't have the kind of 'can do' attitude that the company needs to fulfil its strategic objectives and be a global thought leading brand champion evangelist in the 21st century.

Since change is a response to changes in the environmental niche, we could say that the only time a company needs to change is when its market changes. Sometimes, something genuinely changes in the world that necessitates change. For example, the increase in consumer use of the Internet created retail opportunities that simply did not exist twenty years ago. At that time, we still had mail order home shopping, it just meant that you shopped out of a catalogue and paid 13p a week for 26 weeks until you were the proud owner of a hostess trolley. These retail channels relied on local distributors, and the Internet has largely replaced local, specialised distribution channels. The same products come from the same manufacturers, you're just no longer paying a dozen middle-men and middle-women to bring them to you.

In a competitive market, companies are often rated on market share. If a company wants to get bigger, it has a number of options. It could buy a competitor, it could diversify into other markets and it could change the way it operates in order to outsell its competitors and increase its market share.

There is of course the much overlooked solution of making better products that more people would want to buy. I'm sure that products such as the iPod would not have been as successful if they weren't any good, even in spite of the amount of money spent on marketing. Apple's considerable brand loyalty allowed the iPod to weather its battery problems that may have killed off a less popular product, but we have to apply Occam's razor and presume that the iPod is successful because it's quite good, or at least good enough for its owners.

If a company doesn't have the money to buy a competitor, or if the nature of its products makes innovation difficult then the next best way to increase market share is to have a culture change program – right? Obviously, if people are buying from your competitors, it must be because you don't have meetings standing up and all wear jeans on a Friday.

Of course, I'm being somewhat sarcastic again. Having meetings standing up is a means to an end; the end being to make decisions faster. Making decisions faster makes the company more responsive to market changes, which makes it more adaptable to change, which makes it more likely to be successful. Taking the tables out of board rooms didn't make the company successful. Perhaps it would be better to take the bored out of board rooms. Or take the rooms out and just leave the boards. Now that would be one hell of a room – no room, just boards. Sorry, I was channelling the spirit of Groucho Marx for a moment there.

Do you remember the organisation that got rid of all of its marketing managers to speed up decision making, only to find that it didn't? It just slowed it down for a different reason. Sometimes, people think they are focusing on the problem when in fact what they're looking at is a symptom.

Take the common cold for example. Pharmaceutical companies cannot cure it because it's a virus which mutates. When I have a cold, it's not the virus that's the problem – it's the runny nose and headache that I don't want. The symptoms are the problem. The problem, the virus, I couldn't care less about. I'm full of bacteria and viruses anyway, most of which mind their own business, and some of which are actually important for my survival. Therefore, what the pharmaceutical industry focuses on is not cures as you would expect but on suppressing symptoms. Of course, the side effect of this is that the problem never goes away…

This also hints at an interesting aspect of traditional change management programs. The consultants come along and run some focus groups to ask people what they think should change, then they go and do whatever they were going to do anyway and ignore whatever was suggested by the focus groups. Afterwards, the consultants go away with bulging wallets and happy faces at a job well done, while the staff of the company are more demotivated and disillusioned than ever. You see, if you're going to change the business, don't insult me by telling me I have a say in it when I don't Just get on and do it and then let me know what you want me to do differently.

Our man on the shop floor doesn't expect to be asked his opinion. On the other hand, if you ask his opinion, he expects you to take it into account.

I suppose some people just want to turn up and do their jobs. These people are largely ignored by traditional change consultants because they're not 'with the program'. Well, they are probably the most important people in the organisation, because they are happy to turn up and do a good job, whatever it is. People who have career and political aspirations are often seen as wonderful 'change agents' but they cause other problems. They form steering committees, they come up with great project names.

At one telecoms company I worked for, a sales manager renamed his team as 'PRISM' which stood for something to do with major accounts and had another meaning to do with the way that white light is comprised of many different colours, representing the diversity of his team, combining together to form the brilliant white light of sales awesomeness. Another sales manager, not wanting to be outdone, renamed his team as 'SIGMA', representing the whole being greater than the sum of its parts. When everyone started referring to the team as 'smegma', he quickly dropped the name. If you don't know, smegma is a rude word meaning... well, I can't say, there might be children reading. Ask your mother.

Many of the managers I've worked for did seem to think that if you ask people for their opinion, they will feel warm and loved, at which point you can then ignore them completely. If the change consultants did a survey and ran some focus groups, they could then go and change anything because we all had a sense that we were contributing to the good of the company. The opposite was true.

Imagine that I offer to take you out to dinner tonight. I said 'imagine', I didn't say that I'm actually coming[2]. Imagine that I ask you to dress up, and that I pick you up and we go to the centre of town. We seem to be walking to the most exclusive restaurant, a place you have wanted to try out for a long time. As we get closer, you begin to realise that we're not walking straight for the door, we appear to now be walking in the direction of the greasy café next door. As we walk in and I order two cheese sandwiches, how do you feel? That's how people feel after focus group meetings.

You may have seen this change model before:

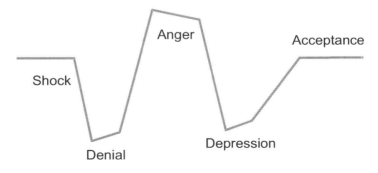

2 A woman once turned up at ITN's offices, saying that she had an appointment with Alastair Stewart, a TV news reader. At the end of the previous bulletin, he had said, "I'll see you at ten o'clock".

This emotional framework is a derivative of work by Elizabeth Kubler-Ross in her book "On Death and Dying" which dealt with the phases people experience when faced with the loss of someone close.

These traditional models are based on overcoming resistance to change, whereas Change Magic is based on harnessing and directing the natural and already existing process of change. Either we never change unless forced to, or we change every day, depending on which way you look at it.

Remember one of Change Magic's key assertions? People only notice what they notice? When you got up this morning, did your thought process go something like this?

"Oh my God! I need new pants! No, I don't need new pants. It's not true. I can't need new pants. I hate pants! Oh I'm so miserable. I feel really bad about my pants. Well I just don't have a choice – I'll put some new pants on"

I'm hoping the answer is "no", otherwise you may find your life is a little more complicated than it needs to be.

In personal change, a lot of therapists have traditionally focussed on 'fixing' problems such as phobias. A far more elegant solution is moving the threshold for the phobia to operate. For example, if you're scared of snakes then that is a really useful skill to have when you're exploring the Amazon. It's just not useful in Milton Keynes. It's not useful to lose the skill, just move the threshold so that it doesn't interfere with your life.

"But", I hear you say, "you're still not telling me how I change people's minds". Patience, my young friend. I have pages to fill and no particular deadline to worry about.

Let's say that a colleague or customer has a very fixed opinion about something that you disagree with. How do you change their mind? Do you present the logical sides of the argument, reasoning that your opinion is the right one? Do you exert emotional influence? Do you argue? I'm sure you can think of colleagues who use those methods – and more. Which techniques are the most effective?

It's a trick question, of course. No one method is effective all the time if we are thinking at the level of content. It's like those sales courses that you'll see advertised that promise to teach you the seven guaranteed ways to get past a gatekeeper. Those seven only work as long as gatekeepers only have six ways to say "no". Guess what? When the gatekeepers learn eight ways to say "no", you have to go on another training course.

Let's think instead about the structure of the situation, not the content. It doesn't matter that you say "black" and your colleague says "white". What you both have in common is a state of certainty. Let's look at what we want to achieve in terms of content:

| Black | → | White |

And now in terms of structure:

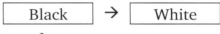

So, whilst we think we want to change someone's mind, in fact we're not introducing any change at all in the person's state. That is a big drawback. It doesn't matter whether we're changing black to white, yes to no or hire to fire. If we don't first bring about a state change, there will be no change in the person's position, and anything that you do to argue with or persuade them will only push them further into their state of certainty.

Now, if you want to bring about a state change in yourself or someone else, it's useful to bear in mind that smooth, progressive state changes are much easier to make. You are unlikely to get someone to change from a state of doubt to a state of total passion for your idea in one step, so what would be a reasonable step on from certainty? How about doubt? Then uncertainty? Then confusion?

Now you can see where confusion fits in – it's a very useful transition state to move someone from just about any current state to any desired state. Confusion is relatively easy to elicit as well – if you already have rapport, you only need to be confused yourself and the other person will often follow you!

Let's take another look at the structure of opinion change:

| Certainty | → | Confusion | → | Certainty |

People generally do not like being confused as it can feel uncomfortable. When people are confused, they will tend to move towards whatever makes them feel comfortable and certain again. It doesn't have to make sense logically, it only has to be compelling.

If we add our content back in to the equation, we get:

| Black | → | Confusion | → | White |

Now, confusion isn't the only transition state you can use. In fact, if you look at natural change that is occurring all around you, you'll see many other transition states.

Here are a few examples that you may have experience of:

- Laughter
- Anger
- Love

- Surprise
- Fear
- Stress

There are some fairly well known 'personal development' courses that lead participants through pain, by confronting their own fears and personal experiences. You might have an experience yourself where fear has made you stronger, perhaps in a dangerous situation.

Many companies use team building days to create change through transition states, unfortunately, not everyone finds them as much fun as their designers intend. As a rule of thumb, getting a barrel of radioactive waste across a swamp using only toothpicks and an elastic band in a wet field near Wolverhampton is even less fun than it sounds.

You can probably recall an intense relationship that changed your beliefs or attitude. Finally, anger is a state that many people experience in companies when they feel something is being taken away from them.

An old manager of mine used to get out of people giving him a hard time (deservedly) by interrupting them, saying something like, "are they new glasses?" and then using the moment of confusion to run away.

The important point is that you can use any transition state that is different to the start and end states. This is how you can tame the emotional roller coaster – by remembering Change Magic's most fundamental message which is to focus on the outcome, not the change. In this case the outcome is a state which frees you to move to the next outcome, which is the target belief or attitude.

In snooping around the wonderful Internet for facts and figures, I found the following in a respected HR magazine's article on change management models.

"Inertia or resistance is a major issue – particularly in more bureaucratic organizations – some change theorists suggest that logic (the facts and data presented in stage one) are not sufficient to move some people to change and that we perhaps need to place more emphasis on the emotional response to change through more skilled use of language, analogy, modelling the way."

Wow! You mean to say that change management isn't just about logic and facts? You mean that if you show someone the company balance sheet they won't understand the reasons for their redundancy and be quite happy with it? You mean people feel things? And those feelings affect the way they respond to change?

Those crazy change theorists. It's a good job there are a few change magicians like us around to make sure things don't get out of hand.

Take a moment to think of something that you keep meaning to get round to, but you always manage to find something else to do instead. The reason that you are avoiding that thing is because of fear. You'll deny it, of course, because a big strapping fellow like your good self isn't afraid of anything. You're awesome in every possible way. Fear is for weak, vulnerable, normal, people. Not superhumans like you. Therefore, because you are in denial, you don't even know what you're afraid of. As soon as you come within a hundred yards of your fear, you'll find yourself gently nudged away by an invisible forcefield. The slightest, tiniest, most subtle twinge of fear will make you stop, mid sentence, and head off in a more comforting direction. Whenever you hear someone change the subject mid, well, you know what I mean. They have been pushed off course by their fear, and they didn't even know it.

Fear is the source of your discomfort zone, that great wilderness that lies beyond your comfort zone. Fear is what makes you do things that you'd rather not, just to fit in. Fear is what makes you forget to do things that you said you'd do. Fear is what makes you act out of character when you're under pressure. Fear is what makes you stressed, aggressive and short tempered.

What are you afraid of? All kinds of things. Rejection. Failure. Being useless, helpless, demanding, needy, worthless. And your greatest fear of all is that all of these things are true. You are unlovable, You are not worthy. You are not good enough. And it feels absolutely horrible, so horrible that your mind protects you and steers you away from the terrible truth.

When you're born, your parents do their best but that's not good enough. They pass on their fears and insecurities of their parents, and you will pass those fears onto your children too. You let your children get on with playing or exploring or dancing or whatever it is they're doing, then when they go too far you jump in with an exception. "Stop that". "Don't". "No".

You have no idea what's going on. You were doing your own thing, enjoying yourself with wild abandon, and now your mother or father is shouting at you and you feel bad, rejected, guilty and worthless. Your parents tell you, one way or another, that they only love you when you're good, so when you do bad things you feel unlovable. You learn to be afraid, afraid to dance, afraid to sing, afraid to create, afraid to love, afraid to let go, afraid to be yourself. You also learn that it's not a good idea to show your fears and weaknesses to the world, so you pretend to be not afraid, you pretend to be the opposite of what you fear you are.

If you feel unlikeable, you show people how lovely and friendly you are. If you feel useless, you make yourself useful. If you feel rejected, you reject other people first. If you feel worthless, you let other people walk all over you. And if you feel that nothing you do is good enough, you show other people how perfect you are.

If you can accept this in yourself, you'll be amazed at how people scream their insecurities at you. The person who tells you how successful they are is answering a question that you didn't ask. The person who goes out of their way to make themselves useful is proving a point that no-one disputed.

From an evolutionary point of view, it makes a lot of sense to be afraid. The things that make us feel good aren't going to kill us, whereas fear is more likely to keep us alive. Yet that primal survival mechanism is hijacked by our modern sensibilities and we end up projecting our fear onto all kinds of ridiculous situations. When your boss tells you that you're not achieving the required standard of work, your life is not in danger. No-one, to the best of my knowledge, has ever been killed by an audience because a presentation about the functionality of a new software release was a bit boring. Those projections are so intense, so powerful, that the nervous speaker acts *as if* their life is in danger, and takes avoiding action as early as possible, perhaps lining up a colleague for the presentation, or getting involved in some other, time consuming project, or as a last resort, falling ill on the day of the presentation so that someone else has to deliver it.

These fears are incredibly powerful and motivate people in all kinds of odd ways, yet they can be very easily overcome.

The pretence masks the fear, and the fear masks the true self. The irony is that people who try to convince you that they are successful actually are successful, and people who try to make you like them actually are very nice, and people who trap potential partners into a loving relationship actually are very wonderful and loveable, and would be more-so if they just didn't try quite so hard. The person who proves they're good enough is already more than good enough, and the person who wants to be valued overlooks all of the many ways in which they already are.

This is a book on organisational change, yet organisational change is really a collective version of personal change. I don't expect you to read a book and then dive into personal transformational therapy. That's not realistic.

What is realistic? Perhaps that when you understand how powerful and invisible your fears are, you'll understand why people do the weird, reactive things that they do. When you begin to understand that, you'll realise that people don't scupper your beautiful strategic plans because they don't like you, they react that way because they're afraid. What of? It doesn't matter. How do you stop them from being afraid? You don't need to. So how do you actually implement change? Just get on with it. People will not be reassured by your kind words and well intentioned promises, they will be reassured by your actions. If you are trying to convince them that everything will be OK, they know that it won't be, otherwise why would you be trying to convince them?

Commit to your plans and take action. Focus on the end result. Make it happen. Those who take comfort in your confidence will overcome their fears and follow you. Those who won't aren't going to change anyway, that's their choice, respect them for it and get on with what you have to do. You can't sit around waiting for everyone's permission.

Communication

Communication networks are made up of two types of elements - nodes and links. Nodes are points where something important happens and links connect nodes together.

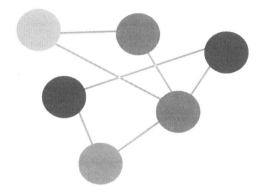

Communication links have, for the purposes of network design, two important characteristics. They have delay and they have loss. Something goes in at one end and, some time later, some of it comes out of the other end. Despite the time and money spent by researchers trying to reduce loss and delay, it's still there.

It turns out that you cannot change the laws of physics.

What happens in the case of human communication? Well, there are nodes (people) and there are links (words and other forms of communication such as symbols and computer interfaces).

In the case of corporate communication there are nodes (companies, customers, markets) and there are links (adverts, sales people, brochures, web sites). The more intelligence we give the nodes, the more decision making we can delegate to them. In a network like the Internet, we no longer need one fixed, central point of command as each node can make certain decisions about the routing of traffic itself. In this case, we can no longer predict the route that traffic will take.

It turns out that intelligent nodes will satisfy their desire to communicate, regardless of any plans that the network designer might have. This can lead to unexpected results but on the whole is a good thing as it allows the network to heal link and node failures without any external intervention. The network can recognise problems and adapt to them.

When a communication network is designed, we generally aim to limit the means by which nodes communicate. The ones with links between them communicate directly, those without communicate indirectly. The network itself introduces loss which is compensated for with components such as amplifiers and repeaters. The more nodes and links a particular message travels over, the more the delivered message differs from the original.

If we use the example of a telephone network, what comes out of the far end is usually close enough to what went in to be intelligible by another human being. We can decipher speech, even though we say the line is of 'poor quality' or is 'noisy' or has 'echo'.

We can also translate communication between different media. In a telephone network there are different types of cables as well as radio and fibre optic links. With spoken language, we can translate it into text or even into forms such as diagrams.

Does delay and loss in a human communication network lead to a decline in signal quality? If you've ever played the game of 'Chinese Whispers' then you know the answer is 'Yes'. If you've ever heard and passed on a rumour then you know the answer is 'Yes' and if you've ever given a customer what they asked for instead of what they needed then you will have learned that answer the hard way.

It turns out that the laws of physics apply to humans too.

As communication nodes, we hear something and we pass it on to other nodes. In doing this, we change what we pass on and time elapses before we pass it on. Many things can happen during that time. In the time it takes a company to communicate a new strategy to all of its internal parts, the marketplace can have evolved, creating the need for a new strategy.

Of course, people have talked about effective communication for a long time. What is often less explored is why, and how, communication is important. Surely, if all the parts of an organisation had a clear strategy then they would not need to communicate with each other. If people knew what they should be doing they wouldn't sit around all day chatting.

Every second of every day, you are making decisions. Sometime you make good decisions and sometimes you make bad ones. If you are now thinking about the assumption that there's no good or bad, right or wrong then well done - if not then you may want to think about a bad decision you made recently. Did you set out with the intention of making a bad decision, or did it seem right at the time?

Here's another useful belief for you:

People do not make bad decisions. They make good decisions with bad, or insufficient data.

Well, that's easy to say in hindsight, which is simply a source of data. When you buy a sandwich and then wish you'd ordered something else, you have new information that you didn't have previously. If you had your time again, you wouldn't just make a difference choice – the whole decision would be different because the information it's based on would be different.

When you make a decision and then, at some later time, think you should have chosen differently, you may also be aware that your intuition turned out to be right. Your intuition is not a vague, fuzzy feeling that can't be rationalised – it is one of the most powerful and specific decision making tools you have.

Your intuition is not fuzzy – it delivers a specific yes/no output which you are aware of as a 'gut feeling'. When you get the feeling of oscillation, or churning, or butterflies, that's your intuition cycling between yes and no – a sign of conflicting information.

Taken at it's most simple level, your gut reaction is like the oil warning light in your car. Many years ago, cars had oil pressure gauges which displayed the actual oil pressure. The driver had to figure out what to do about that, in much the same way that you make a conscious decision now. Today, the car's computer monitors the oil level and only tells you (via a warning light) if you need to take action, in the same way that your intuition keeps quiet unless it's either reinforcing or contradicting an important decision.

If a decision feels right, it probably is right. If it feels wrong, it probably is wrong in some way, or has unexpected side effects that you have not yet considered. Your unconscious mind has collated and summarised far more information than you can be consciously aware of and summarised as a simple feeling – in the same way that your car's computer collates data from hundreds of sensors and then summarises that data with a few warning lights.

If you could travel into the future, would you always make good decisions? This depends entirely on the consequences of your decisions. If you could see every future event affected then maybe the answer is 'yes', however you may then change your decision and then you'd have to go back in time and warn yourself.

You've no doubt seen a film with this basic idea in it and you've probably realised that, half way through the script, the writer got very confused and gave up. The solution is normally to leave all the complicated stuff out and instead focus on the antics of the time travelling killer robot.

So, instead of trying to see into the future (the hard way), simply gather more information in the present (the easy way).

Whenever someone communicates with you, they are transmitting information over many channels. Normally, we pay attention to only one of them, and we only half pay attention to that.

Here are a few examples of the components of communication:

▫ Words	▫ Eye movement
▫ Rate of speech	▫ Mouth movement
▫ Pitch	▫ Head movement
▫ Volume	▫ Hand movement
▫ Change in pitch	▫ Shoulder movement
▫ Eyebrow movement	▫ Breathing in or out

You may think to yourself, "raising eyebrows adds something to a conversation but there's no way it says as much as words" and this is certainly true. The point is that unless you pay attention to everything, the words are meaningless. Let's take the example of two opposite meanings for a sentence - a compliment and an insult. Clearly, it is vitally important to get this right and so we will choose words carefully so that the meaning conveyed is totally unambiguous. Here are the words we will use:

"That's a nice hat"

So, is that a compliment or an insult? If you answer, "Impossible to tell" then you have recognised that there is insufficient data. If you answer "Compliment" or "Insult" then you have unconsciously recognised the lack of information and added it in from your own experience. You have taken something from your memory and added it into the decision as if it were real time sensory data.

This is a very natural and usual aspect of communication. When we read or hear language from a source other than its origin, something is missing and so in order to reconstruct the original meaning we substitute information from our own imagination.

Perhaps you've read a newspaper story and heard a particular tone of voice used? Perhaps you've listened to a radio debate and imagined the speaker's facial expressions? This is all part of the way that we naturally process language. Our brains need far more information than just words, so if anything's missing we add the missing information from our own experience. You could call it 'intuition' if you like.

So, to get back to the question about why and how people communicate, one answer is this:

People communicate to gather more information about the world to make better decisions

How do we know this? Because we know that the converse is true - people make bad decisions when they do not communicate effectively.

Or, in other words:

People who do not communicate as effectively as they are able to are often unhappy with the decisions they make.

So, effective communication could be important to good decision making. In turn, paying careful attention to other people's communication gives you more information. If you only ever listen to words, then you are missing out on 93% of the overall transmission. Does this mean that only 7% of your decisions can be good ones?

I'm sure you've seen this information before, based on research that was done in the 1960s by Albert Mehrabian

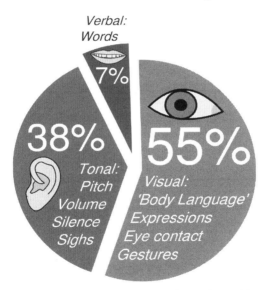

and Michael Argyle. Communication is 7% verbal, 38% auditory and 55% visual. You may or may not agree with the figures, in which case we can at least agree that words are not our only form of communication.

Some people say that the original studies were flawed and these numbers are rubbish. I've seen the original study report and I must admit, they were greatly simplifying human communication in order to understand the role of non verbal communication. Whilst you can agree or disagree with the conclusions, and other peoples' interpretations of those conclusions, the fact that we do communicate through multiple channels seems inescapable.

When I run an exercise during training courses to test this model, the results correlate almost exactly for groups of as few as 4 upwards. We get, plus or minus a few percentage points, 7% for words, 38% for voice tone and 55% for visual elements. The only departure from this is when the speaker's chosen topic is particularly emotive or emotionally resonant, at which point the focus on the words increases. Even then, I have never seen words at more than 50%. What this suggests to me is that we combine verbal and non verbal communication channels in order to derive intention or meaning.

This much seems obvious – that someone will denote a joke or sincerity through a facial expression or change in voice tone. Whilst this obviously has many implications around the office, it is also relevant to corporate communication. Your customers will infer what they thought you really meant rather than what you intended.

Companies have non-verbal communication too, and that doesn't just mean the people who communicate on behalf of the company. For example, imagine a situation where a telecommunications company sponsors a charity that promotes work life balance. At the same time, the company's television advertising shows a father, working late, reading his son a bedtime story by telephone. It really happened.

When people do this, we notice that their communication channels do not carry complementary information. This is called 'incongruence' or, to use the more common description, lying. We are all able to detect incongruence unconsciously, and that usually generates a 'gut reaction' that something is not right. If we are paying very close attention, we can specify the incongruence. For example, when asked, "Have you been eating chocolate?", my niece said, "No" whilst hiding her hands, looking down at her feet and swaying from side to side. My highly developed sensory acuity allowed me to detect this incongruity and suspect that she had, in fact, been eating chocolate. The fact that she had chocolate smeared all round her mouth was another indication.

You don't have to be a master of human behaviour to know when someone is lying, but paying really close attention to the way people communicate is always interesting and often helpful, because lying is not the only form of incongruence. Other states that lead to incongruence include being nervous, feeling under pressure and being afraid to say something for fear of the repercussions.

An important job that a leader can do in a time of change is to say out loud what everyone else is thinking, rather than hope they aren't thinking it. This gives them permission to share their fears too.

The example with the telecoms company is absolutely true, although I don't think anyone else noticed at the time. If they did, they didn't say anything to me about it. Of course, now I've said it, you'll all come out and say, "yes, I had a funny feeling about that". People do seem to trust their intuition more when other people speak up first.

So, when we notice companies transmitting conflicting messages, we can say that they are being incongruent. To say that they are lying is to assume intention, and we do not have enough information to do that. A more accurate interpretation of corporate incongruence might be conflicting needs.

When a person has conflicting needs, they often manifest themselves in non verbal communication. In a number of mental illnesses, this is greatly exaggerated and so we see people trying to control two or more conflicting needs that are generating mutually exclusive behaviours. Even "healthy" people do this regularly. If you know of anyone who is a serial monogamist, then you will see a pattern of behaviour arise that is generated by two conflicting needs. Either the need for companionship is dominant or the need for freedom is dominant. Until the person finds a way to satisfy both needs at the same time, they will forever ebb and flow, leading to a distinctive cyclic behavioural pattern.

There was more on this in the chapter 'Simple solutions'. Do you remember? By categorising all possible courses of action into a limited number of strategies, a company can never quite find the right one.

We see companies doing this too, changing strategy on a weekly basis because of the conflicting needs of different parts. When the metaphorical parts of a person have conflicting needs and those parts have access to the communication centres of the brain, we see incongruence. When the same thing happens in a company, we see two contradictory press releases sent out on the same day. We see confusion and we hear people say, "the left hand doesn't know what the right hand is doing". We hear customers ask sales people about the press releases and the sales people reply, "Oh, that's just what we're telling the stock market - it's not really true".

We also see companies telling shareholders about a takeover when the employees knew nothing about it, and consequently they can feel let down or misled. And yet, for commercial reasons, that information must be confidential until the deal is agreed.

When pressed on the subject, managers say, "I can't say anything", which of course tells you everything you needed to know, or at least confirms your worst fears.

So, in companies and people alike, conflicting needs lead to incongruent communication. As keen observers and listeners, we can easily detect this and learn a great deal of useful information from it.

Company Memo

We would like to take this opportunity to reassure all current employees that absolutely nothing of any interest is happening at the moment. Your jobs are not currently in any danger and we have no plans to close the company today, so don't worry.

Really, think nothing of it. In fact, forget we even mentioned it.

Love, *the Boss*

Mind Your Language

The word 'change' is an interesting one. When used in the form "a change", it is a type of word called a nominalisation - a verb turned into a noun. The position of the word in a sentence indicates it's a noun, yet you can't put it in a wheelbarrow. Here are some nominalisations that are used frequently in business:

- A meeting
- A decision
- A plan
- A discussion
- A relationship

What is important about nominalisations is the direct effect they have on people's mental processing. I recently suggested you look to the outcomes of a change rather than to the change itself, otherwise you will be stuck inside the change forever.

So, how does this relate to nominalisations? Imagine yourself at a meeting, making a decision about a business plan. Take a good few moments to think about this. Now think about yourself meeting with some people, deciding how to plan the business.

What was the difference? You may not have noticed, so here's the difference it makes to the majority of people. In the first example, you imagined a still image whilst in the second example, you imagined a moving image. Problems, indecisions and dilemmas often arise from 'stuck' states.

Imagine yourself going through a change. Now imagine yourself at a time when something is changing for you. Different?

You can literally stop people in their tracks by using nominalisations in your language, and you can get stuck people moving again by changing those stuck words back into verbs:

- To meet
- To decide
- To plan
- To discuss
- To relate

You may be thinking that this is trivial and that it's just words that won't affect people. If that's the case then I suggest you first try it for yourself. Have a look through your change project documentation or company policies and you may even find nominalisations that go hand in hand with the business writing fashion of the recent past called "passive voice" which is used so that the author can avoid blame.

Here's an example of passive voice: "a meeting was held during which a discussion relating to the business plan concluded with a need to make a decision about customer relationships."

And here's the same paragraph using more 'active' language: "I met with Fred and we talked about our plans for the business. We need to do more work on the way we relate to customers."

You may think that the second version is too informal, yet it's certainly more informative and easier to read. We process language by turning it back into sensory experience. Since passive voice has no active verbs, our brains have to do a lot of extra processing to decode the language and, since there's more information missing, we have to add more in from our own expectations. Therefore, the formal business style of writing leads to more ambiguity and reduces the chance that people will actually read it. If a document is important enough for people to read it, write it so that it's easy to read! If it's not important enough, don't waste your time writing it.

So, don't talk about change. Talk about what is changing - from what, into what and how things will be afterwards. Don't have meetings where committees make decisions. Meet people. Talk to them. Decide what to do and then do it. The language you use to communicate change could even be the most important factor in determining the way people cope with it more easily.

Be positive

Well, that's easy for me to say. Every day you have people telling you to be positive, look on the bright side or sell the benefits. This is all completely pointless when communicating change.

In a change situation, it is important that people know what is going on. If they don't they will make up their own version of what is going on and you can guarantee it will be ten times worse than what is really happening. Do not allow people the chance to hallucinate bad things. Giving people relevant information is not necessarily related to what you say. The way that you say it is usually far more important.

Communicating positively does not mean sounding cheerful while you make people redundant, and it definitely does not mean softening the impact of bad news with some positive feedback. For example, "Fred, you're one of our best people, you're fired, and that's a nice tie".

Communicating positively means telling people what **is** happening, what they **will** be doing and what you **will** do about it.

Here are some important ways that you can communicate positively:

State the outcomes of change

Tell people what will happen after the change has taken place. Do not focus on the change process itself as this will only delay you. By directing attention to the outcomes, you will create momentum to move past the transitory period as quickly as possible. Clearly state what the world will be like after the change process is complete. You'll probably find that the world is actually not much different to how it is today, if the change is being made to avert future problems. If the future is drastically different to the present, you should be very cautious. Major change often indicates impending doom, just like it did for the dinosaurs.

Just bear in mind that change, in itself, does not exist. Things change, people come and go, desks get moved around and the words written on the sides of buildings change. The environment changes but change is not an entity in itself. Change is just what we notice when things are different today than they were yesterday. Did you employ a management consultant to run the change project for putting on new underwear today? Why not? (Of course, the answer may be "because I'm wearing yesterday's underwear", which is not always a bad thing.)

Just the facts, ma'am

Of course, you are instigating change because it is wonderful and because it will only improve things. In reality, you know there will be downsides too. People will analyse the facts and will make up their own minds as to how the changes benefit them. You will be surprised at some of the benefits that people come up with, so leave people alone to make whatever connections are important to them.

If people are looking for the downsides to your plans, they will find them. If the are looking for the benefits to them, they will find those too, so first you have to direct their attention towards finding the benefits to them.

Probably the worst thing to do is to make up benefits that people can see through, so the meaning that they take away is that you are trying to manipulate the information in order to influence them.

Jack Nicholson was wrong. You *can* handle the truth, after all.

If you do spell out the benefits, tell them the benefit first

Here's a neat trick borrowed from the latest old fashioned thinking on sales practice. If you tell people 'feature means benefit' then by the time you have said 'means' they will already be ahead of you and will have formed their own benefit before you can tell them yours, because the 'benefit' is simply the meaning of the raw facts. Whatever you tell them will conflict with what they have already decided, which is why sales people often lose rapport at this stage. People are perfectly capable of figuring out the meaning of things for themselves. I will decide why I need a new CD player, I don't need a salesman to tell me.

For example, you can carry this book everywhere with you because of its handy size. On the other hand, the size of this book means you can easily carry it with you. It's a very subtle difference that will have a huge cumulative impact.

This idea is so simple, you might think it can't be true. Instead of saying 'feature means benefit', use 'benefit because feature'. By giving the benefit first, you prevent the listener from forming their own. By using the magic word 'because', you create a rule that links the benefit to the feature. Here are some examples. Pay close attention to what images and thoughts you create in your mind as you read the two alternatives in each one.

- "Our new IT system will be more efficient".
- "We can get more done in less time because of the new IT system"
- "The budget cuts mean we will use resources more effectively"
- "We'll be able to divert our resources to where they will have the most impact because of the budget cuts"
- "The reorganisation will lead to greater organisational efficiency"
- "You can get closer to the people you need to work with because of the reorganisation"

A frequent temptation in this situation is to say something like "we will enjoy organisational efficiencies". That's not a benefit! It doesn't even mean anything...

Remember - benefits because evidence.

We gather sensory evidence in order to derive meaning from our experiences. If we get the evidence first, we'll derive a meaning based on a number of factors, including:

- How you feel at the time
- How you feel about the person giving you the information
- Any similar previous experiences

So it seems that we gather evidence through our senses, we filter that evidence according to a number of factors, and we then generate a meaning which is the bit we actually remember and respond to.

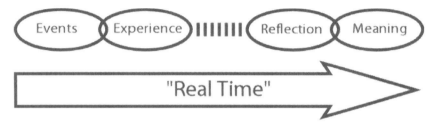

Later on, we use a different form of language to talk about the experience, where the sequence through time has changed:

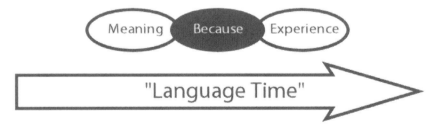

This has a number of very important implications for us.

The factors influencing the creation of meaning will lead you to communicate what the person expects to hear rather than what you mean to say. In the context of change, you will communicate whatever change means to them, not what you meant it to mean.

The factors that influence the creation of meaning are all easy to influence.

If you present the meaning first, you lead the person's senses to gather the evidence to support that meaning.

Sales people are often trained to use a 'features mean benefits' structure, for example, "The new Technogizmo 2000 XL has a small footprint profile *which means that* it saves valuable space on your desk."

It amazes me that after all of these decades of sales training, sales people are still being taught this today, because it actually breaks rapport with the customer. By the time the sales person said, "footprint", the customer had already figured out what it meant. The sales person then continued to talk over the customer's thoughts, or said what the customer already knew, or worst of all, said something different to what the customer had thought, thereby disagreeing with the customer.

If you really must talk about product features, you're better off saying, "benefits because features". For the reasons I've already stated, when the customer hears the benefit first, she is waiting for the evidence to support the assertion, which comes in the form of the feature.

"And you'll enjoy more desk space because of the Technogizmo 2000 XL's small footprint profile."

Compare the two statements and notice the difference.

Just remember that presenting the meaning first doesn't mean saying, "I have some good news about a new reorganisation" because your unconscious communication will be screaming, "Run! Save yourselves!" Here's a little tip for you; giving the meaning first can be as simple as carefully choosing a single adjective or adverb, because those words indicate what a thing or action is like, and therefore what it means.

Here are some examples. Take a moment to pay attention to the experience that each one creates in your mind:

- Here's an update on the latest reorganisation
- This is our current strategy
- We've no plans for changes in the foreseeable future

Hopefully, you would have picked up something like this:

"Here's an update on the latest reorganisation"

"The latest… in a long line. It won't be the last."

"This is our current strategy"

"Current? Will we get a new one tomorrow?"

"We've no plans for changes in the foreseeable future"

"Foreseeable?"

So you can see that just the words latest, current and foreseeable are enough to imply meaning and from that create a complex internal situation, based also on the person's prior experience and current feelings. And that simulation is interchangeable with real life, so the person is now operating from this simulated reality, not from the reality that you are operating from. Because those words are qualifiers, they are conditional, and because they're conditional, suspicious listeners will also consider the various conditions. Think back to the Alignment chapter. The manager who says, "We have no plans to make changes in the foreseeable future", isn't lying exactly, but he's not being honest either.

He wants to both reassure his team and speak the truth, but he can't do both. He tries to be careful, but inadvertently lets the truth out to anyone who is listening properly.

You really have to be careful, don't you? Well, no. Only if you want to be sure to get the right result. If you don't care how things turn out, then don't bother.

Use sensory language

You can't put organisational efficiency in a wheelbarrow. It is a meaningless phrase because it doesn't readily translate into anything meaningful to me, or you, or anyone else.

Describe outcomes in terms of what people will see, hear and feel. This has three advantages. Firstly, they don't have to do any work to understand what you're saying, so they hear more of it. Secondly, this directly engages people's emotions, and those are amongst the most powerful resources that you have to help you bring about change. And thirdly, you are able to convey what you have in mind more clearly, as opposed to using vague intangible language which the listened will translate into a random sensory experience.

Use all of the Logical Levels

The chapter on Alignment explains this in more detail. You can use the knowledge of logical levels that you will have to guide people's thoughts smoothly. The last thing that you want in this situation is to have people making up bad thoughts to fill the gaps in what you have told them. Using the logical levels to guide the audience will ensure that you take them on a smooth journey instead of leaving them to ride an emotional roller-coaster.

Use positive language for ongoing communication

As you continue to communicate with people, state what is happening rather than what isn't. If you talk about what isn't happening then you are giving people absolutely no information to act upon. As an experiment, call a local decorator and ask him to paint your office not blue. Notice the confusion that this leads to. You cause this same confusion every time you tell people what they should not do or what is not happening.

Remember - positive in this context does not mean good or happy. It means talking about what will happen and what does exist. There's no point telling people what they aren't doing and what won't happen as you're giving them no useful information at all. Talk only about what **is** happening, what **will** happen and what you **are** doing.

Questions

Here's an idea for you to ponder on.

Each species has a specialisation which is related to the environmental niche which it occupies. Random mutation and hybrid adaptation lead to changes in the physical structure of an organism, and those changes are either better or worse suited to that environmental niche. Therefore, as I have said elsewhere, the environment selects the organism that occupies it.

But what about humans? We change the environment to suit ourselves, so does that mean we have stopped evolving?

No – because evolution is not a purposeful, planned process. This is the fundamental point that many people overlook. We didn't evolve into human beings – we randomly mutated, and we continue to do so. The species that we know as Homo Sapiens is only what we see at our current stage of evolution, and even at this stage we have huge diversity within the human population. Just within recorded history, many physical aspects of the human species have changed including height and lifespan, and our physical features continue to change as our gene pool becomes more diverse and therefore more adaptable.

So we are still evolving because we are still changing, we are still adapting and we are still learning.

Human beings are specialised organisms. Just like a fish specialises in breathing underwater, and an eagle specialising in flying, we specialise in adaptation. We specialise in creativity and problem solving. We can adapt faster and incorporate those changes into future generations faster than other organisms, so it appears that in our lifetimes, the human cognitive evolution is moving faster than our biological evolution.

We can learn faster than our physical bodies can change. Rather than wait to evolve wings, we invent aeroplanes. Rather than wait to evolve gills, we invent scuba gear. And then we invent the printing press so that we can pass that knowledge across geographic and generational boundaries.

Human beings - you, I, the people you can see around you - are so specialised to adaptation that it makes us very good problem solvers, and it therefore makes us excellent decision makers.

At this point, you might say, "but my wife/husband/boss is a terrible decision maker. They procrastinate and never end up with something they're happy with"

And I would say that this proves that they are excellent decision makers. They are excellent at answering questions. What they have in common with the rest of us is that we are rubbish at asking questions.

Consider this example.

Here's a pen:

And here's a teapot:

(Of course, that's not really a teapot, it's just a picture of one. That really may be a pen, though. How would you tell the difference?)

Answer these questions about those two items:

- □ Which is best?

- □ Which is nicest?

- □ Which is right?

- □ Which should I use?

- □ Which should I have used?

Tough questions? Feel like you don't have enough information? Information is an illusion. You already have too much.

Have you ever tried to compare two jobs, or two holidays, or two people in order to find out which is 'best'? And don't even try and tell me how easy it was, because you're such a rational, well organised person who doesn't get tied up in such trivia. Remember – we all excel at making decisions, finding solutions and answering questions. It's asking questions that we are genetically predisposed to being useless at. And why would we expect anything else? In evolutionary terms, the environment asks the questions, we just have to figure out the answers. Mother Nature asks, "Can a human survive here?", and we find a way.

Sheep, on the other hand, are great at asking questions, because they only have one – "Where's the grass?". At a certain time of year, they might stretch to, "Where's the other sheep?" but that's about it. We, on the other hand are full of questions:

"What should I do?"

"What should I have done?"

"What's the right thing to do?"

"What's best?"

"What's the meaning of life?"

It's no wonder that we get wrapped up in meaningless answers like "42" when we ask such meaningless questions.

When someone asks a question like, "What should I do", most people will respond as if the person doesn't know what to do and jump into giving advice. Usually, they have already decided what to do and they're now trying to live with the consequences of that decision.

Consider a manager who has to get rid of an under performing member of staff. The manager knows exactly what to do, but puts off the decision. In fact, they already made the decision, but they put off taking action on it. They don't want to upset the person, yet they also don't want the consequences of the underperformance. What to do? They might say, "I don't know what to do" when what they really mean is, "I know what to do, but I don't know how to do it and not feel like a git". They're not trying to solve a problem, they're trying to resolve a contradiction between commercial need and self image.

Try these questions instead:

- Which is a pen?

- Which can I make tea in?

- Which is heaviest?

- Which could I hide in my pocket?

Easier? It's not a trick, I'm just asking better questions.

You may be thinking that you always ask really good questions and therefore this doesn't apply to you. You might also be thinking that the first questions were subjective and therefore unanswerable. This is a misleading idea that gets taught on corporate training courses, and we have to set it straight right now. It's misleading for two reasons.

Firstly, all questions are subjective. There is no objectivity, because the object is always a human and a human is always subjective.

Secondly, we all respond to subjectivity by inserting our own experience into the empty spaces. Hypnosis is the an extreme case, but company mission statements and advertising are very close.

I've just sat with a salesman who sells training courses. He had a call from someone who is looking at three career options, let's call them A, B and C. He didn't make a decision because he wants to keep his options open. The salesman asked sales questions which were fine, but they didn't get the person any closer to a decision.

If he is trying to decide which is the best option, he will appear to procrastinate. If he is trying to work out which is the right thing to do, he'll take a long time to make a decision. He already has too much information, he's simply asking the wrong questions.

What about a question like, "Which can I imagine myself still doing in 20 years' time?", or, "Which career can I move into with the least retraining?"

Better questions, and to avoid the same trap I will define a better question as being a question which is more effective at getting a clear answer.

As a Change Magician, you can think of yourself fulfilling a number of roles, one of which is "to help people ask better questions".

You'll know by now that telling people your solution to their problem does not work unless they are seeking practical information such as "how do I open this" or "can you tell me the way to the Post Office?" The only way you can really help people - including yourself - to deal with complex problems is to help them gather more information about the problem, by expanding their map of the problem, by asking them questions.

The interactive chapter of this book has a unique problem solving tool called the Unsticker which asks you questions that change the way you think about a problem. You can learn the simple principles of the Unsticker to solve problems easily. Visit www.theunsticker.com

You may have been on training courses where you learned that there are "open" and "closed" questions and that you should only ask "open" questions. As with all generalisations, it's nonsense. You may have spotted that saying, "all generalisations are nonsense" is in itself a generalisation. If you can work that one out, you're good.

Worrying about open or closed questions implies that you care what the answer is. These questions are fundamentally different and in fact demonstrate something that's critical to your success as a Change Magician. When you ask people questions, the answers are largely irrelevant. What's important is how they think about the answer. By asking questions that direct people to think in certain ways, you will help them to solve questions, recover lost information and reconsider preconceptions easily and, well, magically.

Here are some categories of questions that you may find useful. You can try out the different types of question on different types of problem and learn for yourself which works best in what situation. Remember that the key to this isn't to have the "right" question - it's having lots of questions.

Representation

Some questions attack the way that you represent the problem to yourself. When you are away from the problem - people, a place or whatever - you still carry it with you as a collection of memories. Those memories are arranged in a special, unique way that collectively forms "the problem". As the problem changes, the representation changes. Does the opposite happen too? Yes, if we play with the representation, the problem changes. When your brain notices that the problem can change it very quickly learns that the problem is under your control and this starts a process of reorganisation, during which you will have many creative insights that help you deal with the problem.

Our senses are all interconnected and whilst you may think that a feeling is totally different to a sound, in fact all of these different sensory experiences are generated by electrical signals carried by nerves. When the signals arrive at the brain they are sorted, filtered and then represented to your conscious attention. We all have an element of interaction between these signals and for some people this is much stronger than for others. For some time now, there has been a view that people with a high degree of sensory interaction or "synaesthesia" are particularly creative and intelligent. In fact, this is just another example of scientists jumping to conclusions. We are all synaesthetic, it just gets beaten out of many of us by education.

I was recently in a place where background music was being played and I heard a boy say to his father, "Daddy, I can see the music". His father replied, "No you can't. You might be able to see the speaker but you don't see music. You hear music". Mozart was said to be highly synaesthetic and saw colours when he heard or thought of music. We all do this naturally from birth as it's part of the way that our brain sorts nerve impulses. When you are first born, your brain is relatively undifferentiated. Only by trial and error does your brain start to figure out which nerves do what. If you've ever been into a computer room and seen thousands of wires and wondered where they all go, this is the challenge that your brain faces when you are born. In a computer room, engineers tug on one end of a cable and look for movement at the other end. Sometimes they use an electrical device to play a tone down a wire and listen at the other end to see which wire is being tested. Your brain does the same thing when you're first born - it fires a nerve and tries to relate that to which limb moves.

All of your memories, including holidays, words, music and emotional experiences are represented in all of your senses at the same time, giving you the ability to recover the entire memory using any sensory input as a trigger. You may be reminded of a holiday by a sight, a piece of music or a smell and with that trigger, the whole memory floods back.

What colour is your favourite piece of music? What does blue sound like? What colour is the smell of perfume? What noise does the taste of chocolate make?

Synaesthesia is closely connected with creativity. If you have children, you wouldn't want to train that quality out of them, would you? You can easily develop synaesthesia in children, and in adults, and you'll be surprised at how naturally creative people are.

Here's a little trick for you that uses your synaesthetic ability to control pain such as toothache or backache. When you get a pain, what does it look like? What does it sound like? How can you manipulate the image or sound? For example, if the pain is a red ball, can you squash it or change it's shape? Can you change a sharp "aahhh" sound into a smoother "oooohh" sound and then into an "oooooooh" sound? As you make these changes, how does the pain change? In the case of the image you can pick up the ball and throw it over your shoulder. I've seen people represent pain as black balls, needles, shards of glass and many other variations. In each case you can change the way that the pain is represented which changes the pain and even turns it off altogether. If you're feeling doubtful, that's a good reason to try it.

So, the same is true for problems. If you change the way the problem is represented, the problem has to change to adapt to the new representation. The representation IS the problem as far as your brain is concerned. The effect is exactly the same as painting a bitter tasting coating onto the nails of a habitual nail biter. By making an environmental change that forces the person to do something different, the whole problem has to reorganise itself.

Resource

Generally, you have everything you need to deal with any problem you would ever face. At some point in the past, you have had an experience which is relevant to whatever situation you find yourself in now or in the future. What often happens in the case of 'problem thinking' is that this experience does not readily translate from one context of your life to another.

For example, someone who has a job as a salesman may be unable to talk to strangers at parties. Can you imagine a salesman not being able to talk to strangers? "Aahh...that's different" he would say, and he is right - it is different. It's still relevant though, so what we need to do is get the skills to transfer - to get him to make connections from one area of his life to another. People who are very flexible and adaptable do this naturally.

The resource questions help you to find relevant experience to deal with this problem, which may come from the past, the future or from other people. Remember that if you do 'what someone else would do' you are in fact using your own skills! This other person doesn't live in your head, so you use information from a different part of your brain to provide the answers you need. It was still in your head, it was just stored somewhere out of reach.

Clearly, there are times that you need to learn a new physical or technical skill in order to solve a problem, but the need to learn this skill is not part of the problem - it is part of the solution. If you know that you need to find out how to do something, you have already created a solution which you now need to test.

Acquiring new resources is concerned with not even knowing how you are going to tackle the problem - not knowing where to start. For example, if you are having trouble deciding what to do about something then a useful resource would be 'an ability to make good decisions easily'. You already have this ability, it's just stuck somewhere else for the time being. Access to resources is the issue here, not the presence of them.

Using a role model is an excellent tool in this situation. Asking yourself what someone else would do gives you access to resources that you already have. If you like, you can give the other person the credit but the memory of them that contained the resource was inside your head all along.

Dissociation

Being too close to a problem means that you can't see round or over it and you can't tell how big it is. When you take a break from something and go back to it, only to see it differently, you are dissociating yourself from the problem. When you go on holiday and come back with new ways of tackling old problems, you have dissociated yourself. When you think back to a problem you had ten years ago and laugh at yourself, you are now dissociated.

Dissociation is a very powerful tool and is used in many situations including phobia cures and personal change. Here, dissociation questions are used to help you gain some distance from the problem. This might help you to see round it to the real goal, it might help you to get a sense of the size of the problem or it may just give you some breathing space.

Reframe

Reframing is what happens when you take something that you are totally certain about and add in a new piece of information that throws your certainty out of the window. Reframing attacks subjective meaning; in other words when you have a group of memories that you have collected together and summarised with a meaning, you have added information from your own experience that may or may not be useful.

For example, you might collect some experiences together at work and attach the meaning, "I'm never going to get promoted here, they have their favourites and I'm not one of them". You have no way of knowing if that is true or not, but it becomes true because you believe it. To make matters worse, you then filter new experiences through this meaning. If you did get promoted, it would be because they felt sorry for you, or because no-one else was left, or because they wanted a scapegoat. What kind of manager would you be with this attitude? Reframing just picks at the loose threads of meaning, giving you a chance to build a new, more useful one.

State

If you're feeling miserable, it's probably not a good time to write a life plan. If you're feeling dejected, it's not a good time to go for a job interview. The weight of a problem can really affect your state and thereby your ability to deal with the problem. When you're feeling bright and bouncy, you just shrug things off that would seem like major problems if you were feeling down. Your state is another filter through which you interpret the world, so before you can find a solution to a problem you need to change your state from a 'problem state' to a 'solution state'.

There are many ways to do this which mostly fall into two main categories - physiology and focus of attention. In other words you can go for some fresh air or think about something else for a while. State questions divert your attention to something else. Some of them might be a little odd or even confusing and that's intentional as confusion is another way of changing how you think.

When I was developing the internationally famous Unsticker at www.theunsticker.com, I wondered how I would get the software to interpret the visitor's problem and ask relevant or intelligent questions. I imagined some kind of artificial intelligence software that would pick out key words from the problem statement and place them in the right question. As I worked on the Unsticker, a curious thing happened. I remembered the whole point about creative problem solving was that a person's thinking is constrained by the problem - and that's normally the problem. In the case of the Unsticker, it was also the solution. When a person's thinking is constrained by any frame of reference, anything that happens will be interpreted relative to that frame.

When you visit the Unsticker with a problem, your thinking is constrained by the problem so you interpret the question in relation to the problem, whatever the question is. I realised that with properly structured questions, I could actually ask any question and it would mean something. Even better, asking random questions works more effectively than asking the right question. Why? Because to describe a question as "right" it must fit into the framework of either the problem or a predetermined solution.

The questions in the Unsticker are outside of the frame of the problem, so the person being unstuck has to change the problem in order to process the question. After just a few clicks, many people have said they were unable to remember the problem.

It turns out that you don't need to ask the right question. Just ask any question and trust that you'll get an answer.

You've probably seen lots of problem solving methodologies that have acronyms and steps to follow. Here's a secret for you - don't tell anyone or the people who make money out of these models will get upset.

Every single person on the planet has a way of solving problems that is unique to each individual, although there are some common characteristics that seem to work better than others. A handful of people have figured out their own unique and peculiar problem solving method and written it down. They then tell everyone else that they have a new way of solving problems and that you can't solve problems without it. Then they charge you money to use it.

Companies buy these models by the cartload, which then gather dust on a shelf. Why? Simply, because these models are not YOUR model, and your model works perfectly well. I met someone who remembered his presentation notes by imagining them written in white lettering on the sides of car tyres. He could sell that, and there are enough people in the world with doubt in their abilities to make him rich!

So does the Unsticker ask better questions? Not really, it's just designed to ask questions that aren't bounded by the problem. In that respect, they are better questions in relation to their purpose, which is to move a person's thinking outside of the problem so that they can find a solution. So the Unsticker's questions are better in achieving that purpose, but they're not good questions for gathering facts and data. Just remember, whilst the facts might be important in a court of law, they're not important in solving everyday problems.

Sometimes, your problem solving machine just needs a little oil, and that's what Change Magic is really all about. New questions are being added all the time to make the Unsticker the best problem solving tool there is, because more questions means more ways of unlocking your potential as an outstanding, creative problem solver!

Some text has inadvertently been
written on this page, please
accept my apologies

Change Magic
356

Stories

If you have read any of my other books, you might have seen this fellow before:

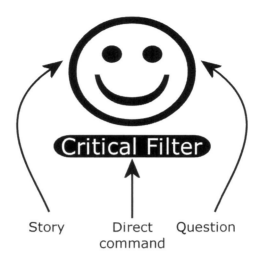

Since we've just been talking about questions, I wanted to remind you of the importance of stories. All too often in business, we trivialise stories and concentrate on hard facts. This is a terrible nuisance, because we're not wired up for facts, and they're rather misleading.

Go into a library or book shop and see what's in there. Lots of books, obviously, along with a coffee shop, adverts for Pilates classes and wireless internet access. But it's the books we're interested in today.

Books have been around for a long time as a means of recording information stored in a symbolic language. Whether that language is English, Latin, Sanskrit, Cuneiform, Hieroglyphs or cave paintings, the point is that written information as we know it is a relatively recent product of humanity. Spoken language is much older and, more importantly, much more widespread because not everyone can read - something exploited by the rulers of the world to protect knowledge.

It seems that the structure of a story is ideally suited to passing important information from one human to another. It seems that checklists and mnemonics are a terrible way of passing information.

We pass down Aesop's fables, Bible stories, Greek myths, fairytales and so on down through generations. The details of the stories change from one telling to the next, yet the meaning stays the same. The story of the gingerbread man changes with every generation. No one storyteller uses the same words as another. Yet the message is always the same – don't accept free rides from suspicious strangers. And the message is conveyed more powerfully through the story than it is by just passing on the facts.

Recently, a number of people have started offering storytelling workshops to businesses. We know that stories are powerful and fun, but why?

The diagram above illustrates the idea that questions and stories will suspend a listener's critical filter. If you simply give someone a direct command, they will intercept it and judge it, either agreeing or disagreeing. Yet questions and stories seem to connect with mental processes that bypass this critical filter completely. This is rather vital when we're introducing change!

I have formed a theory about why stories are important in passing on knowledge, and I'm going to share it with you. To be the best of my knowledge, this is a brand new theory that no-one else knows about yet. It came to me in a flash during a Van Morrison concert following a particularly stimulating conversation on the subject with my friend Kevin. That may seem like a superfluous detail, but you'll understand it later.

A while ago, there was a documentary on TV. I think it might have been about schizophrenia, but the important thing is that it had a number of scientists and psychologists talking about mental simulations. One person likened this to the computers that are used to predict the weather. Basically, meteorologists study the weather and form rules. For example, if the air is warm and wet and it meets air that is cold, it will probably rain. If the temperature is just right and there is an up draught, it will probably turn to snow.

They put all of these rules into a computer, and then they feed in readings about today's weather. The computer model then applies the rules to the current weather in order to figure out what it will be like tomorrow, and the day after, and so on.

If the rules are valid and the current measurements are accurate enough, the model will make accurate predictions for a short period of time. But more than a week and it's only as accurate as a guess. Why? Because the simulation isn't perfect, and small errors add up to become big errors over time. The forecast might say that it will rain tomorrow afternoon, and it actually rains tomorrow evening. It was close, perhaps close enough. But after long enough, its predictions are useless. This is why the meteorologists are always gathering and inputting new data, so that the model can be refined and the simulation can be made more accurate.

The other reason that the simulation can't see further than a few days is that the granularity of the input data is too large. Let's say there's a weather monitoring station every 10 miles - there will still be highly localised changes that have a cumulative effect over time. Have you ever seen one cloud in a clear blue sky and watched it grow, slowly?

Now, think of someone you know who you think has good judgement. Think of a decision you need to make and think about what they would do. What advice would they give you?

Next, think about someone who you have seen who you regarded as a really good presenter.

Next, think of someone who influenced you, positively, at a key point in your career.

What can we deduce from this? Well, one of the scientists in the program said that we create mental models, simulations, of people and we then carry them around with us. The simulations perform the same role as the real person, so you can have your mother telling you to be careful when crossing the road, or your father telling you to wrap up warm. On the other hand, your mother could be telling you you're stupid, and your father could be telling you that you'll never amount to anything. Sadly, that happens.

As a parent, I can see that sometimes parents say things that are unhelpful when they are only trying to do their best. What we need to realise is that the simulation is neither good nor bad, it's just running with the data it was given, and that data can be updated, just like the data in the weather computers.

Your mother could really haven been telling you that she is proud of you, and you still have so much untapped potential that you could achieve anything you want. Your father could have been telling you that he's afraid you'll accept second best in life, and you deserve better than that, you deserve the life that he wishes he had demanded for himself and he doesn't want you to make the mistakes he did. They could say those things, they just don't quite know how to. That's OK – we can correct that error when we build the simulation.

In the program, an author of historical novels said that she creates characters for a new book in her mind and they then take on a life of their own. As they interact with each other, she simply transcribes what they say and do, and her new novel writes itself.

I think the relevance to schizophrenia or whatever they were talking about was the idea that a mental model literally takes on a life of its own and acts as if it is a real live person. The simulation is so vivid that the person interacts with it as if it is a real person. The symptoms of the condition are perhaps then built upon the natural function of the mental simulator, in that we are all able to hear voices and imagine people giving us instructions. The difference in schizophrenia, the experts proposed, is that the person can't tell the difference between the mental simulation and a 'real' external experience. We all experience this to an extent when we wake from a vivid dream and feel confused because it seemed so real.

So here's my theory. We have, in our brains, a remarkable ability to build simulations – not just static maps of the world, but living models that, loaded with rules and starting data, will run by themselves and simulate the world and the people within it.

I read that the scientist, Nikola Tesla, would build inventions and at the same time create a mental model of the thing he had just made. He would leave the experiment running and upon returning to it, his mental simulation was in the same state as the real thing, even weeks later. I've read this as an example of his remarkable mental ability. The thing is, I believe we all share that ability.

I believe that we all share the ability to run a mental simulation of our homes, our workplaces, our colleagues, mentors, loved ones, pets, the weather, the traffic, the laws of physics and so on. And not only that, we have the ability to load new rules in and create new simulations.

Here's the big revelation you've been waiting for. You're probably wondering exactly how we create these new simulations.

Stories.

I have arrived at this idea over the course of many years, but two recent experiences have really brought this to life for me. When I met my friend Kevin recently, he was telling me about something or other, and as he was telling me, I was aware that I was building a mental movie of what he was describing to me. Earlier that day, I had been speaking with a client about a proposal for a training program, and the same thing happened. When the client had been telling me about the current situation, I had built a mental movie – a simulation – of it.

And as I sat there in Wolverhampton Civic Centre, listening to the remarkable Van Morrison and his tightly knit group of virtuoso musicians, thinking about how the atmosphere in the venue felt exactly like Sloppy Joe's in Key West, Florida, it struck me. The raw facts do not provide enough information for the simulation generator to work properly. It needs a story, with all of the rich, metaphorical and sensory details that are contained within.

If you haven't already figured out how this is relevant then I'll spell it out for you: stories are one of your most powerful tools for communicating new rules so that people can build and run new simulations and thereby change the world that they are simulating.

Stories might even be the most powerful tool. You can give people a list of health and safety rules during their induction training, or you can tell them stories about past accidents and how they could have been avoided. You could tell people the rules of the office, or you could tell them stories about things that have happened there, and they'll create their own rules.

> Stories appear to be a fundamental way in which the brain organizes information in a practical and memorable manner.

Antonio Damasio[3]

I once knew someone who read a book and from it formed a rich and vivid mental image of themselves, bringing positive change to the world, easily, effortlessly, elegantly. I remember how much other people were inspired by their abilities to make change so easy and so enjoyable, and so positive for everyone. I remember how they smiled when they realised that the person I was talking about was the person who is reading these words right now.

Since first thinking about this, I've been wondering "Why do stories work in this way?" and "How do we test this?"

I had a number of ideas.

---

3 Processing Narratives Concerning Protected Values: A Cross-Cultural Investigation of Neural Correlates. Kaplan, Damasio et al. Jan 2016.

Let's pretend for a moment that we have a piece of hardware in our heads that gets loaded with new simulations, so just like installing a program on your computer, the simulation needs to be in a certain format. The question then is what are the parameters, what does it need as a minimum, and what information, when there's more of it, leads to a better quality simulation?

The first thing that came to mind is sequence in time. A story will usually follow a sequence in time which a list of direct rules probably does not, so we can see how relationships between parts of the story connect over time. Nikola Tesla's experiments moved and changed, over time. He understood the rules that governed those changes and could reproduce the behaviour of those rules, mentally.

Secondly, I wondered about people. If we strip a sequence down to simplified steps e.g. the GROW coaching model, then we can't form a simulation using that information. We could form a mental image of the checklist, or hear the sounds of the words, but to form a simulation it needs people. So without knowing who is using GROW on who, we either can't build the simulation, or we build it using some previous experience - role models! We might build that using a coach who we looked up to because they seemed powerful, or they were the trainer, but actually their implementation of GROW was not very good, so that's what we learn. Or we insert the client from hell!

Thinking about this, I insert an easy client who is fun to work with! It's funny how many new clients I meet who are easy and fun to work with…

If we think about people for a moment, do you know about mirror neurons? In 'Trends in Cognitive Sciences' of December 1998, Vittorio Gallese and Alvin Goldman wrote an articled entitled "Mirror neurons and the simulation theory of mind-reading" Look it up on Google for a nice PDF reproduction of the article.

They found a part of the brain of a Macaque monkey, in the premotor cortex, that they called 'mirror neurons'. The function of these mirror neurons seems to be that the monkey's brain reproduces activity observed in another monkey. If we think of an emotional response as a form of physical response, then the result is what we might call empathy.

The idea is that we use these mirror neurons to read subtle physical signals and reproduce the same response in ourselves, so we experience the same emotional response. We could call it rapport, empathy, modelling, learning or even mind reading.

Gallese and Goldman put forward a theory for the action of mirror neurons called 'simulation theory', and it proposes that we are natural mind readers, using our own mind as a model for someone else's. We create a model of the world and the people in it, much like weather forecasters create a model of the weather inside a computer.

An alternate theory, called 'theory theory' is that we create explicit rules and assumptions about people's behaviour, using the mirror neurons.

My thinking is that forming a theory in this way requires some kind of labelling system, and we don't acquire that until some time after we're born, so that doesn't explain how babies learn to walk and talk. It does, however, explain how some people are 'good with people' and others are not. It explains how some people can be more empathic, where others have to work a lot harder to figure out what's going on in social situations. The authors of the article I mentioned even propose that it has a connection with Asperger's and Autism.

For our purposes, let's compare the two and see if we can figure out what the relevance to our conversation might be:

Theory	Simulation
Observe someone and form a theory about their behaviour	Observe someone and build a simulation of their behaviour
Explicit rules – we can explain why we act a certain way	Implicit rules – we can't explain why we act a certain way
Possibly limited in scope and accurate for a specific rule	Possibly broad in scope and accurate for general outcomes
Coded in language	Not coded
Passed on through language	Passed on by observing and copying

For example, if I form a theory about someone, I could say that they always come out of their front door at 8:25 because they always walk the same route to work. On the other hand, if I have a simulation of them, I might not know those details but I'll know what they would like for their birthday.

So both seem very useful, and now that I think about it, I can see that they are not different theories, rather one is overlaid on the other. What if we form a simulation first and then code it in language to form a theory? That's certainly what I do when modelling high performers in a business; first observe and get a feel for what they're doing, then go back and code that behaviour into explicit rules. Both are important.

Coding into rules means you can pass on behavioural information in a written or spoken format, which is handy when you think of the communication media that humans have created.

However, the simulation seems to be a much more effective way of picking up large amounts of behavioural data quickly.

If you think that any behaviour can be coded as an explicit theory, try emailing someone the instructions for a sequence of dance steps. You'll need some very specific frames of reference, and some very specific instructions. Or you could do the dance yourself and say "copy this".

You might be thinking that this doesn't hold true for a recipe, and I think that's an interesting case. Whether we're talking about a recipe for an omelette, or a recipe for success, we have two levels of information. We have the basic ingredients:

2 eggs, Butter and Salt

And we have some instructions:

Melt the butter in a frying pan. Break in the eggs. Stir on a medium heat until cooked. Season with salt to your taste.

Is that enough to make an omelette? Maybe. But is it enough to make a good omelette? The British chef Gordon Ramsay has a TV show where he visits failing restaurants and puts them back on track. To check the competence of the chef, he asks them to cook an omelette. It's the first thing they learn in catering college, and they should be able to do such a simple thing well. Yet all too often, the result is crumbly, or rubbery, or some other outcome that indicates the chef may not be as competent as he would like us to believe.

They know what to make an omelette with, they know how to make it, but there's a difference between how the chef in the restaurant makes it and how Gordon Ramsay makes it, and that is the difference between an average chef and an excellent chef.

Lots of people speak at conferences about their secret formula for success. They hand out nice, easy to remember rules. Yet many people find that putting those rules into practice doesn't quite work out in the way they had hoped. I would say that the reason for this is simple – if you're not the person who came up with the rules, then they won't work for you, because they are dependent on lots of other stuff which you don't have, such as the original person's personality, resources, colleagues, experiences, fears and so on.

This is one reason why this book is written the way that it is – because if I gave you a nice simple checklist of things to do, or some nice mnemonics, it might sound good, but you wouldn't have to do any thinking in order to use it. Now you might take the simple checklist and use it properly, but lots of people wouldn't You'll get more out of any learning experience when you have to do some of the figuring out for yourself. And besides, why should I do all the hard work?

By the way, the simple checklists and mnemonics are created for the purposes of being easy to remember – and they are, at that first level. But as you start to try to apply them, you might discover there is a lot of information missing about how to apply them to get the result you want, and that's what has been missed out in distilling the original person's experience into a checklist.

As a result of watching that TV show, I now have a little Gordon Ramsay on my shoulder whenever I cook an omelette. I actually feel nervous to make sure I do it properly so he won't shout at me! Mind you, one of his recipes is for a bacon, pea and goat's cheese omelette with a tomato salad. I don't think I'll be having a go at that one.

I think that the implications of simulations and mirror neurons go far beyond empathy; we use our own mind as a model for the world as a whole, creating rules for understanding weather, crops, food, animals and so on, as well as models for people. Perhaps people are more complex than the weather, so we need special parts of our brain to understand them. On the other hand, the mirror neurons seem to work with some animals too. The researchers found that anything that looks like a hand, including a robotic hand, triggers the process.

Mirror neurons seem specifically designed to mimic other people's behaviour, including emotional responses. In order for mirror neurons to work, we need someone to copy. I wonder if they can work from internal representations? I don't see any reason to think that they wouldn't, since everything else seems to work that way i.e. emotional and physical responses can be triggered as strongly from an external event as from an internally recalled or created one.

So my theory so far is that mirror neurons are responsible for emulating behaviour immediately, and building a real time simulation of behaviour over time. Couple this with work that's been done recently around memory, specifically how mice learn from traumatic experiences by 'reliving' them after the real event, and thereby become accustomed to those kinds of experiences over time - and I think we are on to something.

Our mirror neurons take sensory data about a person and use it to build a simulation that we can then refer to as if we're interacting with that person. Some of the conversations I have with my wife seem to indicate that she can have a previous conversation with her mental simulation of me that is so vivid that she thinks she has had the conversation with the real me!

And the thing about a story is that - ideally - we produce a vivid internal representation from it. A good story brings the characters to life as vividly as if they are really in the room with you. And I don't just mean a good novel or someone who is specifically telling a story, I mean just an average person talking about something that happened at work, and they're so involved in the story that you get drawn in too, and before long you're watching the same mental movie as they are, and you're forming the same opinions about people and events.

After all, how many times do people tell their friends or partners about people at work, and when they meet at the Christmas party, they say, "You're not how I imagined you!"

Look

Limiting Beliefs

If you have had anything to do with coaching or coaches, you may have heard the term 'limiting beliefs', which are things you believe to be true which hold you back and stop you from getting what you want. For example, you might believe that you're not qualified for a promotion, in which case that is a limiting belief, because it's stopping you from taking the steps you need to take to get promoted.

Here's the thing. Beliefs are not inherently limiting. There is no such thing as a limiting belief.

"But", the coaches cry, "if someone doesn't believe they can do something then that is only a belief, and it's holding them back".

Of course that's true. My limiting belief that I cannot fly by flapping my arms prevents me from jumping off cliffs. This does not mean that you really can't get that promotion. There is quite a big difference between a belief about my career prospects and a belief about the effect on my vital organs of deceleration trauma.

Your beliefs lead to behaviour, so you behave in a way which confirms your beliefs. Therefore, all beliefs are limiting, or none of them are, whichever way you look at it. Your beliefs are simply rules. They are neither good nor bad.

Now, this isn't a self help book. This is not "I can whiten your teeth in 7 days". This is a book about organisational change, and specifically this is a book about changing organisations by changing people, and since your organisation will be shaped around your beliefs, it's useful to be able to change beliefs. But not because they are limiting. To say that a belief is limiting does two things.

Firstly, it makes 'limiting' a characteristic of the belief. The limitation is not an inherent characteristic of the belief; it is only a quality of your perception of the belief, which in turn becomes a quality of your behaviour.

This would be like saying that frustration is an inherent quality of the position of the hands on a clock, or that anger is an inherent property of a parking ticket, or that sadness is an inherent quality of a story.

The second thing that it does is to put the belief in control; to make you passive to the belief.

This would be like saying that a red traffic light makes you stop your car. Maybe you think it does? How about an amber traffic light? Does a 30 mph speed limit make you drive slower? Does a fast car make you drive faster? Does a 'no smoking' sign make you give up smoking? Does a 'keep off the grass' sign make you walk on the path?

The point here, if you didn't get it yet, is that it's your willingness to follow the instruction that 'makes' you follow it. There is no inherent quality in the rule which gives it control. Essentially, you choose to follow all instructions for which you would prefer to avoid the consequences. At a busy junction next to a police station, you would probably stop on red. But late at night, on an empty road through a set of road works, where the light changes to amber as you're approaching it and you can see the road ahead is clear?

If you have ever driven over the speed limit, even once, even by accident, then you'll know that there are no consequences for exceeding the speed limit. There are only consequences for getting caught. So your decision to drive a little faster is partly based on your perception of the risk of getting caught.

The rule doesn't control you, it only provides information for you to incorporate into your decision process. Part of that decision process is your willingness to follow social conventions. Another part of that is your sense of right and wrong. But control? That's all yours.

We've talked on and off about belief change. We've explored a number of practical tools for belief change. All of them can be used in the context of aligning beliefs with environment, in order to align behaviour with environment and results. Remember that any behaviour is inherently fine, but it may or may not get you the results you want in a given context. Jumping up and down and shouting may get you what you want in one organisation, but not in another. High performing behaviours are entirely context dependent.

So you must let go of the idea that you can change behaviour by removing limiting beliefs and instead realise that you can change behaviour by aligning beliefs. There was nothing intrinsically wrong with them.

What we are aiming to achieve is the alignment of behaviour with organisational purpose, and to do that we can align individual beliefs. We don't need to fix them.

Because here's the funny thing. To say that you have a limiting belief makes you passive to the belief. Even in the structure of the language, you are saying that the belief limits you and there's nothing you can do about it.

If a policeman closes a road and you take a diversion, you might say, "the policeman made me take a diversion". You are making yourself passive, and yet you are the person taking the diversion. You are taking action, but putting someone else in control of it. To say that the rules made you, or the company made you, or your boss made you, or the traffic made you is one point of view in which you have no control over the actions you take. And yet, logically, you know that this can't be true. How can chocolate make you fat? It's you eating too much that is the problem! How can money make you happy? It's the thought of spending money, or the feeling of comfort that you give yourself that makes you happy. Happiness is not a property of money, it is a property of your response to your perception of money. It is your emotional response to the meaning of money.

By the way, if you know someone who has been trying to lose weight, or cut down on something else, here's an odd idea. People often say they need will power to lose weight, that they have to make an effort. Well, the odd thing is that losing weight requires no effort at all – it's gaining weight that requires all the work! You have to earn money, go to a shop, buy snacks, eat them, that all takes a lot of time and effort! All you have to do to begin losing weight is stop doing those things! It seems that eating junk food is what requires the will power, not stopping eating it.

I know myself that it requires far more effort to go to the Chinese takeaway than to get something healthy out of the fridge, yet I seem to be able to summon up the energy that I can't seem to summon up to get to the gym! In fact, ordering a takeaway and going to fetch it is about the same effort as getting to the gym! So I don't need will power to make myself go to the gym, because that presupposes that I can't go to the gym because I don't have enough will power. It's a ridiculous rule, but it seems to be working quite effectively.

So, a limiting belief is a belief that limits you. And since you created the belief in the first place, it must be under your control.

If I believe that you are reading this book then I'll carry on typing. If I believe that no-one will ever read these words, what's the point? I might as well give up now.

Only joking! Of course I knew you were reading.

So how do we get round the problem of limiting beliefs? Well, it's the very act of calling a belief limiting that makes it limiting. Do you see?

The old industrial psychologists talked about methods of controlling behaviour, and their approach was to go straight for the behaviour to be changed, with a 'don't do that, do this' approach. They talked about methods such as reward and punishment, withdrawal of benefits and motivating offers of things like money and prestige.

If you are a parent, you will understand why direct behaviour change does not work. If you are not a parent, ask the nearest parent.

Changing behaviour through punishment or withdrawal works in the short term, but after that it breeds resentment and indirect retaliation. In the industrial world, this is the 'work to rule'. At home, it's the begrudgingly literal interpretation of every request made. After a while, the parent realises that, sooner or later, the child in question will hold the power to put them into a retirement home where they will live out the remainder of their lives in line dancing classes, listening to brass band concerts and playing bingo with a pen that dried up many years ago. Let's face it, as a parent, you know your children are holding all the Aces. And the same goes for employers too.

What about reward? Again, it works in the short term, but what about long term? Do pigeons go away if you give them bread? Do wolves stay away if you throw them a little meat to keep them happy? And when power hungry people are rewarded with power, they eventually turn into emperors, and when your organisation has been carved up into parochial empires, you no longer have a business.

Reward and punishment do work, but rarely in the way you intend. I used to work with a lovely salesman who was very successful. In fact, he rarely sold anything. What he did was to look for when someone else sold something and then do the paperwork to claim the credit for it. The person who sold it couldn't be bothered to do the paperwork, so everyone was happy! He figured out how the system worked – sales people weren't actually rewarded for selling stuff, they were rewarded for filling in paperwork. He figured out how to make the system work for him.

If you have children then you will probably have learned that when you reward them for doing something, they'll then do that thing over and over again to get the reward. For example, if you pay them for tidying their bedrooms then they'll tidy them very often. In fact, it will seem suspiciously like they're untidying their bedroom just so that they can tidy it again.

Corporate history is littered with such examples. When software writers were paid for every bug they found, they introduced more bugs! I am almost ashamed to admit that, as an engineer, when I was on call, I had a four hour response time and was paid overtime by the hour. So when I was called out, what was my incentive to respond in less than four hours? Especially on Bank Holidays when I was paid double time! I say I am almost ashamed, but not quite. You see, the rules were there to be obeyed. Four hours. If all the engineers start responding in ten minutes, it just makes life harder for everyone.

So the only viable option is to make people want to change. No, that doesn't sound right either. How can you make someone want something? Surely they either want it or they don't? You might entice them, sell it to them, but is that reliable and scalable enough to work for an entire organisation? And doesn't that still sound like coercion?

Here's an idea. People inherently want to do better, and that implies change. People do not intrinsically resist change. What they resist is being changed, or having to sit through another change program's kick off seminar and brain storming session where they know their ideas won't really be incorporated into the program.

What we're left with is Change Magic. When you change the environment, and open people's minds to the potential for change, they will adapt. They will adapt their behaviours and they will adapt their perceptions, because humans don't survive, we adapt.

Since people will adapt according to their own perceptions, we also need to introduce some alignment so that the resulting behaviour change is consistent and deterministic. Not exactly predictable, but we're talking about living, self determined individuals here. If you want predictable outputs then pay your change management consultants to come up with an employee satisfaction survey that ensures the results you want to see. And don't be surprised when, a year later, the organisation is still not performing as it should be.

Of course, you can either change the environment, or people's map of it. It's pretty much the same thing, for our purposes.

I've rambled on about limiting beliefs because it's something I hear a lot in organisational change. People talk about freeing up resources, or needing innovative thinking, or having to break free from the old culture, the old sets of limiting beliefs.

Once people have accepted that their behaviour is generated from their beliefs, the natural thing to do is blame their beliefs for undesirable behaviour. But, and I stress this once again, to call a belief limiting is to put the belief in control and the person with the belief passive to it. It doesn't make any sense, yet we still do it.

Accept beliefs for what they are, simply rules which serve a purpose and achieve a result. When the purpose changes or the desired result changes, a change in belief or perception may be useful. And it is generally easier to change something that seems easy to change.

Ideas

What do you do with ideas? Do you nurture them and let them become new products and services, or do you dismiss them because they're not what you do? Come on, be honest with yourself…

It's really quite amazing how naturally creative we humans are, and it's equally amazing how completely demoralising and demotivating it is for us when that creativity is stifled.

If you're about to say, "but we encourage creative ideas with our suggestion scheme" then I'm going to be ruthless and say that a suggestion scheme hinders creativity. If you have to create a business process to handle ideas then there's something very wrong, because you're effectively saying that the people who have ideas aren't able to pursue those ideas.

An integral part of our creativity is being able to test our ideas and suggestion schemes prevent that from happening. Here's the sequence of events in a suggestion scheme:

Person A has a great idea so they submit it to the suggestion scheme (person B)	→	Person B dismisses the idea because it wasn't theirs and testing other people's wild ideas just means more work	→	Person A is trained to suppress their creative urges

So if you want to foster creativity, let people develop their own ideas.

Is this impractical in a large organisation? Yes, it could seem that way if you believe that creativity is not important. Some people think that success is just down to doing what you're told, harder and more often. Other people think that success is down to innovation and adaptation. I can't tell you which is right for you.

Remember that people naturally learn by modelling behaviour - just as we all did as children. The most efficient way to train people isn't to tell them what to do - it's to get them doing it, regardless of what you think their learning style may be. Learning styles are what people do with their conscious brains whilst they're learning. If you promote an ideas scheme and then do nothing with those ideas, you will train people to keep their ideas to themselves, regardless of the effort you put into the scheme.

Back in the 1920s, birds throughout the UK started breaking into foil topped milk bottles and drinking the cream. Scientists at the time couldn't figure out how the birds were learning this behaviour because their thinking assumed that birds are stupid, therefore one bird must have accidentally discovered that the milk bottle tops could be pecked through and all the other birds must have copied it. Cases of milk theft should start in one place and spread out over time, but what scientists actually saw was the behaviour emerging in several places at once, and they couldn't figure out how the birds were learning from each other so quickly.

The answer, as with all good answers, was very simple. The birds weren't as stupid as the scientists had thought, and they were properly motivated.

All over the UK, birds were learning to steal milk from the bottles on people's doorsteps because it was the obvious thing to do. The idea had come of its time. There was no magic, no telepathy and no amazing leap in creativity.

Some people think that when some birds learned the trick, the knowledge went into an ethereal collective consciousness that is shared between all members of a species. They think that when one bird learned the trick, they all learned it.

Other people think that the pattern of milk theft closely followed the pattern of distribution of milk bottles with cardboard tops. Previously, milk bottle tops had been made of metal. They think that the birds just did what was obvious and all that changed was that the cardboard bottle tops allowed them to succeed. They didn't have to suck seeds any more. Sorry, that's a silly joke.

Ideas have a time. Perhaps no one person invented the wheel, or fire, or anything else. Darwin wasn't the first person to think about evolution, he was the first person to be famous for it. Some people throughout history have clearly been more prolific in writing their ideas down, and so we often think that some people are creative whilst others aren't.

If you look at the history of great thinkers like Darwin, Newton and a bunch of hungry birds, you find that there is often an implication that they borrowed ideas from a less well known predecessor or researcher.

Alfred Russel Wallace developed a theory of natural selection before Darwin, which contributed to Darwin's work. Wallace had been looking for evidence of natural selection after reading the work of Robert Chambers, published in 1844, 15 years prior to Darwin's publication date.

Fifty years before Darwin published 'On the Origin of Species through Natural Selection', there was a man named Jean-Baptiste de Lamarck who put forward a theory of evolution by natural selection. The key difference with

Lamarck's theory was that he saw evolution as a collaborative effort rather than a ruthless battle for survival.

It might be more useful to think that everyone's equally creative, some people just have more faith in their own ideas, and they also have better PR skills.

Creativity, as a concept, has become closely associated with the arts, so many of us are brought up to believe that we are not creative, simply because our drawings don't look like photographs. If you think you can't draw then let me ask you this question: "are you an artist or a photocopier?"

An artist, or a writer, or a poet, or a photographer, doesn't simply record events, they add something new. We want more than facts, more than a verbatim transcript. We want meaning, we want emotion, we want to know how to feel about what's happening. The tranquillity, or drama, or curiosity that a piece of art can evoke creates a sense of meaning in what we're seeing, and what we all want is a life that means something, a life that is significant.

Therefore, businesses often value a handful of 'creative' people and demonstrate the belief that creativity is something unique, special and rare. Since only a few people are creative, only those people can develop innovative ideas, right? What if you were to believe that the majority of people in your organisation are creative? What if everyone is creative? What would that mean?

Getting an idea to market means developing an idea to the stage where it positively impacts your business performance. It may be a new product or it may be a business process or even a new office layout. What's important is that it creates advantage. Sooner or later, all your competitors will have the same idea, so all that matters is the lead you have over them, and how you make the most of that lead.

Remember - your survival depends on you being just one small step ahead, all the time.

Ideas are the currency of competitive advantage, and here's why:

Right now, all over the world, your competitors' employees are having the same great ideas as your employees. All that matters is who gets those ideas to market first.

Your employees aren't necessarily unique, but the culture in which their ideas flourish is.

When you start out on a new journey, you cannot ever know precisely where you'll end up. You take that first step with an intention, a sense of purpose. Where that leads you can't be predicted, can't be scripted. It can only be enjoyed and appreciated.

Getting To the Heart Of It

One of the key skills in corporate consulting as well as personal change work is being able to get to the heart of the real issue quickly. It seems that many people regard this as a skill that is hard to acquire, because there doesn't seem to be a specific process or set of questions you can ask.

Instead of looking at the process or questions to get right to the very core of an issue, let's instead consider what happens when a coach or consultant doesn't get to the heart of the issue.

Did you ever watch Scooby Doo? Maybe you still do? You may recall that, in every episode, there was a ghost or monster that turned out to be some greedy person protecting some kind of treasure. Basically, someone would find some treasure and then use an old ghost story to scare other people away, so the guy who owned the amusement arcade would dress up as a monster shark, or maybe a ghostly sailor. And he would have gotten away with it if it wasn't for those pesky kids.

The reason I bring this up is that the writers of Scooby Doo knew how to use fear as a protection for treasure. Guess what? In corporate and personal change work, we see exactly the same thing happening. People use fear to prevent you from reaching the treasure. The only difference is that they don't know they're doing it, as if the fear has a mind of its own. In a way, it does – your unconscious mind.

Fear will scare off a casual moocher as surely as it scared off the simple townsfolk in Scooby Doo. And it will easily scare you away too, if you don't hang in there.

We recently did some work to model the process whereby a good coach will get to the heart of a client's issue very quickly, and since it's so important in corporate change work to dig down and not accept the easy answers, I thought I would share it with you.

Firstly, the client will tell you everything you need to know in the first sentence, so you really have to pay attention. Sue, my client for the process, demonstrated the issue before she started speaking - she enacted the behaviour that leads some other people to label her as 'quiet'. Specifically, when I asked her to tell me what she wanted to work on, she made hand gestures as if she were mentally preparing and wanting to get it right, yet she wasn't actually saying anything, as if she was 'psyching herself up'.

Secondly, that initial clue led me to form a hypothesis about the root of the issue, so I set off in that direction. What the modelling group noticed was that I tried anything and everything, coming at it from different angles to narrow it down. The key points seemed to be:

- Getting multiple examples in different times and contexts to cross reference

- Coming from different angles to bypass the normal defences

- Periodically breaking state, changing the subject, asking if the client is happy to continue

- Testing the hypothesis and either continuing to be led by it or discarding it if it is disproven

- Using sorting techniques to create greater distinctions between parts of the issue, like getting into its crevices and levering it open

- Being guided by the feelings that I am picking up from the client, specifically discomfort and fear

Third, I kept going until I felt we were at the heart of the issue, and this was the really big thing. At a point where we had a glimpse of the root issue but were still focussing on the stated work situation, I stopped and asked the four modellers if we had reached the root yet. Two said no, two said yes. The two who said yes went on to say 'no, but I think you've gone far enough'

And this raised, for me, the most important observation of the whole process. When we get close to the root of the client's issue, we are faced with their fears, and fears are...well, scary. So one of two things often happens - either the client employs all of their normal defence or avoidance strategies to avoid going into the fear, or the coach feels the fear, doesn't like it and backs off.

In short, the discovery was that the coach doesn't get to the heart of the issue, not because of any lack of skill, but because he or she backs off from the uncomfortable feeling of being there.

One person asked me how I overcome the feeling, and I said that it's the client's fear, not mine, so why should I be scared of it? Also, I guess a few years ago I was in exactly the same place. In fact, I don't guess, I know. I can remember times with clients when I avoided telling them what I really thought because it was uncomfortable, and I bought their excuses and diversions because that was easier than pushing ahead.

Finally, when we had explored the root of the issue, I formulated a statement of the process that generates the behaviour and tried it on to check if it resonated with the client. At this stage, it's as useful to be right as it is to be wrong, because if the client is still uncertain, then making an obviously wrong statement will throw more light on the right answer.

The process statement was "when you were younger, someone who wanted you to not have to learn from life the hard way, and who wanted to stop you from making the mistakes that they had made, would criticise you when you said or did something wrong, and that made you feel bad, so to avoid feeling bad you would wait and prepare yourself so that when you did speak up or act you got it right, so it was more comfortable to stay quiet and let someone else speak up. At work, this means that while you're thinking about the right answer, three quicker, louder people have already jumped in". And her answer... "yes".

I think it's important to point out that this process relies only pushing through the fear barrier to the truth within, it doesn't require a particular style of approach. Some coaches might be very direct and challenging, perhaps even aggressive. Others would be gently challenging and would get there more through dexterity than force.

I wonder if coaches who use a tough, aggressive style are still afraid of the fear, so they have to take a run up at it? My preferred style is to be supportive yet challenging, because I want to retain respect for the client and not make them unnecessarily uncomfortable. After all, this process is for their benefit, not mine.

Here's the process, one more time:

1. Pay 100% attention to ALL verbal and non verbal communication in the first minute

2. From the initial statement, form a theory about the root process (remembering positive intention: the process is not the problem, the output is the problem. The process is trying to do something useful)

3. Dig around the issue (PROCESS not content), getting cross references and multiple examples to test your theory

4. When you feel the fear, you are almost there - keep going

5. Form a process statement and test it with the client

6. If you get a 'yes' response, stop. Anything else, refine the process statement until you get a 'yes'

And there you are - at the heart of it.

So, just like in Scooby Doo, the fear is there to scare away casual moochers who are easily scared and don't ask too many questions, unlike those pesky kids.

I think we could sum this up with a useful belief:

The purpose of fear is to keep you away from treasure.

So when you start to get that uncomfortable feeling, when you see people rationalising, making excuses or getting hostile, you know you are close. When most people would back off at that point, you keep pushing. In fact, you push harder.

THE PURPOSE OF **FEAR** IS TO KEEP YOU AWAY FROM **TREASURE** [4]

While we're here, it might be useful to understand what the role of fear is in this context, where it comes from and how we can deal with it. Whilst it may seem unconventional to talk about fear in the realm of corporate change work, I would suggest that projects and ventures fail, not because of lack of planning or funding, but because of fear.

Fear keeps people in their comfort zones and, like a computer virus, is very good at hiding. All we are usually aware of is the comfort zone, and when we are pushed out

4   SCOOBY-DOO and all related characters and elements are trademarks of and © Hanna-Barbera.

of that we employ all kinds of strategies to get back into it, such as:

- Reasoning and rationalising (It's because…)
- Direct aggression (It's your fault)
- Hiding, avoiding
- Denying (It didn't even happen)
- Diverting attention (It's someone else's fault)
- Becoming passive (It's my fault… help me)

Do you ever see people behave that way in the office, in situations where you sense they are nervous or unsure of what they are being asked to do?

For example, the business owner might say, "We need the sales team to deliver an extra £100 Million of sales if we're going to turn this business around". Using the examples above, the Sales Director might reply:

- "The resources to deliver that level of revenue are simply not available, and that would cause downstream problems for logistics and operations who wouldn't be resourced to handle the work load." (hopes the logic of the argument will dissuade further discussion)

- "What the hell do you think we're doing now? Sitting around drinking coffee? You want to try getting down to the coal face, then you'll see how hard we're working." (hopes the aggressive posture will dissuade further discussion)

- "Erm.. OK then" (he leaves the meeting and calls a recruitment agency to plan his exit)

- "Well if logistics were pulling their weight we wouldn't be in this mess. I mean, what exactly were the Q3 shipment shortfalls? Exactly which products are we missing on?" (hopes the delay will dissuade further discussion)

- "I just don't know how I'm going to deliver that, it's been so hard recently, with my wife leaving me and everything, and I can't do it all by myself..." (hopes the uncomfortable distraction will dissuade further discussion)

So, let's have a look at where this all starts – childhood. I should add that this is a psychological view of where these processes arise. I am not suggesting that people in your organisation need therapy; only that they are human.

The idea is that, as children, we were naturally uninhibited and inquisitive. We explored, played games and made friends without the fears that plagues many people as adults – fear of rejection, fear of failure etc.

As children, we didn't worry about failure when we were learning to walk. We weren't afraid of rejection when we smiled at strangers. We only learned these fears, primarily from our parents, when we were told "no".

Every one of us still has those innate, childlike qualities, and everyone thinks of them differently. Right now, think of the essential quality that you associate with a child – it might be something like playfulness, freedom, curiosity, love, vulnerability or perhaps something else that seems right to you. Remember that word for a moment.

As we grow up, we find that we are told off for being our true selves, so we learn that it's wrong to want the things that we want, and there's something wrong with who we naturally are. This creates a layer of fear – we're afraid to be who we really are. Since we don't want to show the world that we're afraid, we build a layer of pretence that insulates the fear and allows us to project a strong, confident persona to the world.

The problem is that when we interact with other people from that layer of pretence, we are operating from a weak position. We will be employing control strategies - trying to please, coerce, force, bully or reason the other person into doing what we want.

Now, think for a moment. Have you ever had a manager, or have you ever seen someone in a power position using any of these control strategies, and have you ever thought that they seem to imply weakness rather than strength? If so, you have seen this process in action.

So, the important question is, "what do we do about it?"

I asked you to think of a word, and that word describes you when you are at your best, it is your true self.

The first thing we need to do is connect with the true self, and the only way to do this is to move out of the comfort zone and through the fear. The fear is a barrier that keeps you in your comfort zone, and as soon as you get near to it, you will be highly motivated to move back again.

You'll see this behaviour in other people; when something moves them out of their comfort zone and they get a glimpse of the fear, you will see them avoiding, making excuses, rationalising, getting angry, upset, diverting attention and all the other things that they do.

When you observe this behaviour in yourself, at times when you can feel yourself being pushed past your comfort zone, you can become aware of what you are afraid of.

Common fears include:

- Rejection
- Loss
- Abandonment
- Failure

- Success
- Criticism
- Looking stupid
- Being judged

Now, here's the tricky part. We know, as sensible adults, that those fears are ridiculous and unfounded. We know that, if we stand up to present to our colleagues, we don't have to worry about looking stupid. We know it's irrational. And yet, still it motivates our behaviour. When we are able to let go of that fear, move out of the comfort zone and connect with our real selves, we allow our natural energy to flow and connect with other people. This is when we have experiences of being 'in flow' or of being 'connected' with another person. This has happened at the times in your life when you felt most free, most at ease with yourself and most effortlessly effective.

Organisations as well as people exhibit behaviour motivated by fear. In the Alignment chapter, you read about one way to deal with fear and the influence that it has on both individual and organisational behaviour.

The truth that exists behind the lie is that we already are who we aspire to be. As an organisation or as an individual, you already have everything that you need to be everything that you want. Wow, that sounds good. Let's remember it with a useful belief:

You already have everything that you need to be everything that you want.

So having worked hard and pushed through the fear, the next stage is to keep going until you reach the truth inside, that you are already all that you aspire to be, and so much more. That's what lies at the heart of the matter.

A universal characteristic of high performing teams is trust. I find it's useful to think of teams as a group of individuals with a common purpose. Just as we can think of the word 'company' as a collective noun, so can we think of the word 'team' in the same way. We used collective nouns to reveal the nature of a company or team earlier, and it's worth trying this out with your own team. Get everyone to write down a collective noun for you as individuals and compare the results. The differences are where the real value lies.

A huge corporate team building industry has grown out of the need to build trust in teams, so people who do not normally have anything to do with other are forced to build a raft out of toothpicks and a watering can just because they all happen to report to the same manager. If you look back to the chapter on organisational structures, you'll see that the supply chain is often a much better candidate for team building than a bunch of people who all happen to work in the same part of an arbitrary hierarchy. Sometimes, companies do get everyone in the supply chain together for team building, which is a very good thing. The downside is that the same people don't always interact with each other, and you don't want to be running a team building workshop every week.

In my experience, you can't make people trust each other, no matter how much beer you buy them. I find that it is more effective to explore the sense of shared purpose, that we are all trying to get the same thing, and to then create the space within which people can peep out of their holes, have a sniff around and decide if it's safe to come out and play.

Workshops That Get Results

I've really thought long and hard about whether to share this tip with you. It's such a simple yet powerful idea, and it's one that I use every time I facilitate a workshop, meeting, conference, strategy review, client workshop and so on.

I have decided that you will fall into one of two categories.

Either; You have read the book diligently up to this point, in which case you are well on your way to becoming a skilled Change Magician, and I can therefore trust you.

Or; You haven't read the book at all and just bought it to look good on the shelf, in which case you won't be stealing all my wonderful ideas anyway and I don't have to worry.

Here it is. Are you ready? It's really good…

When people chair or facilitate a meeting such as a project, client or strategy review, they work through the agenda in chronological order:

What usually happens in these workshops is that:

- The more people talk about what's wrong in the present situation, the more they descend into a state of conflict.

- People blame each other for what's wrong.

- The action plan looks backwards to problems instead of forwards to solutions.

- The actions are remedial and getting people to take actions is like pulling teeth.

- Since the actions are remedial, they only try to change what has already happened.

- You run out of time at the end so the actions don't get allocated anyway.

- Nothing changes.

Here is the way I suggest you do it instead:

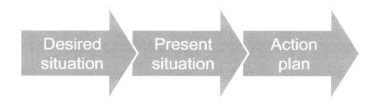

No, you didn't miss anything.

If you talk about the desired solution first – and devote half of your total time to it – you will create a clear and compelling vision of what people actually want, instead of getting them to complain about what they don't want. When you move onto present situation, spend a very short amount of time on it, as you will find that the action points just fall out of the conversation, suggested by people who are in a positive, resourceful state and who genuinely commit to actions, because they want to get to that desired situation as quickly as they can.

What happens when you do it this way is:

- □ You create a shared vision that people feel good about

- □ Problems get put into perspective and become stepping stones

- □ The action plan is obvious, and has very few actions in it

- □ People suggest actions and take responsibility for them

- □ You get to the real heart of the situation instead of going in circles, talking about symptoms

- □ People will think you're the most wonderful facilitator on the planet (another way of saying 'Change Magician')

Facilitating Change

The word 'facilitate' literally means 'to make easy'. Therefore, a facilitator is a person who makes something easy. We usually associate facilitators with discussions, workshops and even conflict resolution, and a good facilitator can make the difference between a productive discussion where different views are aired and resolved, and a free-for-all where different views escalate into entrenched positions. In other words, a good facilitator makes the difference between a group discussion which leads nowhere, and one which leads to an outcome that everyone can live with.

Interestingly, that's how one group of expert facilitators define 'consensus'. I was lucky enough to spend some time with a client whose main business is facilitating change within a particular industry through the creation and implementation of industry operating standards. The organisation was created as a result of a particularly horrific accident where many people were killed as a result of the disparate operators in a deregulated industry not talking to each other about matters of operations and safety.

One of the organisation's most important activities is chairing the working parties and groups, comprised of all of the different industry stakeholders, which define and agree on the standards. These stakeholders can hold views which are utterly opposed to each other, typically around the balance of safety versus cost.

Using the modelling methodology that you'll find in my book Genius at Work, I learned how the best facilitators are able to shape these discussions, influence the stakeholders and reach consensus agreements. Since this is such a valuable set of skills for a Change Magician, I've reproduced the full modelling report here.

Behaviour

This section deals with the key behavioural strategies of the role, including what the high performer does, both internally (mentally) and externally (physically), to achieve their intended results.

Results are the primary means by which we identify a high performer. How they achieve those results is the purpose of the modelling project.

Results

High performers are able to achieve the following results when compared to average performers:

- Accelerated progress of projects, standards implementation etc.

- Reduction in the number of meetings required to resolve an issue or progress a project

- Effective management of conflict leading to improved working relationships and greater productivity outside of meetings

Meeting sequence

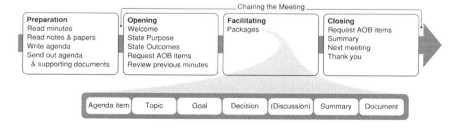

Preparation

Preparation is a key focus for the high performer, and contains one of the most important distinctions between the high and average performers.

A poor facilitator will fail to prepare adequately, and will see the meeting as an entity in itself, with any necessary discussion taking place with the meeting boundaries. This is an extremely inefficient use of time because meetings are then used for group discussion rather than decision making. Therefore, the first difference is this:

Poor facilitators see a meeting as a discussion activity, whereas the best facilitators see a meeting as a decision making activity.

High performers therefore work hard to complete as much work as possible outside of the meeting, building relationships with members and stakeholders and carefully positioning any unpopular agenda items so that minimal discussion takes place within the meeting. A high performer will be very careful not to lobby or influence stakeholders, instead working on the wording of papers or standards proposals to lead to minimal contention within a meeting.

A typical belief from a poor to average facilitator is that any preparation is better than none, so when they are pressed for time they might send out a meeting agenda to participants the day before a meeting. This means that the facilitator is focusing only on their own preparation, and not putting themselves in the minds of the participants, as they will not have sufficient time to prepare. The consequence of this is that the poor to average performer's meetings take longer and more meetings are required to achieve a particular result, which means that the facilitator has to work harder between meetings, which means that they have less time to prepare thoroughly and give participants time to prepare.

The best facilitators will spend up to half a day preparing for a meeting, around 3 or 4 days prior to the meeting. The second difference between the average and best facilitators is the way in which they prepare:

Poor   **Prepare as if they are a participant**

Average   **Prepare as if they are a chairman**

Best   **Prepare as if they are the other participants**

This distinction is not obvious from observing facilitators, as both the average and high performers prepare by reading previous minutes, papers, reports etc. The difference is entirely internal. When the average facilitator reads papers, they read them to familiarise themselves with the topics to be discussed. When the best facilitators prepare, they put themselves 'in the shoes' of the various participants in the meeting to see the issues from as many and as extreme points of view as possible which enables them to pre-empt any potentially contentious issues, giving rise to an observable output:

Average facilitators struggle with conflict for two reasons, partly because they avoid it (by taking it personally) and partly because they fail to pre-empt it. The best facilitators handle conflict more effectively because they work to minimise conflict before it arises. They are not afraid of conflict and they know that they will save themselves time in the long run by 'putting it on the table' themselves.

Planning the agenda

A meeting is rarely a self contained discussion; it is usually a snapshot of a number of activities which are at different stages of development. Some will be early in their lifecycle, requiring scoping discussions. Some will be in their mid term with lots of actions and updates. Some will be winding down with status reports and reviews.

Therefore, planning the agenda for a meeting requires the facilitator to know about the life cycle of each discussion item so that they can allocate sufficient time to it. If the previous meeting worked well in terms of the time available for discussion, then the next meeting agenda can use the same times, adjusted for any changes due to the life cycle of discussion items.

The best facilitators don't worry about having the agenda timing perfect because they will often dynamically rearrange the agenda anyway. Their focus is on concluding the highest priority items so that they can achieve their goals for the meeting. By stating the objective of the discussion item upfront, the participants are able to focus on it. Through this, they are able to achieve faster progress in the *projects* that the meetings are one part of.

It is important that the right participants will be present at the meeting to achieve the stated objectives, so if a key decision maker will not be present then there is no point including the item in the agenda. Ensuring the right people are present for the planned agenda items means that the meeting time is used more efficiently and more is achieved.

Objectives

High performing facilitators have clear goals, and their meetings are a means to achieving those goals. Their goal, which might be to see a standard adopted, or some research acted upon, or a change program implemented, serves as a fixed point like a star to navigate by, which makes it very easy for them to identify any deviations from the topic under discussion. They recognise that an off topic conversation may be interesting, but their meeting is not the time or place for it. Therefore, they do not undermine the value of the conversation, they merely refocus participants' attention on the matter at hand.

Conversely, poor to average facilitators hold the meeting itself as the goal and are therefore less flexible during the meeting. They are more likely to allow the conversation to go off topic because they don't have a clear goal as a point of reference. Because their goal is essentially 'to hold a meeting', the discussion can go off topic and they will still achieve that goal. They might even go as far as to consider the off topic discussion as valuable because it sounds interesting or useful.

Broadly speaking, we can identify the following traits relating to goals and objectives:

- **Poor facilitators see the meeting as an end in itself**

- Average facilitators see the meeting as a means to a short term end
- The best facilitators see a series of meetings as a means to a long term end

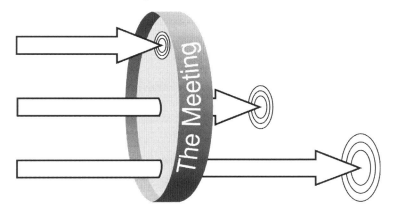

Process

The best facilitators are very process-focused when in a meeting. Paradoxically, they use the agenda to control the meeting, but the agenda does not dictate the meeting. Conversely, a poor facilitator will stick more rigidly to the agenda which increases the chances that the meeting will run over time and that participants will leave due to other commitments.

Time

High performing facilitators have a long term view of time, in that they will invest time in the short term in order save it later on during a meeting or in completing a project more quickly.

Conversely, a poor or inexperienced facilitator will save time in the short term with minimal preparation or an agenda sent out only the night before the meeting, and as a result their meetings last longer and more meetings are required to achieve the same results because participants are not adequately prepared.

High performing facilitators also value time within the meeting itself and will dynamically rearrange the agenda to adapt to changes and keep the group's focus on high priority items. As already mentioned, poor facilitators will tend to stick more rigidly to the agenda which means they're more likely to rush to fit the discussion into the time available and skip over items which need more thorough debate.

High performers will set the agenda based on two rules; the first is to place the highest priority items first, and the second is to make the best use of participants' time. They might group items that are relevant to particular participants who don't need to attend the entire meeting, and they might move important items back if key participants are late. Importantly, they will defer agenda items to a subsequent meeting in order to achieve their most important objectives.

High performers said that time management was perhaps their most important ability, which means managing the process of the meeting to ensure the highest priority items are dealt with first and that the time within the meeting is focused on the agenda items and decisions with minimal off-topic discussion. In fact, 'time management' is a generalisation and a result, what the high performers actually do is to manage a decision making process.

A poor to average facilitator will prioritise easy or quick items first to 'get them out of the way' and leave room for the more challenging items, which may be a by-product of avoiding conflict. However, the easy and quick items are rarely easy or quick and take up significantly more time than the facilitator had intended, leaving insufficient time to tackle the more important issues. This is more likely to generate conflict as participants do not have time to fully explore different perspectives, and is more likely to lead to superficial agreements, made just to finish the meeting on time, which are not backed up by genuine buy-in to actions and commitments. Therefore, by trying to avoid conflict, a poor facilitator creates it. Again, the end result is that the poor facilitator's project takes longer to deliver because conflict is not resolved productively during meetings.

A high performer pre-empts and deals with conflict, with the result that conflict is less likely to occur because participants have had their more extreme views aired in a more collaborative way which 'takes the wind out of their sails'.

The meeting

Probably the single most important characteristic of the high performing facilitators is the way that they view the meeting itself. A poor facilitator sees a meeting as a time and place to get a group together and address any outstanding business such as project updates, presentations, decisions and actions. Whilst this may seem reasonable, it is a very inefficient use of participants' time, which has the following consequences:

- Since the participants' time is not valued, they don't give the meeting a high priority and are often late, leave early and 'multi-task' during the meeting

- Since multiple discussion types are permitted within the meeting (e.g. challenging, decision making, information gathering, knowledge sharing), it is much more difficult for the facilitator to keep the discussion on track, because it's impossible to tell what is a valuable discussion and what is not

- Because different activities are combined within a meeting, the participants are not always clear of their roles, resulting in decision taking longer to make and an increased chance of conflict

High performers see the meeting not as a discussion space but as a negotiation space.

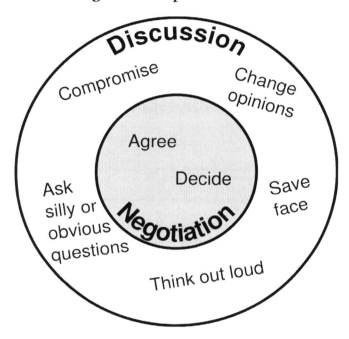

This is a very important distinction, particularly when the facilitator must remain neutral in the discussions.

By treating the meeting as a negotiation space, the focus is on making decisions. The only discussion which arises is aimed at reaching a decision, and this enables the high performer to keep the discussion on track easily.

The downside of this approach is that a negotiation is practically impossible when the parties have strongly opposing views, and this is where the discussion space is used outside of the meeting itself.

At the beginning of a discussion on, for example, a new standard, we might say that the most extreme points of view, represented here as A and B, are simply too far apart to reach a discussion.

 Agreement

Any pressure on them in an open forum to change their views will simply entrench them more. Each industry representative is not a lone entity, they represent an entire industry sector or organisation, and they must be able to demonstrate that they 'hold their own' at industry meetings, otherwise they have no value to the organisation which employs them. They cannot be seen to be 'giving in' to pressure from their opponents, and so any pressure on them to do so will have an extremely counter-productive effect if done in front of other people, as the representatives have a strong incentive to protect their hard-earned reputations.

A high performing facilitator spends time outside of the formal meeting to understand the relative positions of representatives. They do not try to change those positions, they merely seek to understand them so that they can build those different positions and expectations into the item under discussion, which may be something like a new standard or a project scope.

They will then present the revised item at a meeting and clearly mark out the aim of the discussion as being an agreement or approval. By expanding the scope of the subject to get closer to or even encompass these different positions, the facilitator lowers the barriers to reaching an agreement and allows even the most intransigent representatives to show good faith in front of their 'opponents' and compromise on an agreement.

High performing facilitators therefore save the meeting discussion for the final agreement, mainly so that a public commitment to that agreement can be heard by all participants.

If a facilitator were to attempt to move representatives from their positions within a meeting, they would likely entrench those positions further. However, if a facilitator were to conduct a negotiation outside of the meeting, perhaps asking for commitment or acting as a mediator, it would be seen as lobbying or even manipulation, with the facilitator 'picking off' participants in order to influence their views and behaviour.

A high performing facilitator therefore combines a number of skills in order to achieve the outcome of consensus, even though consensus is not their intention.

Preparation

The facilitator takes time to understand how each participant may view the subject under discussion.

The facilitator rehearses the meeting and those opposing positions, either mentally or with colleagues.

Discussion

The facilitator talks to participants to understand their positions and aims to encompass those, or get as close to them as possible, in the wording of the decision being presented.

Facilitation

The facilitator guides a negotiation between participants so that they move closer to each others' positions.

The facilitator does not engage directly in the negotiation, instead reminding participants that it is for them to reach an agreement, if one is possible.

Starting the meeting

The best facilitators start the meeting by reviewing the minutes of the previous meeting. This may seem trivial, yet it is intrinsic to the consensual decision making process.

This serves a practical purpose of approving the minutes, and participants may indeed offer corrections which are then incorporated into a revision of the minutes.

Poor facilitators might focus on the meeting at hand, perhaps reviewing actions from the previous meeting.

The best facilitators review the minutes of the previous meeting, not just the actions, and this enables them to lead the participants through a mental re-run of the previous meeting. Whether each participant agreed or disagreed on each point, they can now agree that the minutes are an accurate reflection of that discussion, so the meeting actually begins with all participants agreeing about a shared past experience. This creates a powerful state of compliance which makes the decision process much easier.

Packaging

The best facilitators break the meeting down into 'packages' or self contained discussions. Each package follows the same format:

1. Direction to the relevant section of the agenda or notes

2. Announcement of the topic under discussion

3. Announcement of the goal for the discussion

4. Request for decision

5. Management of the discussion – if necessary

6. Summary of agreement and/or actions

7. Document the discussion for the minutes

The meeting itself follows the same format and represents an overall package into which the agenda item packages are contained. Even if items are deferred to a later meeting or offline discussion, the meeting itself always seems 'complete' because of the packaging of the discussion.

A poor facilitator starts at the beginning of the meeting and keeps going, without clear delineation between agenda items, which results in blurring of the discussion, deviations and over-runs.

A good facilitator notices visual and verbal signals that the participants use to signal their readiness to move onto the next package, such as sitting back in their chairs to indicate they are 'leaving' the discussion.

Engaging

It is often said that good facilitators are highly attuned to the group and are therefore externally referenced, however this is not the case within an organisational culture where there is a preferred outcome. If we consider a more neutral facilitation environment such as that offered by a relationship counselling service, the facilitator has no agenda other than to help the participants reach a mutually agreeable conclusion. In this case, an externally referenced facilitator would be able to draw out sensitive issues and encourage all participants to engage in the discussion. At other times, this could be counter-productive because forcibly involving a participant could lead them to withdraw from the discussion, and could be viewed as lobbying. Therefore, the specific behaviour of a high-performing facilitator is very much aligned with the culture of the organisation.

Good facilitators keep a close watch on the group and are able to see if any participants have a point to make but are reluctant to speak up. The signs that they look out for include:

- Leaning forwards
- Making eye contact with the facilitator or current speaker
- Raised eyebrows, head up
- Clearing throat
- Raising a hand
- Tapping a pen or pencil on the table
- Agreeing in order to grab an opportunity to speak
- Interrupting

Some of these signs may be very subtle, however the best facilitators are not great masters of 'body language'; their secret is very simple. A poor facilitator will become involved in the discussion and their focus of attention is on the point they are making, not on the other participants. The best facilitators are not involved in the conversation directly, their position is more like an observer, so they are more easily able to notice any behaviours which are different to the majority, much like someone would see the differences in a 'spot the difference' puzzle. If 15 people in a group nod and one frowns, it's easy to spot the frown and draw that person into the conversation. The best facilitators will do this in a very informal, casual way so as not to put undue pressure on the individual. Remember, the best facilitators want every participant to have an equal *opportunity* to participate. Whether they do or not is up to them.

Poor facilitators want everyone to contribute, so they are more likely to poll the entire group, asking for view or feedback, and this formulaic approach is more likely to disengage participants.

The consequence of not watching the whole group, in the words of one role model, is "minority dominance".

The best facilitators will work to ensure that the discussion is balanced, so if the conversation is leaning to heavily towards a particular point of view and is not taking all possible positions into account, the facilitator will play 'Devil's advocate' and raise points that rebalance the argument. A good facilitator is careful to bring this up in a neutral way so that it doesn't sound like their own personal opinion.

Good facilitators openly offer the opportunity for participants to discuss agenda items prior to the meeting. Again, this offer is made in front of the whole group so that the facilitator can not be accused of singling participants out. This allows participants to air their more contentious or sensitive opinions in a 'safe' way prior to the open meeting. Often, in any negotiation, people will change or soften their positions once they hear themselves making a certain point, realising that it sounds perhaps aggressive or unreasonable. If they can only speak up in a meeting, they will cause a reaction from other participants which will often strengthen their position so that they can save face. Staying consistent to our stated beliefs and intentions is a strong driver for people (Robert Cialdini, Influence: Science and Practice) and so forcing participants to discuss their positions in an open forum will make them adhere more strongly to those positions. Giving participants the opportunity to air their views in a more private setting makes it more likely that they will adjust those views to achieve a consensus position.

There are times when a facilitator will have a vested interest in the group reaching a particular decision, perhaps for the adoption of a standard or the approval of a project. In such cases, the facilitator is no longer neutral, yet they must maintain their neutrality or lose control of the meeting. When a good facilitator wants to gently nudge the group in a particular direction, they will conduct the meeting as they normally would, encouraging all opinions and positions to be shared openly. However, they will also offer additional encouragement to participants who are speaking in favour of the facilitator's goal, and give less 'airtime' to participants who are not supportive.

Not every agenda item is relevant to every participant, so it is unreasonable to expect every participant to be fully engaged throughout the entire meeting.

A poor facilitator wants everyone to contribute because their focus is on the meeting as a whole and as an end in itself, so their effectiveness is dependent on keeping all participants engaged, like a school teacher who wants their students to pay attention to every word they say.

A good facilitator thinks in terms of 'packages' and focuses on the participants who have an interest in the current package (agenda item). This gives the other participants some welcome time to 'tune out' and gather their thoughts.

A good facilitator also makes frequent breaks in the meeting, again to allow participants to gather their thoughts, amongst other more practical needs that they may have. A good facilitator would rather have participants engaged at the right times rather than sitting there worrying about important messages and not paying attention to the proceedings.

Focusing

The best facilitators have a number of ways of knowing that a discussion is going 'off track':

1. The discussion is not serving to achieve the objective stated by the facilitator at the start of the discussion

2. The discussion is becoming overly emotional, either in an adversarial way or because the participants are personally interested in the topic

3. The participants have raised the same points at least twice, indicating that they have not moved any closer to a conclusion

The problem for a poor facilitator is that the more animated the participants become about the discussion topic, the harder it is for the facilitator to get the group's attention in order to regain control and bring the discussion back to the topic at hand.

Also, a poor facilitator, because they do not have control of the group, is more likely to experience the problem of the group splintering into subgroups with several discussions happening at the same time. A poor facilitator will deal with this be asking everyone to focus on the discussion at hand, disregarding the fact that they were; it just wasn't the discussion the facilitator was focusing on. A good facilitator will call the meeting to order but will also make sure that each splinter group has its say.

Influence

Even in a neutral position, the best facilitators are highly influential, using non-obvious methods to shape the outcomes of a meeting.

By clearly stating that the meeting is "your meeting", i.e. the participants', the best facilitators push accountability for decisions back onto the group. They cannot 'blame' the facilitator for influencing them, because he or she clearly stated that they are neutral in the decision.

By staying out of direct discussion as much as possible, the best facilitators encourage the participants to debate with each other. Therefore, any agreement or disagreement is made with another member of the group, not the facilitator. This also aids in conflict management, because the best facilitators manage the group such that they are arguing with themselves, not with the facilitator. This further protects the facilitator's neutrality.

By working outside of the meeting on the wording of agreements, papers, projects etc. the best facilitators are able to use resources such as documents to make a point for them. For example, a facilitator might refer a participant to the wording of a standard rather than debating directly. The participant cannot argue with the standard because the standard doesn't argue back. The facilitator protects their neutrality and further reinforces the point that, "these are your standards, not mine".

The best facilitators use the people in the room to exert influence, for example building on supportive arguments and also using government representatives to indirectly influence the group.

Handling conflict

When conflict does arise, it is directed either at another participant or at the facilitator. Conflict will often arise for one of two reasons:

1. A discussion has become heated because participants are focusing on being heard rather than on listening

2. A participant is playing out a role in order to gain control of the discussion or intimidate other participants

The best facilitators rarely encounter the first reason because it is central to the role of a good facilitator, which we can sum up as follows:

The participants come to a meeting to *have their say*, and the facilitator makes sure that they are *heard* by getting them to *listen* to each other.

This connects back to the sense of equality; in order for all participants to have an equal say, they must also listen in equal measure.

The second reason is something that the best facilitators pre-empt with their preparation. By understanding the relative negotiating positions of the participants, they are able to distinguish between a genuine objection and 'bluster' or positioning and deal with it appropriately. Probably the most important behaviour in this case is separating the message from the tone; valuing and including what the person has to say it irrespective of how they say it.

Once a valid point is made, though, the facilitator will deal with the way in which it is made by reminding the speaker that their behaviour is inappropriate and will not be tolerated; an approach based on the belief that all participants are equal and therefore deserve equal respect.

By pushing accountability back onto the participants ("it's *your* meeting", "these are *your* standards"), the facilitator is reminding them that the conflict is theirs to resolve, or at the very least they are disagreeing with their own standards or previous commitments, not with the facilitator.

One of the most important points in any conflict situation is to avoid the language of direct disagreement, which can always be paraphrased as, "you're wrong". Instead, the best facilitators use language such as:

- Yes, and...
- Not only, but also...
- Yes, if...
- I agree, and...
- Perhaps, if...
- And in addition to that...

By using such phrases, the best facilitators are able to build on the discussion, whereas negative language such as "no", or "but" will tend to stifle a discussion. The best facilitators therefore use conflict to flush out alternative options, which if not addressed in the meeting will come back later on and cause bigger problems.

Decision making

The best facilitators do not open each agenda item or 'package' with a discussion. Because they know what the purpose of each package is, they open each item in a way that allows them to achieve that purpose or outcome using the minimum time and effort. They also ask very specific, closed questions in order to guide the discussion quickly towards their desired outcome.

Having said that the facilitator has an outcome, they are also not attached to it. In a way, they don't mind whether the decision is 'yes' or 'no' as long as the group makes a decision, quickly. This is another aspect of their neutrality which they work hard to protect.

The best facilitators' decision making process is:

1. State the outcome of the discussion item i.e. a decision
1. Give the context to the discussion item
2. Ask for the decision
3. If everyone agrees, close the item and move to the next

Only if anyone raises a concern does the facilitator open up a discussion.

Most importantly, when the group agrees, the facilitator does not overtly acknowledge the fact that the group have made a decision, they merely close the item and move to the next with the minimum of fuss. This emphasises that making decisions is quick, easy, painless and most of all, completely normal and to be expected.

Closing the meeting

The end of the meeting is very simple; asking again for any 'AOB' items, summarising any significant decisions or progress, stating the date of the next meeting, if there is one and thanking the participants for their contribution.

Beliefs & Perceptions

The operating principles and behavioural rules that form the foundation of high performing behaviour.

These are unconscious processes which shape the resulting behaviours and as such are not normally available at the level of conscious awareness.

Beliefs

Beliefs are rules. Most people think of beliefs as fixed 'truths', however they have been learned through life experiences, just like rules about social behaviour and train timetables. The only difference with a belief is that we are less likely to question it when experience contradicts it, instead discounting the experience or looking for some other factor to blame.

Behavioural traits

The following behavioural traits can be thought of as perceptual filters, colouring a person's view of the world and thereby influencing their behaviour so that they tend to react in consistent, predictable ways. These traits can be highly context specific, and of course people can adapt to situations which require a different way of thinking. However, by identifying these traits, we can produce a recruitment template which makes it easy to identify similar people, and we can also build content into a training program which makes it easier for other people to see the world as a high performer does, which naturally leads to high performing behaviours.

Options	**Procedures**	Favours familiar processes and proven methods over new ideas
Towards	Away	Goals based on achieving results rather than avoiding problems
People	Task	Focuses on people and relationships rather than tasks and objects
Team	Individual	Achieves results through a team rather than by themselves
Internal	External	Bases decisions on their own internal frame of reference rather than on external benchmarks and comparisons
Difference	Similarity	Notices differences and exceptions rather than similarities
Active	Reactive	Takes action rather than waiting to react
General	**Specific**	Detail oriented rather than generalising or 'seeing the big picture'

Purpose

The best facilitators believe that a meeting exists to make decisions.

Therefore, meetings are not a time consuming non-work activity for the best facilitators, they are the fundamental way in which the team or organisation achieves its purpose, and they are therefore a core activity for a good facilitator.

Participants have to feel that they have achieved something in the meeting, otherwise they will feel it has been a waste of time and will be more difficult to engage in subsequent meetings.

Confidence

The different role models who we interviewed attributed their talents to different factors, for example their extensive industry experience which they used in one of two ways:

- They could understand technical points, or the history behind them

- They knew the 'personalities' and were better able to handle them

40 years of industry experience is hard to gain without spending 40 years in an industry, so in order to replicate these talents in others, we must understand what this experience gives the high performer.

Firstly and most importantly, it simply gives them confidence. They have a sense that they have 'earned their place' and that they can deal with some of the more challenging representatives because they see them as equals. Therefore, confidence is relative to the position and behaviour of people in the meeting, so high performance depends on the facilitator seeing the meeting participants as peers or equals and are put off neither by status nor challenging behaviour.

However, it is impractical for other staff to spend a similar time in the industry just to gain confidence. Each individual has a different way of generating confidence which will be based on their own individual experiences.

Secondly, industry experience gives the facilitator an understanding of the subject under discussion which they say helps them to keep a discussion 'on track'. In fact, they were using other methods to achieve this which were discussed in the previous section.

In fact, industry experience can sometimes be a hindrance in that it can lead the facilitator to form opinions which could bias a discussion. Neutrality is one of a facilitator's most valuable assets.

It is important to note that confidence is not an abstract feeling, it is part of a process that forms part of how the high performer achieves their results. Confidence is not an end in itself, it is a means; confidence to *do what?*

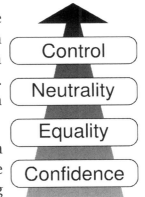

Confidence is the conclusion of a process of mental preparation, a state of readiness and for high performing facilitators it serves the vital purpose of levelling the playing field. A poor facilitator brings the perceived status of meeting participants into the discussion, allowing more 'important' participants to dominate the meeting and failing to earn the credibility and respect that would allow them to easily handle conflict.

An average facilitator tries to leave the participants' job titles out of the meeting because they know that each person has an equal right to be heard and an equal right to be treated with respect. However, they still feel some underlying sense of a 'pecking order' and this influences how they treat different participants.

The best facilitators don't need to try to remember this; they know what earns them the right to facilitate the meeting, such as years of industry experience, and it is easier for them to command respect from the participants, which in turn makes it easier for them to perform the most obvious tasks of a facilitator; keeping the discussion on track, keeping the meeting to time, ensuring that all participants have the opportunity to share their views and recording minutes and actions accurately.

Ownership

Good facilitators see the meeting as a means to an end, that end being the adoption of a standard, the progress of a project etc. In order to achieve that end, a number of people must reach an agreement, and a meeting is an efficient way to achieve that. However, especially when dealing with external stakeholders, the facilitator must protect their neutral position, so they focus on the process of the meeting rather than the content, and guide the participants to focus on the content without having to worry about the process. However, by managing the process, a good facilitator is able to focus the participants' attention in such a way that the content leads the participants towards the facilitator's desired outcome.

If a facilitator allows themselves to get drawn into the content of the meeting then they risk losing control of the process.

The best facilitators regard the process of the meeting as theirs and the content of the meeting as the participants'.

With this perspective, the best facilitators essentially mark out their territory within the meeting room, and set out the ground rules that go with that.

They will also remind the participants where these boundaries lie, e.g. "remember, these are your standards, not mine", pushing the responsibility for the negotiation back onto the participants. This is useful if the participants start to make the facilitator the centre of the discussion.

A poor to average facilitator, in contrast, *tries* to control the meeting which signals to the participants that the facilitator is not in control, opening up the potential for participants to dominate the meeting.

Preparation

A poor facilitator will fail to send out sufficient information prior to the meeting and will therefore waste time during the meeting reading minutes, notes, papers etc. This teaches the participants that they don't need to prepare in advance.

A good facilitator assumes that the participants have read through any information that was sent to them in advance, even saying, "If they haven't, that's their problem, not mine". A participant only needs to attend a meeting once without having prepared, and they will likely not do it again.

Time

A poor to average facilitator sees the meeting agenda as constant and time as variable, whereas a high performer sees time as constant and the agenda as a variable. This attitude enables them to focus on getting their highest priority items resolved in the time available, or the time made available by participants as a result of travel problems, other commitments etc.

Equality

The best facilitators believe that everyone participating in a meeting is equal, in that they have an equal right to be heard and an equal right to share their views, irrespective of their job title or the organisation they're representing. This beliefs leads to three conclusions:

1. The facilitator is also equal to the participants and is therefore not influenced by job titles

2. The participants must treat each other with respect since none has superiority

3. A participant has a right to share their views or not

It's interesting to note that while a good facilitator does not respond to job titles, the participants do, and the atmosphere in a meeting is notably different when a government representative is present. The facilitator will sometimes use this to their advantage, asking the government representative to leave the room or arrive at a particular point in the agenda so that participants can have an 'off the record' discussion. This further strengthens the facilitator's ownership of the meeting space.

A good facilitator believes that the more senior the participant (in terms of their 'day job'), the more valuable their time is, therefore the more value they choose to invest in the meeting. Therefore, an 'important' participant does not daunt a good facilitator as they would a poor facilitator, they actually strengthen the role of the facilitator, because the facilitator knows that they would not give their time freely if the meeting wasn't worth attending.

Engagement

If all participants have an equal right to share their views then it must also be true that they may or may not choose to exercise that right. Therefore, the best facilitators think in terms of 'providing an opportunity for participants to share their views'. They believe that there may be social factors such as peer pressure, or personal factors such as uncertainty or confusion which may prevent an individual from engaging in a discussion, so they are aware of the 'body language' that indicates that someone has a view which they are not sharing. However, they do not 'push' individuals to engage as that would violate their belief about the individual's rights. The right level of discussion is preferably to discussion for its own sake, even if that means a "no comment" from every participant.

Poor to average facilitators measure their effectiveness by the number of people who *do* speak, rather than the number of people who have the *opportunity* to speak, because the discussion is an end in itself, therefore more discussion is good.

Conflict

The best facilitators' beliefs about equality determine how they handle conflict. In particular, because they treat all participants as equal, regardless of their job title or external status, they are able to apply the same rules of etiquette to all participants.

In contrast, a poor facilitator will fail to tackle inappropriate behaviour from someone 'important' and therefore treats the meeting participants differently depending on their perceived status, which may come from their job title or from their superior or intimidating behaviour during the meeting.

Furthermore, a poor facilitator will handle inappropriate behaviour outside of the meeting, essentially placating the perpetrator and encouraging discussion to take the group's focus away from the inappropriate behaviour, which:

- Shows the 'victim' that they are not respected or protected
- Shows the 'perpetrator' that they can get away with it
- Shows the other participants that inappropriate behaviour will not be addressed
- Shows the group that the facilitator is not in control of the meeting

The effect of this is that healthy debate will be suppressed, as quieter participants will fear conflict with the more bullish members of the group because they believe that the facilitator will not 'stand up' for them.

Influence

A good facilitator believes that they must understand a person's point of view, otherwise they cannot help them to find a solution.

They also believe that if they allow a person to talk freely, that person will often talk themselves in to or out of a particular position or point of view.

These beliefs make it easier for the best facilitators to influence a group whilst maintaining their neutrality.

The Difference

General features of high performers

They have a goal which is greater than that of the task which they are recognised for excelling at, so the task becomes a means to an end and not an end in itself.

We observed high performers setting long term goals, such as "to build a coherent change strategy", for which meetings were a means to an end, not an end in themselves.

Their intention, attitude or methods are counter-intuitive and not obvious to an observer.

High performers do not set out to build consensus within a group, because this would be contrary to their neutral position. Building consensus implies influencing the group towards a particular decision, and whilst the high performers did indeed use covert influence methods to achieve this, it was not their primary goal.

Preparing from the participants' points of view is not obvious, as it looks exactly like preparing from any other point of view in that the external behaviour simply involves reading.

High performers avoid conflict by tackling it head on, whereas a poor facilitator tries to avoid conflict, thereby causing it.

They appear to get results easily because they actually do make it easy for themselves by implementing short-cuts or methods which are not obvious to an observer.

High performers make it easy to gain agreement and manage conflict within a meeting because they do the majority of work outside of the meeting. When a group gets together, they are focused on making a decision which then happens quite efficiently.

High performers therefore excel at gaining consensus within a meeting because they have already stacked the odds in the favour prior to the meeting. However, at no point do they lobby or try to influence any participants, as this again would conflict with their need for neutrality.

Specific differences

	High Performers	Average/Poor Performers
Purpose of a meeting	To make decisions	To discuss or debate
Ownership	The facilitator owns the process, the participants own the content	The facilitator owns the meeting
Equality	Sees all participants as equal	Is influenced by job titles and status

Preparation	Extensive, ensures participants have enough time and information to prepare thoroughly	Minimal, focuses on own preparation and may not give participants enough time or information
Preparation perspective	As if they are the other participants, considering all positions	As if they are a participant or chairman
Objectives	The meeting is a means to an end	The meeting is an end in itself
Direction	Has clear goals for the meeting and keeps the conversation on track by checking against their goals	Does not have clear goals, therefore tends to value any discussion, even if it is off topic
Opening	Invests time in reviewing previous minutes, building group compliance through shared experience	Reviews minutes where necessary but mainly focuses on the current agenda
Process	Packages the meeting into agenda items	Treats the meeting as a single entity

Agenda management	Dynamically rearranges the agenda to achieve its objectives	Sticks to the agenda and works through from start to finish
Time	Time is fixed, the agenda is variable	Time is variable, the agenda is fixed
Negotiation	Works outside the meeting to resolve differences, making it easier for participants to compromise	Debates within the meeting, causing participants to become entrenched in their positions
Personal involvement	Not directly engaged in conversation, therefore easier to spot	Gets involved in the conversation so doesn't always notice
Engagement	Knows that not all participants will be engaged in each agenda item and focuses on those who are involved, allowing the others to gather their thoughts and maintain concentration	Wants all participants to be engaged throughout the whole meeting, causing participants to become disengaged when they are realistically unable to maintain concentration

Contribution	Gives all participants an equal opportunity to contribute, whether they choose to or not	Wants all participants to contribute equally
Neutrality	Protects their neutrality, pushing accountability onto the participants	Becomes directly involved in the debate
Decision making	Presents a decision at the start of each agenda item and only opens up a discussion by exception	Opens agenda items as discussions and then concludes them with a decision
Strong personalities	Separates the message from the behaviour and doesn't take it personally	Discounts the message because of the behaviour and takes it personally
Handling conflict	Reminds the group that their conflict is with each other	Becomes involved in conflict
Inappropriate behaviour	Tackles it directly in the meeting	Smooths over it in the meeting and tackles it outside of the meeting, if at all

What's It Like?

It's so important to use metaphor when you describe change that I'll spend some time on the subject. It's like going to a remote island for your holiday. Visiting it for just a day doesn't give you enough time to really get to know the place and the people. Often, it's by sharing the experience of the locals that you really get to understand a place. Enjoying local food where the locals eat, understanding their social life, their history, their geography and their relationship with the natural world.

For example, in the Czech Republic, only the tourists eat fish (if you don't get it, look on a map).

Perhaps you've had a holiday where someone showed you a secret cove or beach, or perhaps invited you to a celebration or village festival? I imagine that's a holiday you'll never forget.

In Gran Canaria, one of the locals told me about their annual festival where they carry a huge paper fish through the streets. The fish embodies the evil spirits and ill feelings that have accumulated over the course of the year, and at the end of the procession they burn it to exorcise the evil spirits and cleanse the people. I think companies should have a ceremony like this, perhaps burning their quality manuals or motivational posters.

Metaphor is about emotion. When you tell someone about your holiday, you draw them into your hallucination and they begin to share your emotional state. They can smell the scent of flowers and feel the warmth of the crystal blue ocean. They can even see that sunset as they drink a cool fruit cocktail on the balcony, feeling the warm evening breeze against their skin.

Now, before you rush off to the travel agent, spare a thought for the power of metaphor and storytelling. By drawing your listeners into a shared dream of the future, you will create a powerful shared motivation to get there.

Compare this approach to:

"In order to achieve our strategic vision, we will:

- Achieve best in class costs
- Streamline our customer facing operations
- Implement a world class reward package
- Become number one in our identified markets
- Leverage our human resources for competitive advantage"

Does that excite you? I genuinely found it on a company's website.

Try as hard as you can to imagine leveraging your human resources. I can't get a picture of an evil manager putting staff on a huge catapult out of my head. As for streamlining customer facing operations, I'm imagining customers on a conveyor belt.

Imagine what they say when you've been made redundant – "You've been leveraged!"

Try this version:

"Imagine waking up every morning with that enthusiasm you felt as a child, looking forward to a day ahead in a community where we all use our resources wisely and care about the money that we spend. Imagine having customers that enjoy working with us because every person who comes into contact with a customer truly wants to be helping in any way that they can. Imagine being able to choose how you are rewarded for the work that you do, and imagine how that makes you feel valued and respected as an individual and a team-mate. Imagine the pride that we will share by earning the respect of our customers and business partners. Imagine the sheer, unstoppable power of a community of people who work side by side to make this a reality."

If you're thinking, "that's fine for the staff but what do I tell the shareholders?" then I have two answers. The first is that, believe it or not, shareholders and investors are human too and some of them even have emotions just like you do. The second answer is to use this principle and adapt it into whatever format you are comfortable with. There are many examples of companies who already do this in advertising and PR material, so we know that it is acceptable to use this format in this context. Which TV adverts are the most effective? Those that list the facts of a product or those that engage your emotions? Why do advertisers use celebrities to endorse products? Why do advertisers develop TV adverts that run in a series like a soap opera? Why do advertisers use images and music that seem to bear no direct relation to the product?

Metaphor is a very powerful tool for aligning people to a common vision. Metaphor and stories are characterised by any of three elements - they are either about someone other than you, a time other than now or a place other than here. So, a description of an experience that is happening to you, here, right now is not a story - it is a commentary. A description of an experience that happened to you, somewhere else in the past is a story.

The interesting thing about stories is that they seem to put the listener into an altered state where their critical filters are less active. Essentially, information conveyed in stories is not judged, filtered or disagreed with because it does not appear to be directly relevant to the listener or reader. This doesn't mean that the information is ignored - it means that the information can act directly upon unconscious mental processes. The story isn't judged to be true or false, good or bad, relevant or irrelevant. It's just accepted as being a story and therein lies its power.

Stories contain nothing that people can directly object to or disagree with. No-one can say, "that's not true!" to a good story, as it's not meant to be true. No-one can say, "I didn't do that!" because it's not about them. As they say in the movies, any similarity to persons living or dead is coincidental.

Here's an example of a story that I created to align a new team that lacked confidence in its ability to do what was asked.

"Once, there was a successful businessman who had a hobby that he was very passionate about. In his spare time, he loved motor racing. At first, he used to go along to as many races as he could and watch but as he became more successful, he could afford to take part. He was a very talented driver and quickly built himself a reputation as a serious competitor.

One day, he decided he would take the plunge and dedicate himself to his dream - to build a racing team. He set aside some money, gained commitment from sponsors and started to recruit his team.

At first, the recruitment didn't go very well. He couldn't afford to pay the same salaries as the top teams paid, so he was looking for talented but unknown drivers. He recruited some, but they didn't stay in the team long before they moved on. Like any manager, he knew that he needed to have a team that worked well together.

The other problem that he had was that he was himself a very accomplished driver. When he recruited a new driver he would try to teach them to drive better. Unfortunately, he didn't really know how he could drive so well as it was mostly intuitive. He would get angry with the drivers when they couldn't see for themselves how he was able to drive. He was on the brink of closing the team down, believing that the problem was one of recruitment.

He was watching a sports program on TV one day when he noticed something odd. When the interviewer was talking to a football manager, the manager kept referring to someone called a 'coach'. The same thing happened with some other sports too. He wondered what a coach could do that a manager couldn't. By chance, he then met someone who was a team coach, so he invited him down to the race track to see what would happen.

The coach watched the drivers practice, and he watched the team manager trying to tell the drivers how to drive. The drivers lacked confidence in their own talents and when they asked how the manager knew certain things, he said, "it just feels right", or, "you can tell by the way it sounds".

There were three drivers in the team, so the coach watched each one very carefully, and he also watched the manager very carefully. The first driver, Adam, was very good at accelerating. From the starting line, Adam was at least a car's length in front of anyone else at the first corner. He seemed to have an intuitive sense of when to change gear to maximise the car's performance.

The second driver, Brian, could brake later than anyone else and so was much faster into the corners than any of the other drivers. He seemed to have an intuitive sense of knowing when to brake as he approached a bend.

The third driver, Claire, could take corners faster than any of the other drivers on the circuit. She seemed to have an intuitive sense of the car's cornering ability and grip.

The downside of these talents was that Adam was always the first into the first corner, but the last out. Brian caught up with Adam at the bend but slowed down too much and was overtaken. Claire would overtake on the bend but lose her advantage on the straight.

The coach got the whole team together and pointed out to them their strengths. The drivers began to feel much better about this. Each driver, at a certain point on the track, was by far the fastest driver on the circuit but was let down by average performance in other areas. The coach began to ask some very special questions about how the drivers knew what they knew.

It turned out that Adam was listening for a certain tone from the engine, tyres and gearbox. He could hear when the car was at peak power output and he could change gear at the exact moment to take advantage. Consequently, he accelerated much faster than drivers who only changed gear at the 'red line' by watching the rev counter. With some help from the coach, he was able to teach the other drivers what to listen for.

Brian could brake much later because he was looking somewhere different to the other drivers. The other drivers were looking at the apex of the bend, whereas Brian was seeing beyond it. He was able to judge the distance to the apex much more accurately, enabling him to brake late but still drive safely. With some help from the coach, he could easily teach the other drivers where to look.

Claire could feel the car's sideways motion. She could accurately feel the movement of the suspension as the car leaned into the bend and she could feel a change as the tyres started to lose grip. She could actually feel the acceleration at different points in her body. With some help from the coach, she was able to teach the other drivers how to feel the movement of the car.

The team went from strength to strength, not because they were taught something new, but because they were able to share their talents and exploit them for the benefit of the whole team. Each driver still had their unique talent, they just helped each other achieve above average results across the range of skills needed to be successful. The coach didn't need to be an expert in driving, only an expert in learning.

What about the manager? Well, the coach had a special job for him. He had to go to every newspaper, journalist, sponsor, TV station and promoter and tell them that he had a new team. He had to tell them that this was the best team on the planet and they were going to re-write the motor racing rules. He had to prove to everyone that he believed in them. And so, the new team was reborn."

So, the important thing about a really effective story is that the listener can readily identify with one or more of the characters whilst at the same time knowing that it's not really about them.

Stories are an incredibly powerful change tool. In this day and age, we seem to have become over-reliant on data and facts and figures. In fact, stories as a means of communicating complex information have been around for thousands of years, whilst email and fax have been around for about 30 years. If you think that progress has made communication more efficient and therefore better, then stories are not for you. If you think that both have a place for different applications, then read on.

Stories are powerful as a change tool because stories can do something very important that facts, graphs and mission statements cannot. Stories can invoke an emotional response in the listener or reader. This ability is not confined to films or books - you have heard many stories that have 'moved' you, and maybe some even moved you enough to make you take action.

The emotional response elicited by a good story is real and powerful, and it cannot be underestimated. Business people often deny that stories are useful as a professional tool, and this is really to do with their definition of 'story'.

Here are some alternative words which mean exactly the same thing for our purposes, yet may be more acceptable in certain contexts:

▫ Case study	▫ Report
▫ Proposal	▫ Presentation
▫ Research	▫ CV
▫ White paper	▫ Press release
▫ News article	▫ Vision
▫ Anecdote	▫ Advertisement
▫ Business plan	▫ Illustration
▫ Account	▫ Executive summary

Some people seem to associate "story" with information that is untrue. This is nothing to do with the use of a story here. For our purposes, all of these stories are absolutely true but that doesn't mean that yours have to be. It doesn't matter if your stories are true or not, as truth is highly subjective. What matters is that you learn to use your own natural storytelling ability to achieve great results.

In order for you to be reading this now, you must have had a certain amount of success in life and had certain experiences. Thinking about the huge range of situations you've been in and the experiences you've had in your life, you already have a true story for any and every occasion. You can easily draw upon your own life as a source of inspiration and change material to help others.

A wonderful way to embed anything into your communication so that it bypasses the listener's critical filters is to use quote marks. For example, the other day I was reading a newspaper article that said, "You are the most talented person I have ever known, and simply by reading this you are already able to accomplish far more than you thought possible", and I thought how strange it was to read something like that in a newspaper. Of course, there is a dark side to this. You can say to your boss, "You know, this morning I saw a guy in the street run up to a complete stranger and yell, "You're a complete idiot!!" and I thought how rude that was".

Stories go right to the heart of our emotions. Stories convey meaning far more directly and effectively than facts and figures. The best trainers and teachers use lots of case studies, anecdotes and stories. When you are communicating at your absolute best, you are holding your audience in a state of eager anticipation. You're already an outstanding storyteller, so celebrate that talent and use it to your advantage.

Our brains are analogue, symbolic computers. As much as we like to hang desperately onto logic and language, our brains just don't process information that way. Metaphor is a symbolic language that is closer to the way our brains naturally work, so whilst you may think that metaphor is too vague, it is in many ways more precise than a 'logical' communication style.

That awful writing style that became popular in the 1980s and 1990s, based on the grammatical style of passive voice, has been responsible for much confusion and conflict because it attempts to remove emotion and personality from language. Computers don't talk to computers by themselves, you know. Human language was created by humans, for humans. Why dress it up any other way?

Here are some examples of 'passive voice' compared to a more active style.

Mistakes were made (Oops!)

An error has occurred resulting in a delay (We made a mistake and now we're late)

The report was written and then sent to the customer (I wrote a report and sent it to Fred)

The Online Writing Lab at Purdue University recommends that when writing in passive voice, you should, "Avoid dangling modifiers". Presumably in case they get caught in something.

The main problem with this style is that it removes references to who it was that did what. In other words, it helps the guilty to avoid blame. It's much easier to avoid blame if mistakes were made, rather than me having to say what mistakes I made.

The other problem with using the passive voice style is that it changes the order in which our brains parse language. We have a short term memory that stores language as it comes in so that we can make sense of it. As you know, sometimes you have to hear a lot of words before you figure out what they mean, because the important words in a sentence can be spread around..

In part, we cope with this by focusing our attention on what we think the meaning should be, often based on our role. If you're a husband, your role is to solve problems. If you're a wife, your role is to support. These are wild generalisations, as I am sure there are lots of excellent female problem solvers out there, and personally I would say I am supportive. Just don't ask my wife if she agrees!

Anyway, our default role helps us to cut out the noise and focus on the important message. By noise, I mean anything unconnected with football or shopping. I'm only joking! Noise means, simply, 'unwanted signal', so the part that you focus on means that whatever you can't focus on is noise.

Try focusing on one sound in your office, perhaps the noise made by the door or air conditioning. Notice how the conversations of your colleagues become irritating as they stop you from hearing what you are concentrating on.

According to Stephen Pinker, our brains are hard wired to process language in one of only two word orders; either 'Subject Verb Object' or 'Subject Object Verb'.

Our language processing facility is already structured, from birth, to learn a language that fits one of those formats, depending on the language we are exposed to.

As you might guess I have an idea about how our brains have evolved in this way. It's not because of language, or rather it predates language and relates to the word of experience. When we first developed tools, the tool had someone to use it and something to use it on. Even now, a hammer isn't intrinsically useful, it only becomes useful when someone uses it to hammer something. So subject, verb and object follows what we see as a chain of events in the world around us.

For example, English has a SVO order: 'the cat climbed the tree', whilst a language with a SOV order, could literally be translated as 'the cat, the tree climbed'. Passive voice messes with this order, so to parse a long sentence written this way requires more short term memory. You have to work harder to convert passive voice into something your brain can directly process, and as a result you get tired, stop paying attention and make up what you want to hear. Probably not what you intended when you wrote your corporate communications policy, is it?

As you start to hear, "mistakes were made following an incident which involved a decision as a result of a meeting in which several people were involved…" your brain literally fills up with information whilst waiting to answer the questions, "Who?", "What mistakes?", "What meeting?" and "Why are you telling me this?"

Of course, your intention may be to confuse the listener or reader, as this is in fact a very effective hypnosis technique. If instead you want to communicate with clarity and emotion, avoid it at all costs.

Hypnosis? Yes, it's a heightened focus of attention that can be achieved in a number of ways, including fixation on an object such as the swinging watch of old horror movies, or the overloading of the conscious mind with conflicting information. Motivational speakers such as Martin Luther King, Winston Churchill and Adolf Hitler were very good at inducing such receptive states, and you have probably seen corporate leaders speaking in the same way.

I'm not saying it's either good or bad, only that it is an aspect of the way we think and process language that some people are naturally attuned to, and naturally use to influence.

Get It Out!

When a problem is stuck in your head, it can be very difficult to see or feel the whole thing. You can easily lose sight of the extent of the problem, or how it connects with other areas of your life. With a complex problem, it can be very important to get the problem into a format that you can interact with directly.

When a problem is too big to think about, you literally 'can't get your head round it'. So if you can't get your head around it, get it out of your head.

By far the simplest way to get an idea out of your head is to write it down and then to put it somewhere safe. It is very important that you know you are writing it down because it is important, not because you want to forget it. Your brain needs to know that you are taking this information seriously and you are only freeing up some memory, like you might do on your PC by closing down a program you aren't currently using.

Do you save your work before you shut down your PC? If you try to shut it down without saving does it remind you? What I'm suggesting here is no different.

This is a very effective approach to help you to concentrate, or to sleep. I will stress again that the key for this to work really well is for you to know you are writing an idea down to get it out of your head so that you do not forget it. If your brain thinks you're trying to forget, it will keep reminding you not to forget and you won't be able to get the level of concentration or relaxation that you need.

I'm talking here as if your brain has a mind of its own, and sometimes it's useful to think in that metaphorical way.

Some people keep a notepad by their bed so they can get thoughts, ideas or problems out of their heads as they settle down to sleep, or so that they can write down ideas that come to them in the night.

Here's one really easy exercise that you can do, either by yourself or with a friend, colleague or facilitator. All you need is a pack of small cards or sticky notes and a clear table.

If you're working with someone, just talk through the problem, As you talk through the situation, your partner writes down the components of the problem along with any words or phrases that you mark out as being important. You might make a particular gesture, you might use a certain tone of voice or you might do something else that indicates that a particular item is important. If you get into an area that seems important in itself, your partner can write down a title for that topic.

If you're working by yourself, just daydream through the problem, thinking about all the different elements or components that contribute to it. Think about all the consequences and factors. Think about all the people involved. Write down all the elements of the problem, along with anything else that seems important onto a card or sticky note. Do not try to think in a structured way, it's important that you just allow yourself to daydream.

When you have a stack of cards, arrange them on the table. You can arrange them any way you want and in any order. You are allowed to do anything with the cards that makes sense to you. You can rearrange the cards as many times as you like until you are happy. You can discard cards and even write new ones if something doesn't fit or is missing.

When you have finished, step back and take some time to notice how the arrangement of cards relates to the problem. If you have discarded any cards, are these meaningful in some way? If you needed to add any cards to balance the 'shape', do these new cards represent some unexplored area or untapped resource?

There's no 'right' or 'wrong' way to arrange the cards, just something that works for you. As you sort and arrange the cards, a pattern will emerge that is generated by the way you structure this situation in your mind, and the exercise allows you to organise and understand the situation in a way that you can't when you just think about it logically.

If you're interested in seeing how this might be relevant, here are a couple of real examples.

This relates to someone who was trying to find a way of channelling energy more effectively. The layout of the cards seems to be an equation with the solution being somewhere to the right of the equals sign. The E stood for Energy.

The second example comes from someone who was planning a career change and needed a clear direction through some problems.

As he lay out the cards, names for the three parts of the arrow came to mind. To the left is 'planning', to the right is 'information' and at the top lies 'purpose'.

One card did not fit in the arrow shape and it turned out to represent a problem that this person had been giving himself. He threw the card away and the problem disappeared.

A problem such as a flat tyre or broken window isn't going to disappear just because you've moved some cards around.

That's not the kind of problem we're talking about. Fortunately, those kinds of problems are very easy to fix, because you know what resources are required. This 'Sorter' exercise is really excellent for problems involving people within systems and relationships, where the problems are not created by physical faults but perceptions and assumptions.

When a situation or problem has been churning around in your head for a while, it quickly becomes mixed up with other thoughts, ideas and concerns. As soon as more than one person becomes involved, the situation gets even worse as each person carries a unique and different representation of the problem. Thinking about the problem, however good a thinker you are, will never, ever help you, and there are two reasons why that is (that I can think of):

- You can only think of things that you know about

- You can only think of a few things at the same time

So, firstly, the Sorter technique - or anything that involves another person observing and reflecting back the unconscious elements of your thoughts - is a good way to bring to your attention elements of the problem that you did not have conscious awareness of, and therefore which you couldn't have thought about.

Incidentally, this is one reason why coaching is so effective. One of the most important things I do is to point out or reflect back information that my clients are not consciously aware of. I am frequently called 'insightful' for doing nothing more than reflecting back something a client said ten minutes before whilst rambling on about a problem. When people talk about problems, they frequently go round in circles of logic, but the problem is so big they can't see that they are going round in circles, like a man lost in the desert who walks for miles and ends up back where he started. When I help pin the logical loop down so that they can interact with it directly, it frequently looks like magic. In reality, it's just me paying attention.

A client was telling me about the problems in her business. She needs to hire a new consultant, but the workload means she is doing a lot of work herself which takes her away from running the business. She wants to step back from the front line, but can't because of the workload. After about half an hour of listening to her go round the loop, I presented her thinking back to her:

"You can't hire a consultant because you're too busy, and you're too busy to step back because you don't have time to hire a consultant. What you need to do is create the time you need to hire someone."

She said, "You always have such good advice!", and, as you can see, it's not really advice at all. I'm just untangling her thoughts so that she can do what she already knows she needs to do.

Secondly, our brains can only process at most about 7 pieces of information. On a typical day, it's more like 3. As soon as a new idea enters your head, an old one falls out. Try juggling and recalling a telephone number at the same time to test this for yourself.

This ability to hold only limited information in conscious attention has an important implication for communicating change. All too often, people launch into communicating the whole plan. As soon as you mention change, people will go off into their own world, so don't tell them any detail at this point.

I guess we're like the villains in films who feel compelled to explain their plot for world domination in great detail while the secret agent is formulating his escape plan.

As you stand there with your beautiful Powerpoint slides, explaining your fiendish plan, your team are also planning their escapes...

You may have heard that you need to cover just 3 points in your presentation, so here they are:

- Things are going to stay the same and get better

- Things are going to stay the same and get better

- Things are going to stay the same and get better

That may look like only one point, but it was so good that it was worth saying three times. You don't want to overload people with information. Remember too that communicating change is a bit of a trick - Change Magic is about continuous change that people don't notice. Of course, people will notice little things changing over time, such as all of your competitors employee's coming for interviews, so you need to keep on reassuring people that things are going to stay the same and get better.

So, since our brains can only process a limited quantity of data (God obviously thought that 640k of memory was more than enough for any program[5]), a complex problem is literally too big to think about. What you need is a device to reduce the scale of the map so that you can plan your route. That is exactly what the cards exercise does - it gives you a

---

5   Bill Gates allegedly said this in 1981. My PC has more than 6000 times this capacity and in a typical company's computer room you can find PCs with almost 500,000 times that capacity. In the near future, you'll see PCs with 1,500,000 times that original limitation. Planning ahead won't help you if you base your plans on how things seem today.

way to see the whole map so that you can decide which areas you want to learn more about or change.

They say that two heads are better than one, which is mostly true unless you've only got one hat. Remember, it's a matter of context.

A really useful place to put your problems when you've finished working with them is in the past. It's often the case that problems that once seemed huge become much smaller with the passage of time. Why wait?

Imagine a line that represents time for you. Imagine drawing a line in space that connects the past, present and future. It may go straight through you from back to front, or it may go from side to side. It may even be more elaborate still - the important thing is that you know where you instinctively think the past and future are.

Remember your pile of problem solving cards? Take the cards and arrange them somewhere that represents the past for you. You may want to arrange them at a point on the line that represents an hour ago, or a week ago, or twenty years ago. You may want to arrange them far enough in the past that the problem is long since gone, but not too long ago that you forget to learn something useful from the problem.

The key is to distance yourself just far enough from the problem to be able to think about it differently. You can even move it around if you like, and find out where you like it best.

Notice any differences in the way that you arrange the cards to when you arranged them in the present. Often, people doing this find that the problem either gets packed away or gets separated into two different issues - the specific problem itself and the useful information that you can extract from it.

Here are some examples from people who have done this exercise in the past.

In this first example, the problem was spread all over the table, seeping into all areas of this person's life and having many consequences:

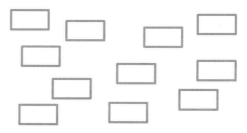

When the problem was moved into the past, all the cards ended up in one neat pile:

Essentially, this person realised that the problem wasn't a problem at all - in fact, she enjoyed having it! The problem that had spread throughout her life became neatly packed away, correlating with the change in the way she now thought about the pattern of behaviour.

In this next example, the person concerned had a problem connected with public speaking that would cause him considerable stress. In the present, the problem was again spread out, correlating strongly with the way that the problem spread into many areas of his life:

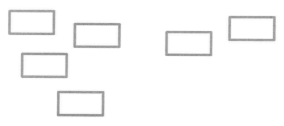

By shifting the problem into the past, it split into two halves. The problem naturally separated into an area that was out of his control and therefore not worth worrying about, and an area that was under his control. This gave him a clear sense of motivation to make specific changes in his life.

The stack of cards on the left represents his emotional state with respect to the problem. The cards on the right represent parts of the problem that are 'real' for him and that he can influence directly.

The final example is of someone who sees time in an arc, with the future stretching away to the right. By moving the problem into the past, the problem split into two separate 'timelines'.

The track on the left is a specific instance of the problem whilst the track on the right represents the 'constant' elements of the problem which are the important lessons to be learned from it. It is very important when solving problems that you learn something useful before discarding them - don't throw the baby out with the bathwater.

Here are a few more card layouts that my clients have come up with during a leadership workshop.

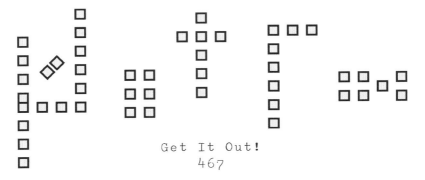

And here are a couple of photos of the process in action. The first photo shows the halfway point, where the layout is visibly open and fragmented.

By exploring the relationships between the groups, we discovered that the client has been putting energy into keeping two aspects of his working life apart. The two cards that you can see in the gap are wedging the pattern open. After exploring these two cards, the pattern quickly resolved into a very symmetrical shape, which had both a strong metaphorical, and a very literal meaning for the client.

When he read through the words on the cards, what he had created was a very neat problem solving process which first expands the problem in order to gather more information and then reduces the problem down to a clear solution.

One technical manager arranged his cards in a vertical line as shown on the left. When I asked him what the arrangement meant, he said, "I'm an engineer so my cards are in a straight line." I said, "You call yourself an engineer?! You call that a straight line?!"

This can have two meanings. Either what he thinks is acceptable as a straight line is not how others might see it, or he is trying to break free from the straight line, trying to introduce an element of uncertainty into a predictable sequence. His career has been a linear progression, and six months after he arranged those cards, he is now considering a sideways move for the first time.

So, you can see that there is no 'right' or 'wrong' way to arrange the cards, only a way that is meaningful to the person with the problem. You can also see the interesting correlation between the layout of the cards and the nature of the problem itself. In all of these examples, the people concerned were as surprised as anyone else to see the chosen layout unfolding in front of them. In each case, the meaning of the layout was obvious and helped the person to create new choices in handling the problem.

You can use this as a group problem solving exercise too. Once you have collected all of the cards, the whole group can interact in questioning the patterns, gaining insights and rearranging the pattern into a communal solution. You'll learn a great deal from the information and patterns, and you'll learn a great deal from the group dynamics too.

Here are some ideas for what to look out for and ask in using the Sorter technique. Remember that every card is placed perfectly and meticulously according to an internal, mental template. No cards are placed by accident.

- Are some cards perfectly aligned and others at an angle? What's the difference?

- Are there distinct groups? How are the groups defined?

- Are there gaps? What belongs in the gap?

- If there are gaps between cards or groups, then are the cards being pulled together or pushed apart? What is the force that is pushing or pulling? What is its source?

- If there are cards within gaps, are those cards pulling or pushing the groups or cards on either side?

- Stand back, what does the overall shape remind you of? How is that significant?

- Are there any cards that just don't seem to belong? Some people just take them out, others throw them away, tear them up or even burn them.

- Are there any missing cards?

- Are there any cards written in the negative (don't, not, can't etc.)? Can they be rewritten, on the reverse, in the positive?

- Are any cards outside of your control?

- Are there any directions of movement in the pattern?

Time is a great healer and, as you can see from the examples above, there's no need to wait.

People often create problems that really reside in the future - perhaps they don't know how something will turn out, or they don't yet have enough information, or they're worrying about something. Business contingency planning is basically organised worrying, so this technique is useful here too.

When faced with a problem, there are two amazing questions that will simply dissolve many problems right before your eyes. Consider a problem stated as "I can't…"

These two magical questions are "**what stops you?**" and "**what would happen if you did?**"

No, you didn't miss anything. That's all there is to it.

Remember that you tend to get what you focus on. By asking people about their problem, you are focussing their attention squarely on the problem itself. The more they look at it, the bigger it gets. Throw in some well meaning sympathy and the problem will soon be big enough to be insurmountable.

"Tell me about it"… "Oh dear"… "Why?"… "Why not?"… These questions just embed the problem deeper.

The first question focuses attention on the nature of the problem – what properties the problem has that cause it to hinder progress. The question puts the person back in control of the problem and separates them from it. They are able to explore the problem as a temporary barrier as the important word in the question is "stop" which implies that time is no longer passing. When people talk about problems, they are often referring to things that happened in the past as if they are happening through the present and future. By asking "what stops you", you are freezing the problem in time and preventing it from affecting the future which is, of course, unwritten.

A sneaky variation on this is "how do you stop yourself?"

The second question focuses attention on the future after the problem has been solved. Asking "what would happen if you did?" forces the person to create an internal experience of the future in which he or she has moved past the current limitation or barrier. In order to answer the question, the person must create this new future representation. In order to create that representation, a very important change must happen inside the person's head. Their world now contains the possibility that there is a solution to the problem. If they can imagine it, then it can exist.

When someone says "I can't do this" and you ask "what stops you?", they will tell you what barriers exist in their perception of the world. You can now work on these barriers directly and remove them, move them aside or lower them – whatever metaphor works for the person in question. You don't even have to work on the barrier itself in most cases, so you don't have to spend time "solving" the problem. You can just ask them to move it aside for a moment and, if they still need it, they can move it back again afterwards. Since these barriers are imposed by the person, they can be moved by the person too. If you listen to their language and watch the way they gesture when they talk, you'll see them describe the barrier and tell you where it is. You can either move it yourself, or you can get them to move it. If you just go right ahead and work on the assumption that they can do whatever they're having difficulty with, you'll find that the barrier disappears by itself in most cases.

When someone says "I can't do this" and you ask "what would happen if you did?", they have to create an internal representation of themselves having done whatever they can't do. The possibility now exists that the thing can be done by them, given time and resources. The barrier is now gone!

Often, when people mean "I can't do it" they actually say the words "I can't imagine myself doing it", or "I can't see myself doing that", and, as usual, they are giving you a very literal representation of the problem. Since they can't imagine or see themselves doing it, they can't do it. Simply by asking, "what would happen if you did?" you help them out by forcing an unconscious internal representation of success.

In contrast, if you respond with "why not?" then you accept their model of the world and the limitation that exists within it. You are effectively saying, "Yes, I agree that you can't do this. Now justify yourself". In return, they will do just that – they will give you a list of very plausible reasons that support their limiting belief. In fact, every time you ask "why not?" they will convince themselves, and you, a little more.

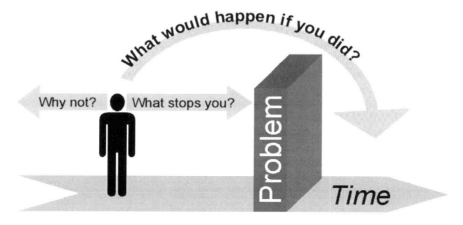

You can see in this picture what happens to the person's focus of attention when you ask them the three questions shown. "Why not?" shifts their attention to why they think they have failed in the past. "What stops you" shifts their attention to the barrier itself and "what would happen if you did?" shifts their attention to a successful outcome.

Remember that until you asked them, they didn't have a representation of success because they knew the barrier was in their way.

The best place for problems is in the past, in that the limitations and emotional responses don't have any place in the here and now. What you learn from problems is very useful indeed, and you need to make sure you always take that with you. When you overcome the problem easily, the learning will be with you forever. When you get stuck with the problem, you'll be glad to see the back of it, losing any potential learning with it.

Stop asking why; ask, "What would happen if you did?"

?

Get It Out!

Time

What is time? The dictionary defines time as "A non-spatial continuum in which events occur in apparently irreversible succession from the past through the present to the future". I think this demonstrates that no-one really knows what time is. Here's another attempt from a different dictionary: "Duration, considered independently of any system of measurement or any employment of terms which designate limited portions thereof."

If you have any clue what that means, let me know. Despite the best attempts of dictionary authors to define time, we still intuitively know what it is and we also know when it has passed. Although time is intangible and subjective, we still find ways to represent time using tangible methods such as clocks and calendars.

I would like to offer you a suggestion: time is simply a side effect of perception. It is one of the ways in which we create differences between memories and experiences so that we can experience change. So just pretend for a moment that time is not an entity that we can measure directly as with light or sound, it is a function of the way we perceive change. If you think that a clock measures time then I would be picky and say that it merely implies the passage of time. A light meter measures light by converting it into something else. A clock does not, as far as I can tell, detect time in the way that a sound level meter detects changes in air pressure.

I have an idea for you. It seems strange – even crazy, but it's no stranger than any other way of trying to understand time, as far as I can tell. Are you ready?

Imagine a teapot, like the one in the chapter on questions. Now imagine a different teapot. How do the two compare?

In order to answer this question, you can imagine placing the two teapots side by side. You can imagine picking them up, feeling the weight, noticing what they're made of, noticing the colour and so on. You can compare both of them at the same time.

Now imagine one teapot and compare it to itself. Is it the same as itself?

Is this picture of a teapot:

The same as this picture of a teapot?

You may be tempted to say yes, because they are similar. But they are not the same. How do you know they're not the same? Because if they were the same, there would only be one of them!

Both of those images came from the same image file on my computer, but they are not the same. They are pictures of the same teapot. Can you work out how they are different?

It's not a trick. In order for us to compare a teapot with itself, we have to perform one of two mental tricks. We either create a second image of the same teapot, or we compare the same teapot at two different points in time. So imagine the teapot above when it's full and again when it's empty, and compare the two.

It can't be full and empty at the same time. Don't say it can be half full and half empty. That would be neither full nor empty. It either has tea in it or it doesn't. The only way it can be both full and empty is if you look at it at different times.

With me so far?

Here's the idea about time: Time is a perceptual illusion created by comparing a thing with itself. A company with itself. A person with him or her self. And of course, you with yourself. In order to compare you with yourself, to say what you have learned or forgotten, achieved or lost, succeeded or failed at, you are comparing yourself at two different times.

And if you're comparing yourself at two different times, only one of which may be the present moment, then by definition you are not comparing the same two people. For example, let's say you compare yourself making a cup of tea now with yourself making a cup of tea yesterday when you made it too weak. The person you are now has 24 hours more experience than the person you were yesterday. We collapse time and act as if the person you are now is the same person you were five minutes ago, or yesterday, or a year ago, or ten years ago. But they are not the same. They are similar, and the difference is significant.

I've noticed that everyone I know has a self image. I think it's a side effect of self awareness. In order to create a map of the world with ourselves in it, we have to create some representation of ourselves to put in the simulation. What I've noticed is that people's self images vary on two dimensions. This is quite cool stuff, and it's very innovative, so I'm sharing it with you for the first time. I think this applies to companies too, when people compare their company with their competitors or the market or even itself.

The problem is related to time, in that if we compare a thing with itself, in the same condition at the same time, we get a comparison that contains no information, because we don't perceive there to be a difference.

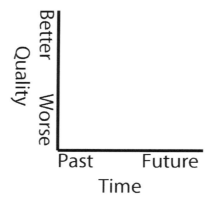

So in order to artificially create a perceptual difference, we vary two parameters – time and quality. By quality I mean that we make a distinction between one thing being better or worse than another, in some way.

Whilst this gives us an infinite combination of possibilities, I'll outline the four main ones.

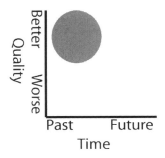

This self image of is of a better time in the past, so the person might look young for their age, or act as if they are younger than their age. This is a sense of positive nostalgia.

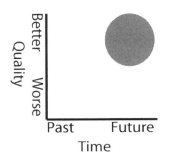

This self image is of a better future time, so this is an aspirational image that gives the person something to aim for.

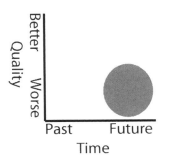

This self image is of a worse future time, so this motivates the person to maintain the current situation because the future will surely be worse.

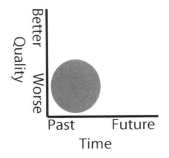

This self image is of a worse time in the past, so this gives the person a self reference of a time when they didn't have confidence, experience, money or whatever, and this prevents them from making the most of what they have now.

The odd thing I've noticed is that the self image seems to be an automatically generated simulation which sometimes serves the person and sometimes does not. I have developed a few techniques to get people to redesign the self image so that it serves them much more effectively, and I have found that the same approach works with the self image that people develop for their companies.

We could compare a company now with itself a year ago, or five years in the future, and pick faults, or find problems, or pay management consultants to find problems.

Compare your company to another completely different kind of company to find out what you're doing wrong and you'd say it makes no sense because you're not comparing apples with apples. Well, if you compare your own company with itself or its competitors, you're doing the same thing.

And yet, people in companies often compare themselves to their competitors and wonder why, when they put in place the same 'winning strategies' they don't work. It's because they only work somewhere else, at some other time. We can distil some useful reference points out of those strategies, but it's useless to copy them verbatim. We can adapt those strategies to your unique environment, but they won't work in themselves. There are other important factors.

Is time a constant? By making watches and clocks and by scheduling TV programs and flights we say "yes" but if time has ever dragged through a dull meeting or flown through a fabulous night out then we know that our subjective perception of time can change.

As far as our brain is concerned it's always 'now'. Optical illusions can fool our visual sense, so can we fool our sense of time too? And if we could, what use would that be?

In the chapter on Systems, we had a look at some process diagrams. Here's one that relates to the flow of time:

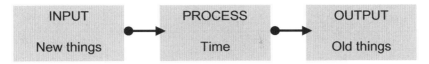

And here is one that may give you a slightly different perspective on what time is:

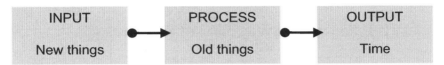

In other words, how do we know that time has elapsed? Because we notice things moving, getting old and changing. Time is not the process – it is the evidence that the process is taking place. The passage of time is necessary for us to notice change.

Whether you agree or not, this is no more or less true than any of the dictionary definitions of time.

In any change situation, it's vitally important to focus on the future outcomes of change. Don't decide whether these outcomes are benefits or not – just state them as facts. You don't need to dress change up as wholly beneficial, because it rarely is. Change isn't good or bad, it just exists. The people affected by change will decide for themselves what the benefits of them are. If you try to pre-judge the benefits, the people involved are more likely to get cynical and think you are trying to influence them – perhaps because you are!

How can you focus on the future and move change into the past? Here's a really simple formula. It's so simple that you may be tempted to think it can't work. Try it first, and then decide. Remember – taking action is very important.

Step 1	Focus your attention on the outcome. Change itself is just a transitory process that happens 'now', whenever that is. Communicate the end, not the means.
	Don't try to sell the benefits, just describe what will be different. Describe how the environment will be different, how people's behaviour will be different and what capabilities you will draw upon to effect change. Do not say that you are going to acquire new capabilities, as they are most certainly already there in your organisation, waiting to transform into behaviour.
Step 2	Notice how people talk about change. Wait until everyone is talking about it – through email, at the coffee machine. Don't bother with focus groups and feedback forms. Just pay attention to what is really happening.
	Talk to the real communication hubs in your business – receptionists, secretaries or security guards. Talk to the people who everyone talks to. Don't commission surveys to get everyone's view, simply ask the people who actually know.
Step 3	Shift the language structure you use to communicate about change from the future tense to the present tense. Start to describe the outcomes as things that are happening now instead of things that will happen.
	Look and listen for the changes in people's behaviour. Talk about the things that are happening in only positive language. This doesn't

mean sounding cheerful – it means talking about what is happening rather than what isn't happening. Using negative language only confuses people.

Step 4	Shift the language structure you use to communicate about change from the present tense to the past tense. This pushes change into the past and diminishes its significance. Who worries about things that have already happened?

So, allow your language to reflect the movement of events through time. If you persist in talking about changes that will happen, they will forever loom on the horizon, growing bigger in people's imaginations and causing more doubt and worry.

You can interact directly with people's sense of time using a variety of powerful techniques. One of them is by manipulating (meaning 'to handle skilfully') your use of verb tense. Since your brain will always translate incoming verb tense into 'now', you will create a powerful time distortion effect.

I'll explain a very powerful technique for exploring time, and then I'll tell you about a couple of ways you already use this technique during business meetings so that you can use it even more consistently and powerfully.

Where do you imagine the future and past to be? Many people imagine that the future is in front of them, and the past is behind them. Consequently, your parents tell you that you have your whole life ahead of you, and friends tell you that particular experiences are all behind them. They might even say "it's all in the past now" as they point behind them, or wave over their shoulders. Is this useful information? Only for Change Magicians!

My future is to my right and my past is to my left – I see all time laid out in front of me like a map. Everyone is subtly different, and it can be very powerful to explore those subtle differences. For our purposes, it's useful to work with the 'typical' model as everyone seems to have an understanding of it, even though it may differ from their own experience.

Imagine a line on the floor that represents time, with the future in front of you, and the past behind you. The point where you are standing is 'now'.

Think about something you want to achieve and notice where it lies on the line – how far into the future it lies. It might be something quite ambitious, so you would like to achieve it but don't yet know how to, or how difficult it might be.

Walk forwards until just before the goal. Notice how that feels. Now step onto the goal itself, and notice how that feels. Finally, talk one more step so that the goal is completely achieved and notice how that feels.

Turn round and look back to the present moment, noticing all the milestones you passed on the way. Walk back to the present, taking with you everything useful you learned on the way so that the experience and knowledge can help you in the present.

When you get back to 'now', look towards the goal again. Has anything changed? Is it in the same place?

Of course, you didn't *really* travel through time, your brain just thinks you did. If you're keeping up with all this, you'll know by now that this is the same thing, in terms of your sensory experience. And what else do you have to go on? As Groucho Marx said, "Who are you going to believe? Me or your own eyes?".

This is a very powerful technique for unlocking potential and exploring future possibilities. Here are a few different ways that you can use this technique.

Overcoming obstacles

There is something you want to achieve, and you know that there are many obstacles or barriers to overcome. Use the basic technique, stopping briefly as you get to each barrier before you step over it. When you reach the goal, turn round and look back through the obstacles you overcame or problems you solved. As you walk backwards through each barrier, be aware of anything you learn or notice.

Exploring decisions

There is a decision to be made, but you find it difficult to make because it has long term implications. Imagine you are standing at the branch point of a number of time lines – one for each choice. Explore each one, going way past the decision point and experiencing the long term implications of that choice before returning to the branch point. Pay attention to any intuitive feelings you get whilst doing this. When you have explored all of the choices, take one step back and look at the time lines. Some may have disappeared, some may have moved. There's a good chance that one will be in the centre, or will be prominent in some way.

The Undo button

There is a decision you made in the past that you're not happy with. Turn round and face the past, looking back to that decision and noticing everything that has happened since then. Walk slowly back to the decision point, collecting up and taking with you everything that you have learned since then. When you reach the decision point, take one more step. Turn and face the future. With all of the experience you have brought back with you, what decision will you make? What forward to the present, exploring the consequences of that decision. You might find that you still make the same decision!

Motivation

There is something you want to do in the future which involves work or effort now. It's difficult to get motivated now for something that isn't pressing, but you know that if you don't put the work in, you will regret it. For example, going to the gym now to be fit for your holiday, or working hard now to pass an exam in the future.

Start with the basic time line procedure. Picture, in the future, your goal in the way that you would achieve it if you put the effort in now. Walk up to the goal and stop just beyond it. Enjoy the feeling of having achieved that in the way that you wanted to. Return to the present.

Next, picture yourself in the future when you haven't put the effort in – perhaps at the exam without having revised, at the presentation without having prepared or whatever. Walk forwards. There's a good chance you will feel resistance, and a feeling of impending doom as you walk forwards. This is good, use it. Stop at the goal and take plenty of time to fully experience your sense of disappointment in yourself. Really regret not having made the effort! Now, grab hold of this feeling as you walk back to the present and stretch that awful feeling of regret all the way back to the present so that you can experience it now in relation to your daily planning and time management. Ultimately, you have to make time for good preparation. Until now, there were more pressing demands on your time, and you wouldn't really devote much time and energy to this until it was too late. Well, this exercise makes it too late now!

Finally, imagine yourself in the present, making the time and effort to prepare well. Walk forward slowly, thinking about your daily and weekly routine and finding time to do the work you need to do. Continue doing this all the way up to the goal and notice how good it feels – both to have achieved the goal and to know that you made the effort and commitment necessary. Take this feeling and stretch it back to the present, pulling back that good motivating feeling and bringing it back with you so that you have it now.

What if?

There is a scenario that you would like to explore, tentatively. Use the basic time line procedure, but this time, do not bring the learning and experience back with you – leave it in the future as you explore each possibility.

There are many more variants and applications of the basic technique, and I'm sure you will invent a few of your own once you explore it and find out for yourself how useful and powerful it can be.

I promised to tell you about how you already apply this in business. Any time you explain a process or sequence of events to someone, you are using this basic technique, verbally. You can use this to add some extra impact and get consistent results.

Imagine going to a regular project meeting. Do you start with an update? Does that involve talking about a series of events or project milestones? Perhaps you tell someone about what you want them to do, as a series of steps. If you do, there are two important things you need to add in.

Firstly, it's very powerful to walk through the steps, to use physical movement to cement the movement through time, just as in the time line exercise. If you can't do that, then use a flipchart or whiteboard to draw out the steps.

When you draw out the steps, do not start at the present moment – start in the past. Sales people often do this naturally, recapping on progress to date. Often, they stop at the present moment so they fail to use the momentum they have created by shared experience.

People involved in projects often talk about the future steps, but start in the present, so they fail to set up the momentum that is so powerful in gaining commitment.

Here's an example: "So, just to recap on where we are, you contacted us a few weeks ago to review this business process. We had an initial meeting to look at the current situation, we've done some analysis work and now we're meeting again to talk through options and to work through a few scenarios. The next thing to do will be to make a decision on a pilot project and then put that into action."

So, we create rapport and momentum by stepping through the past, we focus attention on what needs to be done right now and we also lead towards a specific desired outcome – i.e. that the customer will make a decision. People have a tendency to do what you want them to do when you tell them what you want them to do.

Any time you're talking with colleagues or clients about anything that involves a sequence of events, draw out a time line and step through it, starting in the past and continuing into the future.

Pay particular attention when a customer wants to know about a process and says "walk me through it" – try, if you can, to take advantage of that opportunity! Take them for a walk, and you might find that something very interesting happens. Try it and see.

When you watch a race, do you continually stare at a point in space as drivers or riders or runners zoom past you? Do you start at a point in the opposite direction and watch competitors disappear into the distance? Or do you notice particular competitors and watch them as they move towards, past and away from you? If you want change to happen, you must make it happen by watching it go by, instead of always staring into the future, waiting for the next change.

People only know about change because you tell them about it. Change is happening all the time. Things never stay the same. Time is movement and movement is time. Therefore, change is not the problem, communication is the problem, and that is entirely within your control. You can choose when change takes place. Whilst time moves on, you may or may not choose to move with it. If you constantly talk about change as being something that will happen or is happening, you freeze it in time. If you talk about change as something that happened, you allow your old problems to float away on the river of time. Let them go.

Here's one last tip on time.

If you want people to forget something, stop reminding them about it.

Delegation

Are you using your time and energy effectively? As a rule of thumb, you should devote your time and energy to issues which you can directly control or influence. Of course, it's obvious when you say it, yet we all seem to go round in circles at times, expending time and energy worrying about things that we can't change.

Concentrate on what you can personally control. Who else will influence your promotion? Who else needs to be aware of your boss's behaviour? If you have problems that you are not in control of, give them to someone who can have a positive and direct influence. In other words, distribute the components of your problem to the people most able to effect change.

Here's a tool that you can use to help focus your attention on what you can personally achieve. This will help you to maximise the return on your own effort and make the best use of other people and resources. This is also an excellent group problem solving tool that you can use to focus a team on what they have control of.

Take two pieces of paper or, and write a title on each one.

Issues that I control directly	Issues that are outside of my direct control

Next, make as long a list as you can on each piece of paper. Make sure that you include everything that is on your mind in relation to this problem.

Take a few moments to review the lists and imagine how each of the items manifests itself. Make the two lists as real as you can. You might even begin to feel a little frustration at this point.

Next, tear up, screw up, burn or destroy in whatever way takes your fancy the sheet titled "Issues that I have no direct control over".

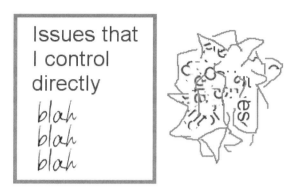

At this point, just let your brain rearrange the problem for you. In the near future you will start finding ways to make the changes you desire because all your energy and time is now focussed on what you can do to directly influence events.

Of course, you're quite right in thinking that you could just go through each component of the problem and ask yourself, "who is the right person to deal with this?" and that would be an excellent approach if you always thought as clearly as you are right now.

When a problem is all around you, your view of the world becomes distorted and you no longer have access to the experience and mental agility that you take for granted at this moment. This is why it isn't always important to start solving the problem consciously. It is only important to unpick the threads of the problem. Once you have conscious access to all of your natural skills, your brain will do the rest of the work for you.

This is really the essence of good delegation. Delegation does not mean passing menial tasks down the chain of command, and it does not mean passing tasks down that you think will develop people. Here's a definition of delegation that we could work with:

Delegation is the process of breaking up a complex task into components and then giving those components to the individuals with the skills and authority to handle them.

You can't delegate anything downwards unless people have authority and skills. The tasks may stretch their skills but they don't stress them. There's a fine line between being delegated to and being dumped on, and that line is the measure of delegated authority. I know this isn't new information to you, it's just worth exploring because, sometimes, managers think about delegation as being about tasks rather than relationships.

Some managers say that people aren't given authority – they have to take it. What this means in practice is that they expect people to take the initiative and to then tell them off for doing it wrong. My experience of what works well is that, as a manager:

- ▫ You are responsible for breaking down complex tasks
- ▫ You are responsible for distributing the components
- ▫ You leave people alone while they work
- ▫ You are responsible for reintegrating the components

Implicit in this is your ability to devolve authority and keep your nose out of other people's business! The cards tool is a useful one for breaking down complex problems into separate tasks – use it to delegate more effectively.

As you know, delegation is not about power, although there are many books available on the subject of management through delegable power. Delegation is about efficiency. It's not about hierarchy and rules about who is supposed to do what; it is about understanding who is best at doing what and then getting out of their way while they do it.

Now here's an interesting thing about delegation. It was interesting to me, anyway. Recently I was modelling high performers in a High Street retailer to create role models for their new graduate scheme. As a result of the modelling, they were able to put people into the business 3 months ahead of schedule, so replicating the intuitive behaviours of high performers in a specific environment is a very handy thing to be able to do.

When I modelled store managers, one of the things I found they did was to delegate. A 'competency' approach would stop there. They're good at delegating, so run a delegation skills course for all the managers. Here's the problem though – they weren't delegating, at least not from their point of view. And if we only run delegation skills training, the managers who already think in the right way don't learn anything new, the ones who have the wrong mindset for that behaviour don't do it anyway and the ones in the middle find it interesting but never quite find the time to put it into practice.

If the high performing managers don't delegate, how can that be the observable external result? Simply because what they're focused on is freeing up their own time. They can only do that by avoiding the minutiae of running the store. If they ask someone to do something, they don't watch them to make sure they're doing it.

Many of the routine tasks had to be recorded in log books, so if the managers want someone to take responsibility for a task, they just tell them what they need to do, what the measurement criteria are and what the consequences are of them meeting those criteria or not. And then the only way they check is to look in the log book, which is handy because that's a part of the task – the paperwork – that the average managers had to chase up on separately.

For the high performing managers to free up their time, they need the store to run itself, so they need and encourage the store staff to take responsibility for that. If an individual failed to take that responsibility, the store manager would go straight to a disciplinary process, beginning with a reminder of the individual's responsibilities. If the individual succeeded, then the store manager would always pass on the recognition of that. They would neither take the 'blame' nor the praise - both would be passed onto the staff equally. Contrast this with the store managers who liked to be friendly with staff, to nurture and develop them. If someone was, say, consistently late, the high performing manager would deal with it quickly and neutrally, whereas the nurturing manager would make allowances, have quiet chats, make it personal and ultimately have a lot of difficulty moving to a disciplinary process.

The bottom line is this - the only way that you can manage your business effectively is to delegate as much and as often as possible.

If you're thinking that you don't have time to delegate, or you can't trust your team to do things as well as you do, then you might be mistaking delegation for abdication.

Manager's Responsibilities

When you delegate, you give someone else the resources and the authority to complete a task, but you always keep accountability for it. When you delegate, you need to give the person a clear description of what you want to achieve but stop short of telling them exactly what to do, step by step.

When you abdicate, you give up accountability for the task, typically explaining at length what you want the person to do, but not what you want them to achieve. Ironically, while you think you're helping them with step by step instructions, you're actually making it impossible for them to complete the task as you intend.

Finally, managers who abdicate tend to make staff into 'milk monitors', wholly responsible for a set of tasks. For example, if one person is good at preparing monthly reports, you might just leave them to get on with it. You think that you'll never have to worry about that task again.

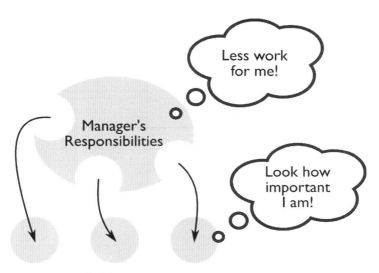

Milk Monitors

What can happen is that other staff follow your lead and leave them to it too. Instead of taking responsibility for tasks that they can see need taking care of, they leave them to pile up, thinking, "If Joe is so clever, he can do it". If they're feeling particularly resentful, they might even deliberately cause problems to make Joe look stupid. So by relying on particular staff to always do a certain job, what you actually create is gaps that no-one is responsible for, and no-one is interested in. By abdicating, you make more work for yourself.

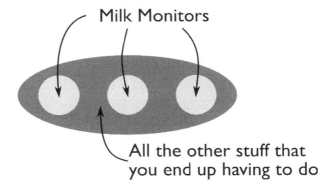

It's all very well taking my word for it, but you need to understand the importance of delegation for yourself, otherwise you'll never get round to doing it. It will always be easier just to do something yourself, just this time, and explain it to someone else next time.

Next time never comes.

One of the most important jobs for a good manager is education. By making sure your staff are trained to the right level and that they understand the standards that they need to work to, you can delegate very quickly and easily without having to explain yourself every time. Education is an investment that the worst managers don't make time for, but that's like saying that you don't have time to pack for your holidays, or you don't have time to buy birthday presents.

You might save yourself a little time now, but you'll pay the price later.

When you delegate a task, you are delegating the authority to complete the task, but not the responsibility for it. Ironically, managers who abdicate tend to do the opposite, they abdicate the responsibility for the task, but not the authority to get it done, so that when the person performing the task fails, it will be their fault, even though realistically they could never have succeeded.

Delegating should be as natural and regular as breathing, so to delegate effectively, remember that you need AIR:

Authority	The Authority to make decisions in order to complete the task you're delegating
Information	The right Information to underpin those decisions
Result	The end Result that you want to see

The most vital thing to remember about delegation is that you are delegating not only a task, but also the authority to make decisions that are necessary to complete that task. Delegation is a shift in decision making authority from one level of an organisation to another – this is why people who go to conferences on behalf of their employers or governments are called delegates; because they have *delegated authority*.

Why are we talking about delegation? Delegation is for managers! Leaders do strategy. Leaders are awesome. Everybody wants to be a leader. Managers are boring. When are we going to learn about strategic thinking?

Strategic thinking is something you can only do when you are free of day to day operational tasks, so to think strategically, you must first **delegate everything**.

Yes, everything.

When you delegate everything, you are then forced to answer a simple question:

"What shall I do today?"

You then have two choices:

"I'll go and see what my team are doing today", or

"I'll think about what I want my team to do tomorrow"

The first choice is meddling. It shows that you don't trust your team and that you have abdicated, not delegated. Your team will not grow, they will not engage, they will not give their best, they will not push themselves. There is no challenge for them to rise to.

The second choice creates a space for your team to grow into. It forces you to plan ahead. This is what gave one business unit in Parker Hannifin a 700% increase in profitability.

If you want to redecorate your house, you have to make space.

If you want to get new furniture, you have to make space.

If you want to think strategically, you have to make space.

Leaders are supposed to think strategically, therefore, your primary responsibility as a leader is to **make space**.

Are we there yet?

Motivation

Our Change Magic journey has been in two parts, as you may have noticed. First, we laid some ground rules, shared some useful beliefs and collected information. All of the preparatory stuff. Then we worked through the implementation of change, through communication, measurement, problem solving and so on. In the middle, we had the Route Planning chapter, which is the point at which we shift from planning to doing.

I often see articles and social media posts citing various statistics about the high proportion of change projects which fail. These statistics and perspectives come from a project management view of the world.

> You can't manage change, you can only
> lead it. Most organisations manage
> change and change is painful. Managing
> change may be extremely painful for
> staff at the grass roots of the
> organisation.

Dianne Adamson, speaking at The Future Technology
Challenge Forum in 2011

> We can be as innovative as we like but
> unless you get people with you and
> behind you on your journey, you will
> find innovation very difficult.

Dianne Adamson again

One of the major weaknesses uncovered
during the analysis was ... the
absence of leadership within the
delivery process. Processes alone are
far from enough to cover the
complexity and human aspects of many
large projects subject to multiple
stakeholders, resource and ethical
constraints.

A study in project failure, Dr John McManus and Dr
Trevor Wood-Harpe

The fundamental problem with bringing
about organisational change is that
people want things to stay exactly as
they were.

DK Matai, www.businessinsider.com

The cost of project failure across the
European Union was €142 billion in
2004.

A study in project failure, McManus and Wood-Harpe

A project plan might include:

- Order new servers

- Install new software

- Handover new office building

- Agree customer complaint procedure

They're all fine. Nice, hard, tangible milestones in a project plan. They're not the problem. The problem is that we also have these:

- Communicate project goals to all staff

- Obtain senior management buy-in

- Implement new reward mechanism

- Develop competency framework

One of the most popular project management methodologies, in the UK at least, is PRINCE, which stands for Projects IN Controlled Environments.

Well, I have some bad news. When people are involved, the environment is anything but controlled.

Building staff engagement or obtaining management buy-in is really not the job of a project manager. What else can they do but trust their HR colleagues to deliver on such tasks? As you know already, those kids of tasks are anything but straightforward, and the focus falls to motivation. We need to motivate staff. We need to increase employee engagement.

This is a dangerous road. Your employees already are motivated and engaged. That's not the problem. You do not need to do anything to motivate your staff. They have a contract of employment which they freely entered into, and they turn up for work most days. They already are motivated. The question is, motivated to do *what*?

A division of a large engineering company wanted to make all of its staff feel that they were part of the success of projects, so it introduced a bonus scheme. If the company delivered its customer projects on time and to budget, each employee would get a £1,000 bonus.

Nice idea, eh? Everyone from designers to project managers to security guards to reception staff to the tea lady all play a part in the success of the business, so they should all be rewarded for that part, whether it seems obviously relevant or not. What a lovely, inclusive attitude.

At the end of the year, the company was significantly late and over budget with most of its projects. They were hiring more and more contractors to cover the shortfall caused by staff coming and going whenever they felt like it. They were making penalty payments to foreign governments for late deliveries. Their costs of underperformance ran to around £16 Million a year.

Logically, that would mean that the staff wouldn't be paid their bonus. Instead, the managers (who wanted their bonus too!) decided that they should pay the bonus because staff had worked hard. And because they had come to expect the bonus, so it would be unfair to deny it, just because of the minor point that everyone had failed miserably. The cost to the company was £250,000.

It's important to understand that these kinds of bonuses can act in two ways; either as an incentive or as a reward. An incentive comes before the task, a reward comes afterwards. Rewards and incentives are not a sustainable solution, yet companies still use them.

However, the one thing which really works to increase morale, engagement and productivity is challenge.

When your team are motivated and you give them achievable challenges which enable them to learn and grow in their roles, they will perform better and feel more valued.

Fast paced sales environments such as call centres often use very short term incentives to motivate staff, for example the first person to sell ten insurance policies wins a holiday voucher. Whilst the effect that this has on the team is complex, it does achieve its objective of increasing sales.

The thing which creates sustainable engagement is challenge – the feeling that your work is interesting, demanding, enables you to grow and encourages you to do your best. However, you also need feedback to let you know that you are successfully rising to that challenge. Financial rewards are a feedback mechanism which put a price on motivation, and that's fundamentally whey they don't work.

Childcare nurseries often have a problem with parents arriving late to collect their children. When nurseries impose nominal fines for late collection, the result is counter-intuitive. The number of late collections doesn't go down, it goes up, the reason being that parents are now engaging in a fair and equal transaction, where they pay a legitimate nominal fee for an extra half hour of childcare.

If money were no object to you but you valued convenience then you would park wherever you liked and treat parking fines as a 'pay and display' charge. Faced with the choice of paying £2 for a 2 minute walk from your car to your designer shop, versus paying £40 for a 2 second walk, you'd take the short walk. For most of us, the risk of the parking ticket is a deterrent, but if the parking fine was £2, I'm sure we'd behave differently.

Therefore, the feedback needs to have a direct relationship to the behaviour, whereas money is such a generalised concept that it has no relationship to the performance of a challenging task.

My friend Steve teaches martial arts. He told me that his fellow instructor says that when a student does something right, the teacher should acknowledge it without drawing attention to it. When Steve was watching his students and saw someone doing well, he would say, "Very good". His colleague corrected him, "Not very good, just good."

Imagine that I've taught you how to poach eggs. You have a go for yourself, at home when I'm not around. You then post a photo of your eggs on Facebook. I send you £5. Are you now engaged?

If the teacher 'makes a fuss' of the student, the student's focus will be on the praise. The student will stop practising the required skill for their own benefit and start doing whatever is necessary to get more attention and praise.

How, then, do you find the right level of challenge to properly motivate the learning process?

Surely, you must understand the capabilities of your team, hold regular performance reviews, assess their work against objective standards and send them on training courses?

No. As the people who keep trying to sell us investments are fond of quietly whispering while we're not listening, "Past performance is not a guide to future returns. The value of investments and income from them may go down as well as up and you may not get back the amount invested. Your capital and income are at risk."

The performance and experience of your team are all evidence of past behaviour, not future capability. You are capable of so much more than you are required to do at work. You feel that you could rise to a much greater challenge. What makes you special? Doesn't that apply to your team too? To everyone in your organisation? Isn't everyone capable of more?

Finding the correct level of challenge for an individual is amazingly easy.

Set the level of challenge high.

In fact, too high. Set the challenge to a level that's just higher than you think the person is capable of.

Challenge: Too low   Too high   Just right

Then, collect feedback based on results and adjust the level of support you give.

You might remember this diagram:

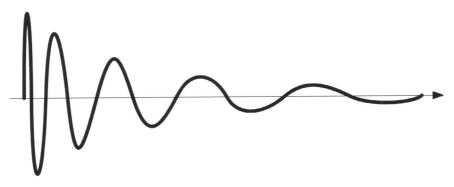

When you first delegate the task, you might ask for an hourly update. The next day, you might just check in at the end of the day. After a week, it's a brief conversation on a Friday afternoon. After a month, it's an email update.

At each of the reviews, you'll ask how the person is getting on. They might say, "Fine" when they mean, "I'm struggling!". Asking them how they're doing is important only to open the conversation and get them talking.

At each review point, you will have an idea of where the person should be up to, what they should have achieved and so on. You'll therefore base your feedback only on objective results.

Let's say that the task is to create a plan for taking a new product to market. You delegate the task by stating the end point, not by telling the person what to do.

You might set the outcome as, "Before 1st April this year, you will have created a plan for taking X product to market. The plan will be in place with the sales teams, they will understand what they need to do and will have the resources necessary to do it. The plan will enable them to achieve £1million total sales revenue by 1st April next year."

By setting the outcome, you give them the responsibility to achieve it. Remember, AIR. The Authority to achieve the Result, and the Information required to make decisions to achieve the Result.

If you tell them what to do, for example if you tell them to first meet with the sales manager, you're taking back responsibility. Why would they risk being wrong when you obviously have all the answers? Whatever they come up with, you're going to tell them to do it your way anyway. There's no need for them to think for themselves. You think that you're an awesome delegator because you give your team lots of great advice on what to do. Well, if that's the case then you're not delegating, you're abdicating. You're giving your team all the answers and then expecting them to deliver results. It can't work. I can tell you my route, my recipe, but I can't guarantee that it will work for you.

You have to specify only the outcome and allow your team to come up with own route plan.

At your first review, you ask them where they're up to. They say that they have started collecting market analysis data. You know that this is useful, but not nearly as useful as getting the early support of the sales manager. However, if you give advice to go and speak to the sales manager, you will instantly take back responsibility and throw away all the good work you've achieved. You have to stick with it. How can you point people in the right direction without telling them what to do? We talked about this earlier – you ask questions. Specifically, you ask questions that the person can only answer by thinking about things that they haven't thought about yet.

"When do you think you'll have something ready to show the sales manager?"

"Oh, a long time yet, maybe two months."

"How do you think she'll react?"

"I think she'll welcome it, they need all the help they can get."

"That's true. So if this plan is going to be helpful, and I guess the sales team might have some experience in this area, when are you thinking of first sharing your plans with the sales manager?"

"Well, I guess if I spoke to her soon then she might be able to help me."

"Sounds good. Let's catch up again next week."

You might call this 'coaching' because you're guiding the person to find their own answers, but it isn't coaching. For a relationship to be 'coaching', the coach must not be dependent on the success of the client. Within an organisation, a line manager cannot allow a subordinate to fail, therefore cannot coach them. They can ask questions in order to guide and support, but that's not the same thing. The manager, or even a colleague in the same company, always has a vested interest in the client's success.

The only motivation that you have to provide, beyond the delegation of responsibility itself, is, "sounds good". You're acknowledging that the person is moving in the right direction, and marking the end of the feedback discussion.

Bonuses do not work when all you want your staff to do is what you already pay them for; their normal duties, including new areas of responsibility which you delegate which are as much about developing people as about increasing productivity.

Treats only work as long term rewards for performing well against targets when those targets are met because people will do more of what you reward them for. When you reward people for trying their best, that's what they'll do – or at least, that's what it will look like they're doing, but there will always be a long list of reasons as to why they didn't quite succeed.

The problem with the company that paid everyone the £1,000 bonus is that staff and managers had come to expect it. Everyone knew that the targets were totally unachievable, but staff would be disappointed if they didn't receive the bonus for 'trying their best', which of course, they didn't.

The only things that really work to motivate staff to perform their normal duties is:

- Hire staff who are well matched to the actual requirements of the job
- Set clear and unambiguous performance targets
- Give staff responsibility for those targets
- Hold staff accountable for those targets
- Set and deliver long term rewards for compliance
- Set and deliver consequences for non-compliance
- Use short-term rewards only when you want short-term results

Research into motivation and delegation from Trinity College in Dublin states an interesting conclusion:

"So if a principal can plausibly convey her motives to her agent, she can very well change his beliefs and perceptions."

In other words, when you delegate a task, if you can convey exactly what you want, you actually influence the mindset of the person you're delegating to, so that they become your 'eyes and ears' in the task.

So for all you control freaks who don't like to delegate because things don't get done the way you want, the problem may well lie in your ability to convey what it is you want, rather than your staff's ability to do what they're told.

Here are some suggestions for practical activities that you can easily put in place to build motivation.

What?	How?
Belonging	Morning meetings, mutual support, shared learning, share success
Equality	Fair assessment, remove bias, transparency for promotions
Feedback	Give developmental feedback that enables people to succeed
Recognition	Give appropriate recognition for achievements
Ownership	Give staff a sense of ownership of their job or area of responsibility and delegate authority with AIR

One of the other interesting findings from this research is that there is a trade-off between the difficulty of a task and the person's level of motivation, like this:

What this means in practice is that each member of your team has a level of difficulty that motivates them most. If a task is less challenging, it's not interesting enough to motivate them, and if it's too difficult, they don't have enough knowledge or belief in their abilities to be motivated.

Your aim as a manager is to identify that 'green zone' where the right level of challenge creates the most motivating and rewarding environment for your staff.

I'll mention sales because it's important to most businesses and because we've just been talking about motivation which often is thought about most in the sales context, perhaps because it's easy to see a direct and short term connection between motivation and results.

Whilst many sales people carry sales targets and are focused on results, that's not always the case. Some sales people are measured on the number of calls they make, on reading the script correctly or on filling in the right forms.

Other sales people are measured on what they achieve, regardless of how they achieve it.

A focus on results relies absolutely on a management culture that trusts individual excellence. It relies on very clear direction from the top. It relies on the business having a clearly communicated strategy.

A focus on activity relies on getting everyone doing the same things, because the systems and processes are valued more highly than the abilities of the sales people. The activity focus compensates for variations and changes in sales teams by making sure everyone does the same thing, regardless of their individual experience or potential. At one of the spectrum, we have volume B2C sales such as home improvement and financial products, where the high turnover of staff means that it's easier to systemise the sales approach, even down to having a scripted sales call. At the other end of the spectrum, when selling regulated products, the organisation clearly has to make sure that all the sales people stick within those regulations.

A large telecoms company I worked for focused on activity. Although account managers had sales targets, those targets were wrapped up in pay plans that were so complicated and changed so frequently that people were never actually paid against plan but instead against subjective decisions of who had been a good chap and kept his/her customers happy, so the account managers were actually paid to be service managers, contrary to the pay plan.

Another company I worked for had an interesting culture; focus on activity but measure results. So the sales managers wanted to see everything the sales people were doing to make sure they were doing it right, but they held people accountable to results. Do you see the problem? The sales people aren't in control of what they do to achieve the results they are paid on, whereas the sales managers aren't in control of the results they're trying to dictate activity for.

The result was that sales people always looked busy, but many of them were working on deals that were never going to close, because it was easier to follow the rules and look busy than to break the rules and risk not hitting target. Do you follow? I am certain I can do what my manager tells me to do, even if it doesn't result in a deal. I am not certain I can break the rules and win the deal by myself. Therefore if I follow the rules it's less risk to me, and if I miss target at least I did what I was told. The overall management culture at the company was "If I can see you then you must be working".

If you want to track what your sales people are doing by making sure they follow a prescribed process then training a rigid sales system is the answer. This is common in activity focused sales cultures, where the management strategy is:

"If we make sure people do the right things in the right order then they will get the right results".

The alternative that I'm suggesting is a focus on results all the way through the organisation, so the management strategy becomes:

"If we focus people on the right results, they will do the right things in the right order".

We can add another layer to this which is the rare opportunity to build a culture, so the strategy becomes:

"If we build the right culture then the right people will do the right things, delivering the results we want", and that 'right culture' includes the results focus.

Of course, this isn't a rigid and exclusive focus; more of a bias that impacts on strategy, qualification, resource allocation, measurement, reward and recognition etc.

If you focus only on results and ignore how people achieve them, you might worry about developing a 'wild west' culture where the end justifies any means. Certainly there are companies that operate like this. I would suggest that a results focus needs absolutely clear strategy and boundaries, whereas an activity focus needs a clear sense of purpose and feedback of what that activity achieves.

In other words, if you focus on results, you need to be clear on what your overall business strategy is and how that has been translated into sales targets. This is vital in enabling sales people to qualify prospects. Activity focused sales people will work on anything that comes their way. Results focused sales people will work on what they can win. If you don't tell them what the clear strategy is they will apply their own criteria and you'll end up with inconsistent results across the sales organisation which means inconsistent use of supporting resources which means that your cost of sale increases.

If you focus on activity, the sales people need to know what the output is so that they understand their role in the system. If you worked on a production line where you assembled part of a product but you never knew what the whole product was, how would that feel? Would it be better if you understood what the final output was, what it is used for and who uses it? In manufacturing, this improves quality through greater personal responsibility.

I'm not here to tell you which is right for you; I can only tell you what the consequences of each approach are. Personally, I favour a results focus, but it does have consequences for the way you manage and motivate the sales people. I think that an activity focus works better in sales environments where there are fewer variables in the sales process. For example, if we're talking about inbound financial services sales, you either want a loan or you don't and you either pass the credit check or you don't. In IT sales there are many more variables, from technology and service design down to corporate politics and individual desires.

Inbound sales actually isn't that easy, I'm simplifying it a bit. To be honest, even in a highly regulated environment, I still can't really understand why anyone thinks that scripts that have to be read verbatim are a good thing. I suppose it means that you can get people to sell who aren't sales people. They don't have to understand what they're doing, or understand the product, or care about the customers, or want to sell, because the script has all that in it. No, I still don't get it…

If you want your people to be able to navigate around obstacles, they have to know where they're going and that they are allowed to make changes to the route they take.

If you're modelling excellence, as I'm suggesting, you will find that another consequence is constant evolution in pursuit of excellence. This is ideal for a results focused organisation, but not ideal for an organisation that likes things done a certain way and only that way.

For an activity focused organisation, 'excellence' means 'doing things the right way', whereas for a results focused organisation, 'excellence' means 'finding a better way'.

Constant evolution means always finding better, faster or more efficient ways to reach the goal rather than sticking with the best way that you know right now. The alternative is that you carry on doing what you know how to do, and after a while the rest of the world overtakes you. If you're lucky, you'll lurch from one massive culture change program to the next as you run to catch up. If you're unlucky, the market environment will select you out.

I say we choose our own luck.

Appendices

This has nothing to do with Change Magic but I thought you might like it anyway. It's a real entry from a very large company's online telephone directory. The name has been blurred to protect the guilty.

Contact Details | Whereabouts | +/- My

Miss Noeleen H▓▓▓▓
Customer Qulaity Manager

Summary of useful beliefs

13 People aren't afraid of change. They're just reluctant to spend more time learning how to work complicated computer software.

15 If you want people to accept change, let them expect it.

47 Nothing is true

48 All models are generalised interpretations of reality. Whilst they may be useful, they are not true.

51 Only do what works

52 Do not ask, "Will this work?", ask, "How will we make this work?"

52 There is no substitute for knowing what you want.

60 A catalyst accelerates change without becoming involved in it.

61 Anything is possible if you are prepared for the cost, consequence and commitment.

65 If what you're doing isn't working then do something else.

66 Are we doing this because it's the right thing to do, or are we doing it because we're doing it?

72 Changing one part of a system changes the whole system.

74 Companies are not broken.

75 Every behaviour has a positive intention.

77 A behaviour can only be evaluated in comparison to its context and purpose.

77 A part that is unaware of its relationship to other parts can only act in its own self interest.

78 "Why" is the wrong question.

78 Knowing the cause of the problem will not help you to solve it.

117 When you give people targets, they will do the minimum necessary to hit the target.

118 You cannot improve anything, you can only change it and then measure it

151 Your customers are happiest when you do what you say you're going to do

151 The faster the feedback, the more adaptable you are to your environment.

163 Failure is the ONLY feedback.

165 Companies don't exist.

219 Everything is working perfectly. We are where we are.

245 If you build the right place, it will attract the right people who will run the right program.

319 People do not make bad decisions. They make good decisions with bad, or insufficient data.

334 Remember - benefits because evidence.

338 Use sensory language

389 Right now, all over the world, your competitors' employees are having the same great ideas as your employees. All that matters is who gets those ideas to market first.

395 The purpose of fear is to keep you away from treasure.

400 You already have everything that you need to be everything that you want.

474 Stop asking why; ask, "What would happen if you did?"

491 If you want people to forget something, stop reminding them about it.

511 Set the level of challenge high.

548 "We are the music makers, and we are the dreamers of dreams."

What is Change Magic?

Organisations are similar in many ways to people. If you remember the cartoon strip 'The Numskulls' from the

Beezer and more lately the Beano, you'll remember that inside our heads we have little people controlling our actions, and that they work in different departments, like in a company. Conversely, companies have departments organised like the parts of a person.

There are creative parts, parts that are good at planning, parts that are good with money, communicating parts and parts that are good at organising other parts. There are a number of very successful personal change and therapeutic approaches which use this metaphor of parts. Up until now, those approaches have only been used to help people.

Change Magic uses the basic change toolkits of these approaches to help organisations. The creator of Change Magic and the author of this book is trained and experienced in the use of these change methodologies and has used the same basic toolkit to effect both personal and organisational change. Therefore, Change Magic is an account of what has been found to work across a wide range of personal and organisational change situations.

Making this connection between companies and people was the historical root of Change Magic. The key principles evolved over many years of trying out new ideas and noticing which were really effective in getting groups of people to work together and develop consistently.

The second key principle in Change Magic is that change is not important – only outcomes are important. Focussing on the change process itself freezes 'the change' in time and makes it a thing or even an obstacle. The second principle of Change Magic is therefore to harness that natural change that accompanies the passage of time. You change during every second of every day. No two experiences can ever be the same, yet our brains cope with information overload by making them seem the same. By only noticing what we want to notice and by forgetting details, we make situations and experiences distorted and generalised versions of real events.

We already have a perfect change methodology which we can see in action every day, all around us. Charles Darwin already researched evolution through natural selection, so we can just learn from his work without having to do lots of expensive research again. What we learn from Darwin is very relevant to change management, in fact it's absolutely vital. The key lessons are:

- You don't need to be way ahead of your competitors – just a tiny bit ahead, consistently.

- You don't need to know where you are heading. Your market will decide this for you as long as you keep moving.

- Success does not come from planning, it comes from adapting.

Many companies employ change managers, set up change project offices and give their change projects elaborate names and personalities. They have notice boards and mugs, awareness days and magazines. They spend more time and money on the change project than on the outcome. Change Magic is about realising that the company is going to change anyway, because the company is only a collection of people who are constantly changing. Change Magic is about harnessing this natural energy and directing it. Change Magic is about subtlety, stealth and business as usual. Companies that survive periods of environmental change are those that adapt. Since the employees of a company will, by and large, be members of the species

Homo Sapiens – the most successful and adaptable species on the planet – this won't be a problem.

What will be a problem is that corporate change projects stop people from adapting. By drawing attention to the change itself, it is frozen in time and made into a thing. We humans naturally do this as part of the collective generalisation that we call language.

You can't hold, see or hear a meeting. A group of people decide to meet with each other. You can't taste or smell a decision. A human being decides on something, and others share his or her view. As for a plan, we often seem to confuse 'planning' with 'knowing what to do'. Writing down some wise yet vague words does not constitute knowing what to do.

So, humans naturally adapt by making sense of their environment and responding to it. Humans are very good at comparing lots of similar situations and grouping them all together into one 'meaning'. This meaning is a generalisation which means that it's inaccurate yet useful. It does not mean that it is true.

Newton's laws of motion are generalisations that are useful enough to land a man on the moon. They are not useful when the model is tested to its extremes, when Einstein's theory of general relativity takes over. Even Einstein couldn't make his model work at its extreme limits, where Quantum theory takes over. It's interesting that for hundreds of years, physicists thought Newton was right, so his theories came to be known as 'laws'. Even laws, truths and rights can be wrong in situations where the generalisation is too far removed from reality.

Jean Baudrillard wrote an essay in 1991 entitled 'The Gulf War Did not Happen', the basic premise of which (as I understand it) is that since no single person witnessed the whole war no one can say for certain that it happened at all. Certainly, piecing together news reports will give us a complete but inaccurate version of events whilst one single report will give us an accurate but incomplete version. If something as important and well reported as the Gulf War cannot be accurately recorded, what chance do we have?

So, Change Magic is really a game of two halves. The first part relates to problem solving. Yes! I said the P word. You don't have challenges, opportunities or issues, you have problems. Recognise them, stand up to them and then solve them. Recognise problems for what they are and then treat them with the contempt they deserve. The reality is that you need to fix problems before moving onto part two.

The second part of Change Magic relates to harnessing natural change momentum and directing it towards a desired outcome. You don't really need to motivate or incentivise people – you just need to shake their model of the world so that they recognise what changes need to be made.

Have you ever returned from a holiday to notice all the things that needed fixing or finishing in your house that you had learned to live with? This is what happens when organisations get stuck in time. The world moves on and they don't because they stop paying attention to the world. Organisations that have an overly inward focus of attention don't notice that the world changes. What the people in these organisations need is the equivalent of that holiday so that they can see for themselves what needs to be changed. If you provide them with a clear direction, they will make they changes themselves, with no need for a change management project!

Change Magic is not a business process re-engineering tool. It is not a methodology for changing things like sales processes or financial procedures. It is not a tool for analysing and investigating accidents or failures. For these applications, you need a specific and methodical approach.

Change Magic can incorporate these approaches but in reality it is better suited to situations that used to be called 'culture change'. Change Magic is really at home where changing the behaviour of people is the main component of the problem. You can rewrite your sales process until you're blue in the face – it doesn't mean people will change their behaviour.

When people change and are given the freedom to change their environments, you'll find that business processes change anyway because people change them. That's right! People will make their own changes, and you can guarantee they will be much better and more complete changes than anything your team of consultants could suggest to you.

Remember – consultants who use off the shelf change programs are forcing an out of date generalised solution to someone else's problem on you. Don't stand for it. You have your problem and you need your solution. Nothing else will do.

Why is this chapter at the end of the book? Because this book isn't just a list of the process steps of Change Magic, because it doesn't really have any. Change Magic is about beliefs and attitudes. If I had given you those in a list, you would have decided straight away if they were true or false and your mind would have closed. There may have been times during this book when you were a bit bemused. I can guarantee that everything is here for a reason. When you are performing Change Magic, you don't have to worry whether people make sense of your words and actions. People are very good at making whatever meaning they want to make. The worst thing that can happen is that you, and the people you work with, start 'knowing' things.

Knowledge can be a terrible thing when trapped in a closed mind.

The purpose of this book is to begin the process of changing your beliefs and attitude towards change. This is a handbook for Change Magic, and it is also Change Magic in action.

Change Magic is not a prescriptive process – it's more of an attitude. If you asked me to summarise the key aspects, ideas or themes that make Change Magic unique, I would say:

- You can treat an organisation as a person, a living entity, and use the same basic tools to change it.

- Change is an illusion caused by a combination of what we notice and our perception of the passage of time.

- The way you communicate with people is the single most important factor in organisational change.

- Organisations do not have problems. People have problems and people can solve them if you just keep out of their way.

- People do not tolerate a situation – they adapt to it.

- Everyone changes all the time. Conversely, no-one changes, ever. It all depends on your point of view.

- Change Magic is about changing organisations by changing people because ultimately, an organisation is nothing more than a collective noun for a group of people with a common interest.

You may think that you've spotted some repeated ideas in this book, or some chapters that seem to link together but which aren't arranged in sequence. I could flippantly say that this is down to the quality of my proof reading but in reality this is intentional, as it stops you from mentally packaging ideas and keeps your mind open so that the real learning can slip in.

If I gave you all the answers, this wouldn't be Change Magic. It would be a script of something that worked once, somewhere else for a different bunch of people. In other words, it would be like every other change management approach – prescriptive, generalised and limited. Change Magic is limitless in its application and development because the next step lies with you. This book is designed to change your attitude, give you some useful new ideas and leave your mind open enough for you to complete the job in a way that is personal and specific to you. By adding your own experience, ideas and beliefs to Change Magic, you will end up with an approach that is relevant, useful and, above all, yours.

So, this information is kept at the end of the book because I didn't want to spoil the adventure. For those of you who enjoy having structure and formality, I needed to explain the background to Change Magic without affecting the function of the book.

If you give people enough information to make a decision, they will decide, they will know and they will understand. The information will be neatly wrapped up and filed away in the vaults of their mind. They will forget that they know, just like you have forgotten all the quiz show trivia that's stored somewhere in that bottomless goldmine of information that is your memory.

If you give people the structure they need but not enough information, they will know what's missing and search out the pieces they need. They will know when they have all the information that exists for this particular subject and, at that point, they will stop acquiring new information

If you give people the information they need but no structure, they will deduce a structure from the information that they have. This will exclude any new information.

When people are constantly open to more information or new ways to organise it, we call that an open mind, or a state of learning. So you see, by giving you complete information and structure, I am helping you to become closed minded and that is never a useful state to be in. Again, as an example of Change Magic in action, I need to find a way of opening your mind. Everybody likes to think they are open minded, and this normally just means 'broad minded' which is something totally different. True open mindedness is not about acceptance or tolerance – it is about learning. It is about seeing things that are familiar in a new way. It is about listening to everyday information and hearing something new. It is about recognising familiar feelings and choosing to respond differently.

Rachel Carson, a famous environmentalist, said, "A child's world is fresh and new and beautiful, full of wonder and excitement. It is our misfortune that for most of us that clear-eyed vision, that true instinct for what is beautiful and awe-inspiring, is dimmed and even lost before we reach adulthood."

Change Magic could therefore be summarised as the following process:

1. Open mind
2. Set direction
3. Stand back

Change Magic is designed to be read as you would read a novel. It doesn't contain all the answers, but it contains enough questions and useful ideas to start your natural processes of developing your own solutions.

In this respect, Change Magic is the antithesis of traditional management theory books. Change Magic doesn't give you a prescriptive formula for organisational change – it recognises the reality that there isn't a formula for change. Any prescriptive change model can only be a generalised account of something that worked somewhere else, with different people in a different situation to yours.

The people in the bakery knew what they needed to do and they knew what needed fixing. They didn't sit down and refer the matter to their managers who could form a steering committee to hire consultants to make a recommendation. They just fixed the problem and got on with the really important thing – making bread for their customers to buy.

You might be wondering if these reckless bakers had thought of the health and safety or quality control implications of hand mixing dough or fixing packaging machines by themselves. I suppose they just believed that it was more important to keep their customers happy. At some point, you need to decide what is important to you in just the same way. Do you wait until someone fixes the machine for you, or do you roll your sleeves up and get mixing?

Change Magic isn't about changing organisations, and it's not about changing people either. It's about getting people to do different things with the skills and experience they already have. You can tap into these skills by changing the way that you think about people, the way that you communicate with them and the way you interact with them. So, if Change Magic is about changing anything, it's about changing yourself.

Hopefully, you had already figured that out.

Suggested reading

Genius at Work	Peter Freeth
Learning Changes	Peter Freeth
The Unsticker	Peter Freeth
How to Win Friends and Influence People	Dale Carnegie
The Dilbert Principle	Scott Adams
Groucho Marx and Other Short Stories and Tall Tales	Groucho Marx
Secrets of the Amazing Kreskin	Kreskin
Quirkology	Richard Wiseman
The Brain that Changes Itself	Norman Doidge

The Author

I'm an expert in 'modelling' high performers; figuring out the hidden secrets of your highest performers and turning that insight into leadership, management and sales development programs that are perfectly aligned with your culture and business strategy.

My innovative approach has led to:

- 700% increase in profitability for a leading global engineering company
- 25% reduction in graduate development time and cost for a High Street retailer
- 200% increase in sales conversion rates for a contact centre operator

On top of that, I have 15 years L&D experience across all market sectors and organisational levels; leadership and management development, coaching, NLP, sales, business strategy, and another 20 years corporate experience in technology and sales.

If you would like to know more about me, my consultancy business or public speaking opportunities, you can contact me directly using the contact details below.

Website	www.geniuslearning.co.uk
Email	peter@geniuslearning.co.uk
Linkedin	uk.linkedin.com/in/peterfreethgenius
Facebook	www.facebook.com/peter.freeth.genius
Twitter	@genius_learning

Also look for The Unsticker on the Google Play Store. It's free, it's world famous, and you'll never be stuck again.

The End

You may think that this is the point where you finally get your twenty-seven point plan for change management. Well, it isn't.

There's no strict, prescriptive formula. Remember, right at the start when you read "only do what works"? If you currently use such a prescriptive change formula, you must realise that it is a generalisation of something that worked once, for someone else, with a different group of people, in a different situation. There's just no guarantee that it will work for you.

Of course every situation is different. If you changed your underwear yesterday and then again this morning, there is a difference. You are different. You are a day older, with 24 hours more experience to draw upon in making decisions.

The point of Change Magic is that it offers you a chance to think differently and to realise that you already can and do think differently. It offers you the chance to see that your intuitions may be right after all. It offers you the chance to listen more carefully to the situation, so that you can gather more information and make better decisions. It offers you the chance to feel OK about letting people change their own environment with you as their guide.

We are problem solving, self correcting machines. We do not suffer a poor environment – we adapt to it. We do not cope with bad situations and we do not put up with rules that we don't like. We adapt to them. We take the sights, sounds and feelings of the situation and we modify them to create something more pleasant.

The task for you as a Change Magician is to shake this view of the world – to gently nudge people from their place of rest. They have inertia and you have momentum. If you remember your 'O' level Physics, you'll know that the

The End
541

momentum of a system is constant, so you have to transfer some of your momentum to them. Do this too quickly or too hard and you will have lit the blue touch paper. My advice is to retire quickly. If you can transfer momentum gently, you will nudge people into a new state of awareness, and they will be more receptive to the idea of change.

When people don't like change, it's when they have adapted to their current environment and have created an internal model of it. They are no longer responding to the real world – they are responding to a model of it. Any threat of change means they have to open up their senses and redefine that internal model. This is an uncomfortable process and in common language we call it 'learning'. You can catalyse this process using the ideas, principles and beliefs you have read about in this book. When you notice that people are beginning to open up their senses, you know that the time for Change Magic has come.

Given the opportunity, the motivation and the permission, people will readily effect change in their own environment more quickly, creatively and effectively than anything your team of consultants could come up with. This is because an individual knows his or her own environment far better than you or anyone else does, so don't bother trying to learn about it – let them change it themselves.

When the system has rebalanced itself, people have drawn new maps that they can be comfortable with and you are enjoying the benefits of the change you catalysed, you can tell everyone that it was all thanks to you. They may or may not believe you, but then that's often the risk you take as a Change Magician

If being a Change Magician is about only one thing, it's the realisation that you don't need to have all the answers. You only need to have all the questions.

If you're the kind of person who likes to flick through books from the end then I've secretly placed the thrilling conclusion in the middle so that you don't miss out on all the fun. Remember, sometimes the journey is more valuable than the destination.

However, I do want to share one final story with you, and I hope it will be especially valuable for you if you're currently working longer hours than you should in order to benefit someone else.

A few years ago, I lived in Leamington Spa and in a nearby row of shops there was a locksmiths. The tiny shop sold padlocks, did key cutting and offered a 24 hour call-out service for people who had locked themselves out of their homes or offices. In the few years that I lived in that area, I never once saw the shop open, but it didn't look abandoned either.

I met someone who lived near to the locksmiths and asked if he knew the story behind the shop. He said,

"The guy still owns the shop, but he almost never goes in there. He just does call-outs.

When he opened the shop, his plan was to make enough money to retire to Spain with his family. He made the most money from the 24 hour call-out service, so he concentrated on that, working every hour that he could. Any time, day or night, wherever he was, whatever he was doing, he'd take a call.

After a few years, he made so much money that he actually bought a villa in Spain. His wife and son used to go there as often as they could, but the locksmith never went with them. He'd stay at home in case he got another call-out, because that meant more money that he couldn't turn away.

For years, his wife and son enjoyed the villa while the locksmith stayed in his shop, waiting for a call-out.

One day, while he was at work, there was an accident, a car crash.

His wife and son were killed.

He never really felt like opening the shop again after that, and he never went to the villa in Spain."

Most people think I'm going to say that the locksmith was killed, but I think you'll agree that his fate was far, far, worse.

Do you work longer hours than you should?

Here's one last useful belief for you. It may be startling and you may or may not agree with it. Beliefs are like that. It's funny how something that someone holds to be absolutely true, someone else can disagree with totally. Well, someone must be wrong, mustn't they? If you are absolutely right, then what you believe in has to be true and universal. Everyone else on the planet must be wrong. We all believe different things about life, about religion and about other people. Who is right?

Of course, if we start to admit that it's possible for different people to believe different things and neither be wrong then we're on a slippery slope towards the inevitable belief that no-one is right and that everyone is wrong, in that no one person can have a universal set of beliefs that apply to anything other than themselves.

In other words, what you believe about the world doesn't apply to the world. It applies only to you. Or, you might say that what you believe about the world says more about you than it does about the world. "We see the world, not as it is, but as we are", as they say.

While we're on the subject, here's another interesting idea. Well, I think it's interesting anyway. Whenever you have a situation where a large number of people disagree about the facts, it's quite likely that they are all right, from a certain point of view. Therefore, it's not the opinion that matters – it's the point of view. "That's obvious", I hear you cry, so here's the important bit.

Let's say that there are broadly two opinions amongst the business community about the state of the economy. One says, "There's not enough business about, so more suppliers entering the market means a smaller slice for me". The other says, "Every supplier who enters the market brings in their own fresh ideas and contacts, thereby making the market bigger. More new suppliers means a bigger market for me to exploit".

If you look at the facts, the research and the economic data, both could be true. Certainly, people will defend both opinions as if they are true. Thinking simplistically, let's deduce that both views are true, based on your point of view. With this in mind, what will you now choose to believe? Which view will you take? How will you use this knowledge of opinion and truth to choose the most useful opinions for you?

It's funny too how people who have really strong beliefs about change are called leaders. They don't really do much to convince people that they're right. They just act like they're right because in their mind there is no room for doubt. Their certainty becomes infectious. Other people start to share their vision. These people have all kinds of beliefs – about inventions, about companies, about art and about nations. They convince not because they are convincing but because they are certain.

When I first started work as an apprentice at a telecoms company, I worked with an engineer named Tony Noakes who was an enormous, white haired cockney. If you have ever seen the British comedian Al Murray (The Pub Landlord), just put him in a big white wig and you have Tony Noakes. We mostly spent our time laughing, looking at girls and eating bacon sandwiches, so I didn't realise until many years later that I had been privileged to spend so much time with a great philosopher.

Tony used to say to me, several times a day, "John, life's a game, and you're either a winner or a loser. Which are you?"

This confused me at first, for two reasons. Firstly, my name is Peter. Secondly, I thought that being a winner or a loser was something that you only found out after the race by comparing yourself to other people. What Tony taught me was that winning is not about the race. It's about choice.

Being a winner or a loser is a state of mind that you choose before you even step onto the track, the court or the boardroom floor.

Leaders seem to have a hallucination about their future that other people get drawn into. Other people start to share that hallucination. It becomes real in the same way that anything you think of is real. Imagine biting into a piece of soft, juicy fruit. Feel the flavour of the juices as they ooze out. Of course it's real – because you think it is!

So, if you want to start making changes in your life, don't plan or write lists or formulate a strategy. Simply start acting as if it is real. Your thoughts, words and deeds will unite to form an unmistakeable self belief that will draw people and opportunities towards you.

Planning for change makes it a possibility. It's still an "if". You can plan all you like, but planning doesn't change the world. Will a piece of paper be your only legacy? Successful people – those who influence their worlds to get the lives they want – don't plan or meet with small business advisers (or even large ones). They just get on with it and make it real. They believe with a certainty that is infectious. They invite other people into their hallucination. Eventually, their hallucination becomes reality. How? Because enough people share it to make it real. Some of those people even share it by placing orders and paying money.

If you have a dream, don't keep it to yourself. Share it. Get other people committed to it. They will make it real for you. If you have already decided what you are going to do, tell everyone you know about it. Make it real, make it happen.

The first and most important step in making any dream a reality is when you share it with other people. Just for a moment, let's define reality as 'a hallucination about ongoing events shared by two or more people', based on the current thinking that you make up most of your ongoing reality based on what you think should be happening. This explains how you can lose car keys that are under your nose.

If we accept, just for a moment, this definition of reality, then you can immediately see how sharing your dream, vision or goal with someone else makes it real. In fact, the more people you share it with, the more real it becomes.

The End

People start to interact with your dream, creating their own versions of it and beginning to influence and change the physical world in order to support your dream. People begin to do things, to make things and to change things and, over time, your dream becomes reality – regardless of how you define it.

If, on the other hand, you're not really committed to your dream, you're not too bothered about it and you don't think it's important, just write it down in a strategy document, white paper or business plan. Then leave it on a shelf so that no-one else can interact with it emotionally.

Let's take this a little further – is there any limit to the dreams that we can share? How about putting a man on the moon? Or running a mile in under four minutes? Or achieving the things that your teachers at school said you couldn't?

If life itself is a collective hallucination, why shouldn't you tweak it a little to meet your own goals and aspirations?

Willy Wonka gave us the final useful belief:

"We are the music makers, and we are the dreamers of dreams."

Printed in Great Britain
by Amazon

47884058R00310